Computing and
Programming with Java

Computing and Programming with Java

Rowan Jordon

Larsen & Keller
www.larsen-keller.com

Computing and Programming with Java
Rowan Jordon
ISBN: 978-1-64172-153-0 (Hardback)

 Larsen & Keller

Published by Larsen and Keller Education,
5 Penn Plaza,
19th Floor,
New York, NY 10001, USA

Cataloging-in-Publication Data

Computing and programming with Java / Rowan Jordon.
 p. cm.
Includes bibliographical references and index.
ISBN 978-1-64172-153-0
1. Java (Computer program language) 2. Computer programming.
I. Jordon, Rowan.
QA76.73.J38 C66 2019
005.133--dc23

Table of Contents

Permissions

Index

Preface

Java is a programming language that is specifically designed to have minimal implementation dependencies. It is built as an object-oriented language. Its syntax is largely influenced by C++. Java applications are compiled to bytecode. They run on any Java virtual machine. It is the most widely used language for Client-Server web applications. It plays a crucial role in mobile operating systems. This book is a compilation of chapters that discuss the most vital concepts in the field of Java. It is compiled in such a manner, that it will provide in-depth knowledge about the techniques of computing and programming with Java. In this book, constant effort has been made to make the understanding of the difficult concepts of Java programming as easy and informative as possible, for the readers.

A short introduction to every chapter is written below to provide an overview of the content of the book:

Chapter 1 - Java is a computer-programming language. It is designed to run on all Java enabled platforms, without recompilation. This is an introductory chapter, which will introduce briefly the important concepts central to Java programming such as Java syntax, clone, Java concurrency, Java bytecode, Java performance and real time Java, besides many others; **Chapter 2** - Java derives its syntax from C and C++ mostly. It is an object-oriented language. This chapter elucidates the programming basics of Java such as leap year program, binary program, bouncing ball program, factors program, etc. to develop an easy understanding of Java programming; **Chapter 3** - The Java platform is a set of programs that enables the development and operation of programs using the Java programming language. Such platforms include an execution engine, a compiler and a set of libraries. This chapter discusses in detail all the varied types of Java computing platforms along with important aspects such as Java card, java development kit, etc.; **Chapter 4** - The compiler used for the Java programming language is known as the Java compiler. It produces Java class files that contain platform-neutral Java bytecode. There are different types of Java compilers such as Jikes, Javac, Graal, GNU compiler for Java, etc. which have been discussed in comprehensive detail in this chapter; **Chapter 5** - In programming, an API or application programming interface refers to a set of tools and protocols for building software. The topics elaborated in this chapter, such as Java Advanced Imaging, Java Persistence API, Java Naming and Directory Interface, Java 3D, etc. will help in providing a comprehensive understanding of Java APIs; **Chapter 6** - Computer programming has undergone rapid developments in the past decade, which has resulted in the development of significant tools and techniques in the field of Java programming. This chapter discusses such diverse aspects including Java collections framework, Java Class Library, Java applet, Java servlet and JavaServer Pages, besides others.

Finally, I would like to thank my fellow scholars who gave constructive feedback and my family members who supported me at every step.

Rowan Jordon

Introduction to Java

Java is a computer-programming language. It is designed to run on all Java enabled platforms, without recompilation. This is an introductory chapter, which will introduce briefly the important concepts central to Java programming such as Java syntax, clone, Java concurrency, Java byte-code, Java performance and real time Java, besides many others.

Java Programming Language

Java is a programming language that produces software for multiple platforms. When a programmer writes a Java application, the compiled code (known as bytecode) runs on most operating systems (OS), including Windows, Linux and Mac OS. Java derives much of its syntax from the C and C++ programming languages.

Java is a general purpose, high-level programming language developed by Sun Microsystems. The Java programming language was developed by a small team of engineers, known as the Green Team, who initiated the language in 1991.

Today the Java platform is a commonly used foundation for developing and delivering content on the web. According to Oracle, there are more than 9 million Java developers worldwide and more than 3 billion mobile phones run Java.

In 2014 one of the most significant changes to the Java language was launched with Java SE 8. Changes included additional functional programming features, parallel processing using streams and improved integration with JavaScript. The 20th anniversary of commercial Java was celebrated in 2015.

Java is an Object-Oriented Language

Java is defined as an object-oriented language similar to C++, but simplified to eliminate language features that cause common programming errors. The source code files (files with a .java extension) are compiled into a format called bytecode (files with a .class extension), which can then be executed by a Java interpreter. Compiled Java code can run on most computers because Java interpreters and runtime environments, known as Java Virtual Machines (VMs), exist for most operating systems, including UNIX, the Macintosh OS, and Windows. Bytecode can also be converted directly into machine language instructions by a just-in-time compiler (JIT). In 2007, most Java technologies were released under the GNU General Public License.

Java on the Web

Java is a general purpose programming language with a number of features that make the language well suited for use on the World Wide Web. Small Java applications are called Java applets and can be downloaded from a Web server and run on your computer by a Java-compatible Web browser.

Applications and websites using Java will not work unless Java is installed on your device. When you download Java, the software contains the Java Runtime Environment (JRE) which is needed to run in a Web browser. A component of the JRE, the Java Plug-in software allows Java applets to run inside various browsers.

Principles

There were five primary goals in the creation of the Java language:

1. It must be "simple, object-oriented, and familiar".

2. It must be "robust and secure".

3. It must be "architecture-neutral and portable".

4. It must execute with "high performance".

5. It must be "interpreted, threaded, and dynamic".

Editions

Sun has defined and supports four editions of Java targeting different application environments and segmented many of its APIs so that they belong to one of the platforms. The platforms are:

- Java Card for smartcards.

- Java Platform, Micro Edition (Java ME) – targeting environments with limited resources.

- Java Platform, Standard Edition (Java SE) – targeting workstation environments.

- Java Platform, Enterprise Edition (Java EE) – targeting large distributed enterprise or Internet environments.

The classes in the Java APIs are organized into separate groups called packages. Each package contains a set of related interfaces, classes, and exceptions. Refer to the separate platforms for a description of the packages available.

Sun also provided an edition called PersonalJava that has been superseded by later, standards-based Java ME configuration-profile pairings.

Execution System

Java JVM and Bytecode

One design goal of Java is portability, which means that programs written for the Java platform must run similarly on any combination of hardware and operating system with adequate runtime support. This is achieved by compiling the Java language code to an intermediate representation called Java bytecode, instead of directly to architecture-specific machine code. Java bytecode instructions are analogous to machine code, but they are intended to be executed by a virtual machine (VM) written specifically for the host hardware. End users commonly use a Java Runtime Environment (JRE) installed on their own machine for standalone Java applications, or in a web browser for Java applets.

Standard libraries provide a generic way to access host-specific features such as graphics, threading, and networking.

The use of universal bytecode makes porting simple. However, the overhead of interpreting bytecode into machine instructions made interpreted programs almost always run more slowly than native executables. Just-in-time (JIT) compilers that compile bytecodes to machine code during runtime were introduced from an early stage. Java itself is platform-independent and is adapted to the particular platform it is to run on by a Java virtual machine for it, which translates the Java bytecode into the platform's machine language.

Performance

Programs written in Java have a reputation for being slower and requiring more memory than those written in C++. However, Java programs' execution speed improved significantly with the introduction of just-in-time compilation in 1997/1998 for Java 1.1, the addition of language features supporting better code analysis (such as inner classes, the StringBuilder class, optional assertions, etc.), and optimizations in the Java virtual machine, such as HotSpot becoming the default for Sun's JVM in 2000. With Java 1.5, the performance was improved with the addition of the java.util.concurrent package, including lock free implementations of the ConcurrentMaps and other multi-core collections, and it was improved further with Java 1.6.

Non-JVM

Some platforms offer direct hardware support for Java; there are microcontrollers that can run Java bytecode in hardware instead of a software Java virtual machine, and some ARM based processors could have hardware support for executing Java bytecode through their Jazelle option, though support has mostly been dropped in current implementations of ARM.

Automatic Memory Management

Java uses an automatic garbage collector to manage memory in the object lifecycle. The programmer determines when objects are created, and the Java runtime is responsible for recovering the memory once objects are no longer in use. Once no references to an object remain, the unreachable memory becomes eligible to be freed automatically by the garbage collector. Something similar to a memory leak may still occur if a programmer's code holds a reference to an object that is no longer needed, typically when objects that are no longer needed are stored in containers that are still in use. If methods for a nonexistent object are called, a "null pointer exception" is thrown.

One of the ideas behind Java's automatic memory management model is that programmers can be spared the burden of having to perform manual memory management. In some languages, memory for the creation of objects is implicitly allocated on the stack or explicitly allocated and deallocated from the heap. In the latter case, the responsibility of managing memory resides with the programmer. If the program does not deallocate an object, a memory leak occurs. If the program attempts to access or deallocate memory that has already been deallocated, the result is undefined and difficult to predict, and the program is likely to become unstable or crash. This can be partially remedied by the use of smart pointers, but these add overhead and complexity. Note that garbage collection does not prevent "logical" memory leaks, i.e., those where the memory is still referenced but never used.

Garbage collection may happen at any time. Ideally, it will occur when a program is idle. It is guaranteed to be triggered if there is insufficient free memory on the heap to allocate a new object; this can cause a program to stall momentarily. Explicit memory management is not possible in Java.

Java does not support C/C++ style pointer arithmetic, where object addresses and unsigned integers (usually long integers) can be used interchangeably. This allows the garbage collector to relocate referenced objects and ensures type safety and security.

As in C++ and some other object-oriented languages, variables of Java's primitive data types are either stored directly in fields (for objects) or on the stack (for methods) rather than on the heap, as is commonly true for non-primitive data types. This was a conscious decision by Java's designers for performance reasons.

Java contains multiple types of garbage collectors. By default, HotSpot uses the parallel scavenge garbage collector. However, there are also several other garbage collectors that can be used to manage the heap. For 90% of applications in Java, the Concurrent Mark-Sweep (CMS) garbage collector is sufficient. Oracle aims to replace CMS with the Garbage-First collector (G1).

Syntax

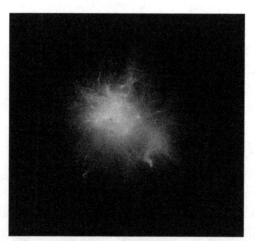

Dependency graph of the Java Core classes (created with jdeps and Gephi).
The most frequently used classes Object and String appear in the centre of the diagram.

The syntax of Java is largely influenced by C++. Unlike C++, which combines the syntax for structured, generic, and object-oriented programming, Java was built almost exclusively as an object-oriented language. All code is written inside classes, and every data item is an object, with the exception of the primitive data types, (i.e. integers, floating-point numbers, boolean values, and characters), which are not objects for performance reasons. Java reuses some popular aspects of C++ (such as the printf method).

Unlike C++, Java does not support operator overloading or multiple inheritance for classes, though multiple inheritance is supported for interfaces.

Java uses comments similar to those of C++. There are three different styles of comments: a single line style marked with two slashes (//), a multiple line style opened with /* and closed with */, and the Javadoc commenting style opened with /** and closed with */. The Javadoc style of commenting allows the user to run the Javadoc executable to create documentation for the program and can be read by some integrated development environments (IDEs) such as Eclipse to allow developers to access documentation within the IDE.

"Hello World" Example

The traditional "Hello, world!" program can be written in Java as:

```
class HelloWorldApp {
    public static void main(String[] args) {
        System.out.println("Hello World!"); // Prints the string to
the console.
    }
}
```

Source files must be named after the public class they contain, appending the suffix .java, for example, HelloWorldApp.java. It must first be compiled into bytecode, using a Java compiler, producing a file named HelloWorldApp.class. Only then can it be executed, or "launched". The Java source file may only contain one public class, but it can contain multiple classes with other than public access modifier and any number of public inner classes. When the source file contains multiple classes, make one class "public" and name the source file with that public class name.

A class that is not declared public may be stored in any .java file. The compiler will generate a class file for each class defined in the source file. The name of the class file is the name of the class, with .class appended. For class file generation, anonymous classes are treated as if their name were the concatenation of the name of their enclosing class, a $, and an integer.

The keyword public denotes that a method can be called from code in other classes, or that a class may be used by classes outside the class hierarchy. The class hierarchy is related to the name of the directory in which the .java file is located. This is called an access level modifier. Other access level modifiers include the keywords private and protected.

The keyword static in front of a method indicates a static method, which is associated only with the class and not with any specific instance of that class. Only static methods can be invoked without a reference to an object. Static methods cannot access any class members that are not also static. Methods that are not designated static are instance methods and require a specific instance of a class to operate.

The keyword void indicates that the main method does not return any value to the caller. If a Java program is to exit with an error code, it must call System.exit() explicitly.

The method name "main" is not a keyword in the Java language. It is simply the name of the method the Java launcher calls to pass control to the program. Java classes that run in managed environments such as applets and Enterprise JavaBeans do not use or need a main() method. A Java program may contain multiple classes that have main methods, which means that the VM needs to be explicitly told which class to launch from.

The main method must accept an array of String objects. By convention, it is referenced as args although any other legal identifier name can be used. Since Java 5, the main method can also use variable arguments, in the form of public static void main(String... args), allowing the main method to be invoked with an arbitrary number of String arguments. The effect of this alternate declaration is semantically identical (to the args parameter which is still an array of String objects), but it allows an alternative syntax for creating and passing the array.

The Java launcher launches Java by loading a given class (specified on the command line or as an attribute in a JAR) and starting its public static void main(String[]) method. Stand-alone programs must declare this method explicitly. The String[] args parameter is an array of String objects containing any arguments passed to the class. The parameters to main are often passed by means of a command line.

Printing is part of a Java standard library: The System class defines a public static field called out. The out object is an instance of the PrintStream class and provides many methods for printing data to standard out, including println(String) which also appends a new line to the passed string.

The string "Hello World!" is automatically converted to a String object by the compiler.

Example with Methods

```
// This is an example of a single line comment using two slashes


/* This is an example of a multiple line comment using the slash and
asterisk.

 This type of comment can be used to hold a lot of information or de-
activate

 code, but it is very important to remember to close the comment. */


package fibsandlies;

import java.util.HashMap;


/**

 * This is an example of a Javadoc comment; Javadoc can compile doc-
umentation

 * from this text. Javadoc comments must immediately precede the
class, method, or field being documented.
```

```
  */
public class FibCalculator extends Fibonacci implements Calculator {
    private static Map<Integer, Integer> memoized = new HashMap<Integer, Integer>();


    /*
     * The main method written as follows is used by the JVM as a
starting point for the program.
     */
    public static void main(String[] args) {
        memoized.put(1, 1);
        memoized.put(2, 1);
        System.out.println(fibonacci(12)); //Get the 12th Fibonacci
number and print to console
    }


    /**
     * An example of a method written in Java, wrapped in a class.
     * Given a non-negative number FIBINDEX, returns
     * the Nth Fibonacci number, where N equals FIBINDEX.
     * @param fibIndex The index of the Fibonacci number
     * @return The Fibonacci number
     */
    public static int fibonacci(int fibIndex) {
        if (memoized.containsKey(fibIndex)) {
            return memoized.get(fibIndex);
        } else {
            int answer = fibonacci(fibIndex - 1) + fibonacci(fibIndex - 2);
            memoized.put(fibIndex, answer);
            return answer;
        }
    }
}
```

Special Classes

Applet

Java applets were programs that were embedded in other applications, typically in a Web page displayed in a web browser. The Java applet API is now deprecated since Java 9 in 2017.

Servlet

Java servlet technology provides Web developers with a simple, consistent mechanism for extending the functionality of a Web server and for accessing existing business systems. Servlets are server-side Java EE components that generate responses (typically HTML pages) to requests (typically HTTP requests) from clients.

The Java servlet API has to some extent been superseded by two standard Java technologies for web services:

- the Java API for RESTful Web Services (JAX-RS 2.0) useful for AJAX, JSON and REST services, and

- the Java API for XML Web Services (JAX-WS) useful for SOAP Web Services.

JavaServer Pages

JavaServer Pages (JSP) are server-side Java EE components that generate responses, typically HTML pages, to HTTP requests from clients. JSPs embed Java code in an HTML page by using the special delimiters <% and %>. A JSP is compiled to a Java servlet, a Java application in its own right, the first time it is accessed. After that, the generated servlet creates the response.

Swing Application

Swing is a graphical user interface library for the Java SE platform. It is possible to specify a different look and feel through the pluggable look and feel system of Swing. Clones of Windows, GTK+, and Motif are supplied by Sun. Apple also provides an Aqua look and feel for macOS. Where prior implementations of these looks and feels may have been considered lacking, Swing in Java SE 6 addresses this problem by using more native GUI widget drawing routines of the underlying platforms.

Generics

In 2004, generics were added to the Java language, as part of J2SE 5.0. Prior to the introduction of generics, each variable declaration had to be of a specific type. For container classes, for example, this is a problem because there is no easy way to create a container that accepts only specific types of objects. Either the container operates on all subtypes of a class or interface, usually Object, or a different container class has to be created for each contained class. Generics allow compile-time type checking without having to create many container classes, each containing almost identical code. In addition to enabling more efficient code, certain runtime exceptions are prevented from occurring, by issuing compile-time errors. If Java prevented all runtime type errors (ClassCastException's) from occurring, it would be type safe.

Class Libraries

The Java Class Library is the standard library, developed to support application development in Java. It is controlled by Sun Microsystems in cooperation with others through the Java Community Process program. Companies or individuals participating in this process can influence the design and development of the APIs. This process has been a subject of controversy. The class library contains features such as:

- The core libraries, which include:

  o IO/NIO

  o Networking

  o Reflection

  o Concurrency

  o Generics

  o Scripting/Compiler

  o Functional programming (Lambda, Streaming)

  o Collection libraries that implement data structures such as lists, dictionaries, trees, sets, queues and double-ended queue, or stacks

  o XML Processing (Parsing, Transforming, Validating) libraries

  o Security

  o Internationalization and localization libraries

- The integration libraries, which allow the application writer to communicate with external systems. These libraries include:

  o The Java Database Connectivity (JDBC) API for database access

  o Java Naming and Directory Interface (JNDI) for lookup and discovery

  o RMI and CORBA for distributed application development

  o JMX for managing and monitoring applications

- User interface libraries, which include:

  o The (heavyweight, or native) Abstract Window Toolkit (AWT), which provides GUI components, the means for laying out those components and the means for handling events from those components

  o The (lightweight) Swing libraries, which are built on AWT but provide (non-native) implementations of the AWT widgetry

- o APIs for audio capture, processing, and playback

- o JavaFX

- A platform dependent implementation of the Java virtual machine that is the means by which the bytecodes of the Java libraries and third party applications are executed

- Plugins, which enable applets to be run in web browsers

- Java Web Start, which allows Java applications to be efficiently distributed to end users across the Internet

- Licensing and documentation

Documentation

Javadoc is a comprehensive documentation system, created by Sun Microsystems, used by many Java developers. It provides developers with an organized system for documenting their code. Javadoc comments have an extra asterisk at the beginning, i.e. the delimiters are /** and */, whereas the normal multi-line comments in Java are set off with the delimiters /* and */.

Implementations

Oracle Corporation is the current owner of the official implementation of the Java SE platform, following their acquisition of Sun Microsystems on January 27, 2010. This implementation is based on the original implementation of Java by Sun. The Oracle implementation is available for Microsoft Windows (still works for XP, while only later versions are currently officially supported), macOS, Linux, and Solaris. Because Java lacks any formal standardization recognized by Ecma International, ISO/IEC, ANSI, or other third-party standards organization, the Oracle implementation is the de facto standard.

The Oracle implementation is packaged into two different distributions: The Java Runtime Environment (JRE) which contains the parts of the Java SE platform required to run Java programs and is intended for end users, and the Java Development Kit (JDK), which is intended for software developers and includes development tools such as the Java compiler, Javadoc, Jar, and a debugger.

OpenJDK is another notable Java SE implementation that is licensed under the GNU GPL. The implementation started when Sun began releasing the Java source code under the GPL. As of Java SE 7, OpenJDK is the official Java reference implementation.

The goal of Java is to make all implementations of Java compatible. Historically, Sun's trademark license for usage of the Java brand insists that all implementations be "compatible". This resulted in a legal dispute with Microsoft after Sun claimed that the Microsoft implementation did not support RMI or JNI and had added platform-specific features of their own. Sun sued in 1997, and, in 2001, won a settlement of US$20 million, as well as a court order enforcing the terms of the license from Sun. As a result, Microsoft no longer ships Java with Windows.

Platform-independent Java is essential to Java EE, and an even more rigorous validation is required to certify an implementation. This environment enables portable server-side applications.

Use Outside the Java Platform

The Java programming language requires the presence of a software platform in order for compiled programs to be executed.

Oracle supplies the Java platform for use with Java. The Android SDK is an alternative software platform, used primarily for developing Android applications with its own GUI system. The Eclipse IDE platform supports Java, but provides its own GUI system SWT.

Android

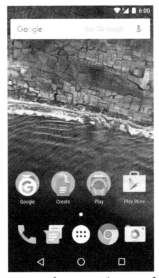

The Android operating system makes extensive use of Java-related technology.

The Java language is a key pillar in Android, an open source mobile operating system. Although Android, built on the Linux kernel, is written largely in C, the Android SDK uses the Java language as the basis for Android applications. The bytecode language supported by the Android SDK is incompatible with Java bytecode and runs on its own virtual machine, optimized for low-memory devices such as smartphones and tablet computers. Depending on the Android version, the bytecode is either interpreted by the Dalvik virtual machine or compiled into native code by the Android Runtime.

Android does not provide the full Java SE standard library, although the Android SDK does include an independent implementation of a large subset of it. It supports Java 6 and some Java 7 features, offering an implementation compatible with the standard library (Apache Harmony).

Resource (Java)

A resource is data (images, audio, text, and so on) that a program needs to access in a way that is independent of the location of the program code. Java programs can use two mechanisms to access resources: Applets use Applet.getCodeBase() to get the base URL for the applet code and then extend the base URL with a relative path to load the desired resource, for example with Applet.getAudioClip(url). Applications use "well known locations" such as System.getProperty("user. home") or System.get Property("java.home"), then add "/lib/resource", and open that file.

Methods in the classes Class and ClassLoader provide a location-independent way to locate resources. For example, they enable locating resources for:

- An applet loaded from the Internet using multiple HTTP connections.

- An applet loaded using JAR files.

- A Java Bean loaded or installed in the CLASSPATH.

- A "library" installed in the CLASSPATH.

These methods do not provide specific support for locating localized resources. Localized resources are supported by the internationalization facilities.

Resources, Names, and Contexts

A resource is identified by a string consisting of a sequence of substrings, delimited by slashes (/), followed by a resource name. Each substring must be a valid Java identifier. The resource name is of the form shortName or shortName.extension. Both shortName and extension must be Java identifiers.

The name of a resource is independent of the Java implementation; in particular, the path separator is always a slash (/). However, the Java implementation controls the details of how the contents of the resource are mapped into a file, database, or other object containing the actual resource.

The interpretation of a resource name is relative to a class loader instance. Methods implemented by the ClassLoader class do this interpretation.

System Resources

A system resource is a resource that is either built-in to the system, or kept by the host implementation in, for example, a local file system. Programs access system resources through the ClassLoader methods getSystemResource and getSystemResourceAsStream.

For example, in a particular implementation, locating a system resource may involve searching the entries in the CLASSPATH. The ClassLoader methods search each directory, ZIP file, or JAR file entry in the CLASSPATH for the resource file, and, if found, returns either an InputStream, or the resource name. If not found, the methods return null. A resource may be found in a different entry in the CLASSPATH than the location where the class file was loaded.

Non-System Resources

The implementation of getResource on a class loader depends on the details of the ClassLoader class. For example, AppletClassLoader:

- First tries to locate the resource as a system resource; then, if not found,

- Searches through the resources in archives (JAR files) already loaded in this CODEBASE; then, if not found,

- Uses CODEBASE and attempts to locate the resource (which may involve contacting a remote site).

All class loaders will search for a resource first as a system resource, in a manner analogous to searcing for class files. This search rule permits overwriting locally any resource. Clients should choose a resource name that will be unique (using the company or package name as a prefix, for instance).

A resource bundle is a set of key and value pairs, stored as a resource, that is commonly used to allow the localization of an application. For this purpose different resource bundles with a common set of keys are used to store translations for the messages and user interface texts of an application.

Final (Java)

While inheritance enables us to reuse existing code, sometimes we do need to set limitations on extensibility for various reasons; the final keyword allows us to do exactly that.

Final Keyword in Java

Final in Java is very important keyword and can be applied to class, method, and variables in Java.

Final is often used along with static keyword in Java to make static final constant and you will see how final in Java can increase the performance of Java application.

Final is a keyword or reserved word in Java and can be applied to member variables, methods, class and local variables in Java. Once you make a reference final you are not allowed to change that reference and compiler will verify this and raise a compilation error if you try to re-initialized final variables in Java.

Final Classes

A final class cannot be subclassed. Doing this can confer security and efficiency benefits, so many of the Java standard library classes are final, such as java.lang.System and java.lang.String.

Example:

```
public final class MyFinalClass {...}


public class ThisIsWrong extends MyFinalClass {...} // forbidden
```

Final Methods

A final method cannot be overridden or hidden by subclasses. This is used to prevent unexpected behavior from a subclass altering a method that may be crucial to the function or consistency of the class.

Example:

```java
public class Base

{

    public         void m1() {...}
    public final void m2() {...}


    public static         void m3() {...}
    public static final void m4() {...}

}


public class Derived extends Base
  {
      public void m1() {...}   // OK, overriding Base#m1()
      public void m2() {...}   // forbidden

      public static void m3() {...}   // OK, hiding Base#m3()
      public static void m4() {...}   // forbidden

  }
```

A common misconception is that declaring a method as final improves efficiency by allowing the compiler to directly insert the method wherever it is called. Because the method is loaded at run-time, compilers are unable to do this. Only the runtime environment and JIT compiler know exactly which classes have been loaded, and so only they are able to make decisions about when to inline, whether or not the method is final.

Machine code compilers that generate directly executable, platform-specific machine code, are an exception. When using static linking, the compiler can safely assume that methods and variables computable at compile-time may be inlined.

Final Variables

A final variable can only be initialized once, either via an initializer or an assignment statement. It does not need to be initialized at the point of declaration: this is called a "blank final" variable. A blank final instance variable of a class must be definitely assigned in every constructor of the class in which it is declared; similarly, a blank final static variable must be definitely assigned in a static initializer of the class in which it is declared; otherwise, a compile-time error occurs in both cases. (Note: If the variable is a reference, this means that the variable cannot be re-bound to reference another object. But the object that it references is still mutable, if it was originally mutable.)

Unlike the value of a constant, the value of a final variable is not necessarily known at compile time. It is considered good practice to represent final constants in all uppercase, using underscore to separate words.

Example:

```
public class Sphere {


    // pi is a universal constant, about as constant as anything can
be.
    public static final double PI = 3.141592653589793;


    public final double radius;
    public final double xPos;
    public final double yPos;
    public final double zPos;


    Sphere(double x, double y, double z, double r) {
        radius = r;
        xPos = x;
        yPos = y;
        zPos = z;
    }


    [...]
}
```

Any attempt to reassign radius, xPos, yPos, or zPos will result in a compile error. In fact, even if the constructor doesn't set a final variable, attempting to set it outside the constructor will result in a compilation error.

To illustrate that finality doesn't guarantee immutability: suppose we replace the three position variables with a single one:

```
public final Position pos;
```

where pos is an object with three properties pos.x, pos.y and pos.z. Then pos cannot be assigned to, but the three properties can, unless they are final themselves.

Like full immutability, the use of final variables has great advantages, especially in optimization.

For instance, Sphere will probably have a function returning its volume; knowing that its radius is constant allows us to memoize the computed volume. If we have relatively few Spheres and we need their volumes very often, the performance gain might be substantial. Making the radius of a Sphere final informs developers and compilers that this sort of optimization is possible in all code that uses Spheres.

Though it appears to violate the final principle, the following is a legal statement:

```java
for (final SomeObject obj : someList) {
    // do something with obj
}
```

Since the obj variable goes out of scope with each iteration of the loop, it is actually redeclared each iteration, allowing the same token (i.e. obj) to be used to represent multiple variables.

Although it also appears to break the intent of final variables, modifying the value from another class (by getting the reference via a public getter method and changing its value) does change the value of the referenced object. For instance, according to the semantics of the final keyword, the following unit test should output "68", while in fact it outputs "82" and throws an assertion exception:

```java
package test;

import java.sql.Date;

public final class TestFinal {


    private final String name = "Andrew";

    @SuppressWarnings("deprecation")

    private final Date dob = new Date(Date.parse("07/20/1968"));

    public String getName() {

        return name;

    }


    final public Date getDob() {

        return dob;

    }

}


package test;

import static org.junit.Assert.*;
```

```
import java.util.Date;

import org.junit.Test;

public class TestFinalTest {


    @Test

    public void test() {

    }


    @Test

    public void changeDate() {

        TestFinal testFinal = new TestFinal();

        Date initialDate = testFinal.getDob();

        initialDate.setYear(82);

        Date finalDate = testFinal.getDob();

        System.out.println(finalDate.getYear());

        assert(finalDate.getYear() == 68);

    }

}
```

The reason for this is that declaring a variable final only affects the reference, not the value of the variable, and Java always passes by value, which creates a different reference to the same value in the second class. That the value of the private field can be changed without a public setter implies that encapsulation is weak at best, and shouldn't be counted on to protect key values, even in combination with the final keyword.

Final and Inner Classes

When an anonymous inner class is defined within the body of a method, all variables declared final in the scope of that method are accessible from within the inner class. For scalar values, once it has been assigned, the value of the final variable cannot change. For object values, the reference cannot change. This allows the Java compiler to "capture" the value of the variable at run-time and store a copy as a field in the inner class. Once the outer method has terminated and its stack frame has been removed, the original variable is gone but the inner class's private copy persists in the class's own memory.

```
import javax.swing.*;


public class FooGUI {
```

```
public static void main(String[] args) {
    //initialize GUI components
    final JFrame jf = new JFrame("Hello world!"); //allows jf to be
accessed from inner class body
    jf.add(new JButton("Click me"));


    // pack and make visible on the Event-Dispatch Thread
    SwingUtilities.invokeLater(new Runnable() {
        @Override
        public void run() {
            jf.pack(); //this would be a compile-time error if jf
were not final
            jf.setLocationRelativeTo(null);
            jf.setVisible(true);
        }
    });
}
}
```

Blank Final

The blank final, which was introduced in Java 1.1, is a final variable whose declaration lacks an initializer. A blank final can only be assigned once and must be unassigned when an assignment occurs. In order to do this, a Java compiler runs a flow analysis to ensure that, for every assignment to a blank final variable, the variable is definitely unassigned before the assignment; otherwise a compile-time error occurs.

C/C++ Analog of Final Variables

In C and C++, the analogous construct is the const keyword. This differs substantially from final in Java, most basically in being a type qualifier: const is part of the type, not only part of the identifier (variable). This also means that the constancy of a value can be changed by casting (explicit type conversion), in this case known as "const casting". Nonetheless, casting away constness and then modifying the object results in undefined behavior.

Further, because C and C++ expose pointers and references directly, there is a distinction between whether the pointer itself is constant, and whether the data pointed to by the pointer is constant. Applying const to a pointer itself, as in SomeClass * const ptr, means that the contents being referenced can be modified, but the reference itself cannot (without casting). This usage results in behaviour which mimics the behaviour of a final variable reference in Java. By contrast, when applying const to the referenced data only, as in const SomeClass * ptr, the contents cannot be modified (without casting), but the reference itself can. Both the reference and the contents being referenced can be declared as const.

In C++, const is a soft guideline that programmers can easily override by type casting a const reference to a non-const reference. Java's final is a strict rule such that it is impossible to compile code that directly breaks or bypasses the final restrictions. Using reflection, however, it is often possible to still modify final variables. This feature is mostly made use of when deserializing objects with final members.

Java Annotation

One word to explain Annotation is Metadata. Metadata is data about data. So Annotations are metadata for code.

Java Annotation is a tag that represents the metadata i.e. attached with class, interface, methods or fields to indicate some additional information which can be used by java compiler and JVM.

Annotations provide data about a program that is not part of the program itself. Annotations have no direct effect on the operation of the code they annotate.

Annotations are decorators that are applied to Java constructs, such as classes, methods, or fields, that associate metadata with the construct. These decorators are benign and do not execute any code in-and-of-themselves, but can be used by runtime frameworks or the compiler to perform certain actions.

Annotations have a number of uses, among them:

- Information for the compiler — Annotations can be used by the compiler to detect errors or suppress warnings.

- Compile-time and deployment-time processing — Software tools can process annotation information to generate code, XML files, and so forth.

- Runtime processing — Some annotations are available to be examined at runtime.

Built-in Annotations

Java defines a set of annotations that are built into the language. Of the seven standard annotations, three are part of java.lang, and the remaining four are imported from java.lang.annotation.

Annotations applied to Java code:

- @Override - Checks that the method is an override. Causes a compile error if the method is not found in one of the parent classes or implemented interfaces.

- @Deprecated - Marks the method as obsolete. Causes a compile warning if the method is used.

- @SuppressWarnings - Instructs the compiler to suppress the compile time warnings specified in the annotation parameters.

Annotations applied to other annotations (also known as "Meta Annotations"):

- @Retention - Specifies how the marked annotation is stored—Whether in code only, compiled into the class, or available at runtime through reflection.

- @Documented - Marks another annotation for inclusion in the documentation.

- @Target - Marks another annotation to restrict what kind of Java elements the annotation may be applied to.

- @Inherited - Marks another annotation to be inherited to subclasses of annotated class (by default annotations are not inherited to subclasses).

Since Java 7, three additional annotations have been added to the language.

- @SafeVarargs - Suppress warnings for all callers of a method or constructor with a generics varargs parameter, since Java 7.

- @FunctionalInterface - Specifies that the type declaration is intended to be a functional interface, since Java 8.

- @Repeatable - Specifies that the annotation can be applied more than once to the same declaration, since Java 8.

Example

This example demonstrates the use of the @Override annotation. It instructs the compiler to check parent classes for matching methods. In this case, an error is generated because the gettype() method of class Cat doesn't in fact override getType() of class Animal like is desired. If the @Override annotation was absent, a new method of name gettype() would be created in class Cat.

```java
public class Animal {
    public void speak() {
    }


    public String getType() {
        return "Generic animal";
    }
}


public class Cat extends Animal {
    @Override
```

```
    public void speak() { // This is a good override.
        System.out.println("Meow.");
    }


    @Override
     public String gettype() { // Compile-time error due to mistyped
name.
        return "Cat";
    }

}
```

Custom Annotations

Annotation type declarations are similar to normal interface declarations. An at-sign (@) precedes the interface keyword. Each method declaration defines an element of the annotation type. Method declarations must not have any parameters or a throws clause. Return types are restricted to primitives, String, Class, enums, annotations, and arrays of the preceding types. Methods can have default values.

```
    // @Twizzle is an annotation to method toggle().
    @Twizzle
    public void toggle() {
    }


    // Declares the annotation Twizzle.
    public @interface Twizzle {
    }
```

Annotations may include an optional list of key-value pairs:

```
    // Same as: @Edible(value = true)
    @Edible(true)
    Item item = new Carrot();


    public @interface Edible {
        boolean value() default false;
    }


    @Author(first = "Oompah", last = "Loompah")
```

```
    Book book = new Book();


    public @interface Author {
        String first();
        String last();
    }
```

Annotations themselves may be annotated to indicate where and when they can be used:

```
    @Retention(RetentionPolicy.RUNTIME) // Make this annotation acces-
    sible at runtime via reflection.

    @Target({ElementType.METHOD})        // This annotation can only be
    applied to class methods.

    public @interface Tweezable {
    }
```

The compiler reserves a set of special annotations (including @Deprecated, @Override and @ SuppressWarnings) for syntactic purposes.

Annotations are often used by frameworks as a way of conveniently applying behaviours to user-defined classes and methods that must otherwise be declared in an external source (such as an XML configuration file) or programmatically (with API calls). The following, for example, is an annotated JPA data class:

```
@Entity                                                // Declares this
an entity bean

@Table(name = "people")                                // Maps the bean
to SQL table "people"

public class Person implements Serializable {

    @Id                                                // Map this to the
primary key column.

    @GeneratedValue(strategy = GenerationType.AUTO) // Database will
generate new primary keys, not us.

    private Integer id;


    @Column(length = 32)                               // Truncate column
values to 32 characters.

    private String name;


    public Integer getId() {
        return id;
```

```
    }

    public void setId(Integer id) {
        this.id = id;
    }

    public String getName() {
        return name;
    }

    public void setName(String name) {
        this.name = name;
    }
}
```

The annotations are not method calls and will not, by themselves, do anything. Rather, the class object is passed to the JPA implementation at run-time, which then extracts the annotations to generate an object-relational mapping.

A complete example is given below:

```
package com.annotation;


import java.lang.annotation.Documented;
import java.lang.annotation.ElementType;
import java.lang.annotation.Inherited;
import java.lang.annotation.Retention;
import java.lang.annotation.RetentionPolicy;
import java.lang.annotation.Target;


@Documented
@Retention(RetentionPolicy.RUNTIME)
@Target({ElementType.TYPE,ElementType.METHOD,
        ElementType.CONSTRUCTOR,ElementType.ANNOTATION_TYPE,
        ElementType.PACKAGE,ElementType.FIELD,ElementType.LOCAL_VARI-
ABLE})
```

```
@Inherited

public @interface Unfinished {
    public enum Priority { LOW, MEDIUM, HIGH }
    String value();
    String[] changedBy() default "";
    String[] lastChangedBy() default "";
    Priority priority() default Priority.MEDIUM;
    String createdBy() default "James Gosling";
    String lastChanged() default "2011-07-08";
}
package com.annotation;


public @interface UnderConstruction {
    String owner() default "Patrick Naughton";
    String value() default "Object is Under Construction.";
    String createdBy() default "Mike Sheridan";
    String lastChanged() default "2011-07-08";
}
package com.validators;


import javax.faces.application.FacesMessage;
import javax.faces.component.UIComponent;
import javax.faces.context.FacesContext;
import javax.faces.validator.Validator;
import javax.faces.validator.ValidatorException;

import com.annotation.UnderConstruction;
import com.annotation.Unfinished;
import com.annotation.Unfinished.Priority;
import com.util.Util;


@UnderConstruction(owner="Jon Doe")
```

```java
public class DateValidator implements Validator {


    public void validate(FacesContext context, UIComponent component,
Object value)
        throws ValidatorException
    {

        String date = (String) value;

        String errorLabel = "Please enter a valid date.";

        if (!component.getAttributes().isEmpty())

        {

            errorLabel = (String) component.getAttributes().get("er-
rordisplayval");

        }


        if (!Util.validateAGivenDate(date))

        {

            @Unfinished(changedBy = "Steve",

                value = "whether to add message to context or not,
confirm",

                priority = Priority.HIGH

            )

            FacesMessage message = new FacesMessage();

            message.setSeverity(FacesMessage.SEVERITY_ERROR);

            message.setSummary(errorLabel);

            message.setDetail(errorLabel);

            throw new ValidatorException(message);

        }

    }

}
```

Processing

When Java source code is compiled, annotations can be processed by compiler plug-ins called annotation processors. Processors can produce informational messages or create additional Java source files or resources, which in turn may be compiled and processed, and also modify the annotated code itself. The Java compiler conditionally stores annotation metadata in the class files, if the annotation has a RetentionPolicy of CLASS or RUNTIME. Later, the JVM or other programs can look for the metadata to determine how to interact with the program elements or change their behavior.

In addition to processing an annotation using an annotation processor, a Java programmer can write their own code that uses reflections to process the annotation. Java SE 5 supports a new interface that is defined in the java.lang.reflect package. This package contains the interface called AnnotatedElement that is implemented by the Java reflection classes including Class, Constructor, Field, Method, and Package. The implementations of this interface are used to represent an annotated element of the program currently running in the Java Virtual Machine. This interface allows annotations to be read reflectively.

The AnnotatedElement interface provides access to annotations having RUNTIME retention. This access is provided by the getAnnotation, getAnnotations, and isAnnotationPresent methods. Because annotation types are compiled and stored in byte code files just like classes, the annotations returned by these methods can be queried just like any regular Java object. A complete example of processing an annotation is provided below:

```java
import java.lang.annotation.Retention;
import java.lang.annotation.RetentionPolicy;


// This is the annotation to be processed
// Default for Target is all Java Elements
// Change retention policy to RUNTIME (default is CLASS)
@Retention(RetentionPolicy.RUNTIME)
public @interface TypeHeader {
    // Default value specified for developer attribute
    String developer() default "Unknown";
    String lastModified();
    String [] teamMembers();
    int meaningOfLife();
}


// This is the annotation being applied to a class
@TypeHeader(developer = "Bob Bee",
    lastModified = "2013-02-12",
    teamMembers = { "Ann", "Dan", "Fran" },
    meaningOfLife = 42)
```

```java
public class SetCustomAnnotation {
    // Class contents go here
}


// This is the example code that processes the annotation
import java.lang.annotation.Annotation;
import java.lang.reflect.AnnotatedElement;


public class UseCustomAnnotation {
    public static void main(String [] args) {
        Class<SetCustomAnnotation> classObject = SetCustomAnnotation.class;
        readAnnotation(classObject);
    }


    static void readAnnotation(AnnotatedElement element) {
        try {
            System.out.println("Annotation element values: \n");
            if (element.isAnnotationPresent(TypeHeader.class)) {
                // getAnnotation returns Annotation type
                Annotation singleAnnotation =
                        element.getAnnotation(TypeHeader.class);
                TypeHeader header = (TypeHeader) singleAnnotation;

                System.out.println("Developer: " + header.developer());
                System.out.println("Last Modified: " + header.lastModified());

                // teamMembers returned as String []
                System.out.print("Team members: ");
                for (String member : header.teamMembers())
```

```
            System.out.print(member + ", ");
         System.out.print("\n");


         System.out.println("Meaning of Life: "+ header.mean-
    ingOfLife());
            }
      } catch (Exception exception) {
         exception.printStackTrace();
      }
   }
}
```

Use Cases for Annotations

Annotations are very powerful and Frameworks like spring and Hibernate use Annotations very extensively for logging and validations. Annotations can be used in places where marker interfaces are used. Marker interfaces are for the complete class but you can define annotation which could be used on individual methods for example whether a certain method is exposed as service method or not.

In latest servlet specification 3.0 a lot of new Annotations are introduced, especially related with servlet security.

HandlesTypes – This annotation is used to declare an array of application classes which are passed to a ServletContainerInitializer.

HttpConstraint – This annotation represents the security constraints that are applied to all requests with HTTP protocol method types that are not otherwise represented by a corresponding HttpMethodConstraint in a ServletSecurity annotation.

HttpMethodConstraint – Specific security constraints can be applied to different types of request, differentiated by the HTTP protocol method type by using this annotation inside the ServletSecurity annotation.

MultipartConfig – This annotation is used to indicate that the Servlet on which it is declared expects requests to made using the multipart/form-data MIME type.

ServletSecurity – Declare this annotation on a Servlet implementation class to enforce security constraints on HTTP protocol requests.

WebFilter – The annotation used to declare a Servlet Filter.

WebInitParam – The annotation used to declare an initialization parameter on a Servlet or Filter, within a WebFilter or WebServlet annotation.

WebListener -The annotation used to declare a listener for various types of event, in a given web application context.

WebServlet – This annotation is used to declare the configuration of an Servlet.

Clone Java Method

In Java, whenever we assign an object reference to another, it is just a bit by bit copy of the memory address, so any changes made using first object reference will be reflected in others and vice versa.

For Example:

```
MyClass mc = new MyClass();

MyClass mc_1 = mc;
```

In the above snippet, any changes made to using mc object reference will be seen by mc_1, and the reverse is also true. What if you need an object reference, which is a copy of another object, but you want that both objects should not interfere their state, i.e. they independently modify their instance variables, which should not seen in other object references. In short, they should have different memory addresses, but the same state when getting copied. Afterward, they can modify their state as needed. This is where cloning comes into the picture.

The object cloning is a way to create exact copy of an object. The clone() method of Object class is used to clone an object.

The java.lang.Cloneable interface must be implemented by the class whose object clone we want to create. If we don't implement Cloneable interface, clone() method generates CloneNotSupportedException.

The clone() method saves the extra processing task for creating the exact copy of an object. If we perform it by using the new keyword, it will take a lot of processing time to be performed that is why we use object cloning.

Classes that want copying functionality must implement some method to do so. To a certain extent that function is provided by "Object.clone()".

clone() acts like a copy constructor. Typically it calls the clone() method of its superclass to obtain the copy, etc. until it eventually reaches Object's clone() method. The special clone() method in the base class Object provides a standard mechanism for duplicating objects.

The class Object's clone() method creates and returns a copy of the object, with the same class and with all the fields having the same values. However, Object.clone() throws a CloneNotSupportedException unless the object is an instance of a class that implements the marker interface Cloneable.

The default implementation of Object.clone() performs a shallow copy. When a class desires a deep copy or some other custom behavior, they must implement that in their own clone() method after they obtain the copy from the superclass.

The syntax for calling clone in Java is (assuming obj is a variable of a class type that has a public clone() method):

Object copy = obj.clone();

or commonly

```
MyClass copy = (MyClass) obj.clone();
```

which provides the typecasting needed to assign the general Object reference returned from clone to a reference to a MyClass object.

One disadvantage with the design of the clone() method is that the return type of clone() is Object, and needs to be explicitly cast back into the appropriate type. However, overriding clone() to return the appropriate type is preferable and eliminates the need for casting in the client (using covariant return types, since J2SE 5.0).

Another disadvantage is that one often cannot access the clone() method on an abstract type. Most interfaces and abstract classes in Java do not specify a public clone() method. As a result, often the clone() method can only be used if the actual class of an object is known, which is contrary to the abstraction principle of using the most generic type possible. For example, if one has a List reference in Java, one cannot invoke clone() on that reference because List specifies no public clone() method. Actual implementations of List like ArrayList and LinkedList all generally have clone() methods themselves, but it is inconvenient and bad abstraction to carry around the actual class type of an object.

Alternatives

There are alternatives to clone(), notably the use of a copy constructor - a constructor that accepts as a parameter another instance of the same class - or a factory method. These methods are not always adequate when the concrete type of the cloned object is not known in advance. (However, clone() is often not adequate either for the same reason, as most abstract classes do not implement a public clone() method.)

Also the use of serialization and deserialization is an alternative to using clone.

clone() and the Singleton Pattern

When writing a class using the Singleton pattern, only one instance of that class can exist at a time. As a result, the class must not be allowed to make a clone. To prevent this, one can override the clone() method using the following code:

```
public Object clone() throws CloneNotSupportedException {

    throw new CloneNotSupportedException();

}
```

This is only necessary if a superclass implements a public clone() method, or to prevent a subclass from using this class's clone() method to obtain a copy. Classes don't usually inherit a public clone() method because Object doesn't have a public clone() method, so it is usually unnecessary to explicitly implement a non-functional clone() method.

clone() and Class Hierarchy

To provide a properly cloneable object of any type, the clone() method must be both declared correctly and implemented correctly according to the convention described in Object.clone().

1) Every type that needs to be cloned must have a public clone() method in its own class or a publicly accessible clone() method in one of its parent classes.

Example:

To invoke clone() on varY1, which is of type Y, then Y or a parent of Y must declare a publicly accessible clone() method. Here, it is the parent class X that provides the public clone() method.

```
public class X implements Cloneable {
        public X clone () throws CloneNotSupportedException {
                return (X) super.clone ();
        }
}


public class Y extends X { }


public class Z extends Y { }


public class test1 {
        public void function () throws CloneNotSupportedException {
                Y varY1 = new Z ();
                Y varY2 = (Y) varY1.clone ();
        }
}
```

2) Every class that implements clone() should call super.clone() to obtain the cloned object reference. If the class has any object references that must be cloned as well (when deep copying, for example), then the clone() method should perform any required modifications on the object before returning it. (Since Object.clone() returns an exact copy of the original object, any mutable fields such as collections and arrays would be shared between the original and the copy - which in most cases would neither be expected nor desired.)

Example:

Since class Z contains an object reference, its clone() method also clones that object reference in order to return a deep copy of the original.

```java
public class X implements Cloneable {
        public X clone() throws CloneNotSupportedException {
                return (X) super.clone();
        }
}


public class Y extends X { }


public class ObjectABC implements Cloneable {
        public ObjectABC clone() throws CloneNotSupportedException {
                return (ObjectABC) super.clone();
        }
}


public class Z extends Y {
        private ObjectABC someABC;

        public Z clone() throws CloneNotSupportedException {
                Z newZ = (Z) super.clone();
                newZ.someABC = someABC.clone();

                return newZ;
        }
}


public class test1 {
        public void function() throws CloneNotSupportedException {
                Y varY1 = new Z();
                Y varY2 = (Y) varY1.clone();
        }
}
```

Potential Pitfalls

If every class in a hierarchy implements a clone() method, all of these functions will be called upon cloning, adding some overhead. Over many iterations, this overhead could become significant.

With complex object graphs, deep copying can also become problematic when recursive references exist.

It is not always appropriate to have multiple copies of the same object floating around. If the purpose of a specific clone() implementation is not fully understood by consumers, it may unintentionally break the "single object, multiple references" paradigm.

clone() and Final Fields

Generally, clone() is incompatible with final fields. Because clone() is essentially a default constructor (one that has no arguments) it is impossible to assign a final field within a clone() method; a compiler error is the result. Where the value of the field is an immutable object this is okay; just let the 'constructor' copy the reference and both the original and its clone will share the same object.

But where the value is a mutable object it must be deep copied. One solution is to remove the final modifier from the field, giving up the benefits the modifier conferred.

For this reason, some programmers suggest to make the objects in the hierarchy Serializable, and create copies by serializing the old object and then creating a new object from the resulting bit-stream, which handles final data members correctly, but is significantly slower.

Alternatively, one can return a completely new object from the current objects fields, which can be done first calling the constructor, and later assigning non final fields. Another alternative method is actually making the idea formal : creating a copy constructor that takes an instance. In fact that is what is recommended over clone by some people.

Java Syntax

A syntax for any language is the set of rules by which the language is governed and ruled, written and interpreted.

Java has many features and own set of syntax rules, structure, and programming paradigm. The Java programming paradigm is based on Object-Oriented Programming. The syntax for Java language is derived from C and C++, and that is the reason for Java syntax looks very similar to C codes.

When we consider a Java program, it can be defined as a collection of objects that communicate via invoking each other's methods. Let us now briefly look into what do class, object, methods, and instance variables mean.

- Object – Objects have states and behaviors. Example: A dog has states - color, name, breed as well as behavior such as wagging their tail, barking, eating. An object is an instance of a class.

- Class – A class can be defined as a template/blueprint that describes the behavior/state that the object of its type supports.

- Methods – A method is basically a behavior. A class can contain many methods. It is in methods where the logics are written, data is manipulated and all the actions are executed.

- Instance Variables – Each object has its unique set of instance variables. An object's state is created by the values assigned to these instance variables.

Basics

Identifier

An identifier is the name of an element in the code. There are certain standard naming conventions to follow when selecting names for elements. Identifiers in Java are case-sensitive.

An identifier can contain:

- Any Unicode character that is a letter (including numeric letters like Roman numerals) or digit.

- Currency sign (such as ¥).

- Connecting punctuation character (such as _).

An identifier cannot:

- Start with a digit.

- Be equal to a reserved keyword, null literal or boolean literal.

Keywords

abstract	continue	for	new	switch
assert	default	goto	package	synchronized
boolean	do	if	private	this
break	double	implements	protected	throw
byte	else	import	public	throws
case	enum	instanceof	return	transient
catch	extends	int	short	try
char	final	interface	static	var
class	finally	long	strictfp	void
const	float	native	super	volatile
				while

1. ^ Keyword was introduced in J2SE 1.4

2. ^ab Keyword is not used

3. ^ Keyword was introduced in J2SE 5.0

4. ^ Keyword was introduced in Java SE 10.0

5. ^ Keyword was introduced in J2SE 1.2

Literals

Integers	
Integers	
binary(introduced in Java SE 7)	0b11110101 (0b followed by a binary number)
octal	0365 (0 followed by an octal number)
hexadecimal	0xF5 (0x followed by a hexadecimal number)
decimal	245 (decimal number)
Floating-point values	
float	23.5F, .5f, 1.72E3F (decimal fraction with an optional exponent indicator, followed by F)
float	0x.5F0F, 0x.5P-6f (0x followed by a hexadecimal fraction with a mandatory exponent indicator and a suffix F)
double	23.5D, .5, 1.72E3D (decimal fraction with an optional exponent indicator, followed by optional D)
double	0x.5FP0, 0x.5P-6D (0x followed by a hexadecimal fraction with a mandatory exponent indicator and an optional suffix D)
Character literals	
char	'a', 'Z', '\u0231' (character or a character escape, enclosed in single quotes)
Boolean literals	
boolean	true, false
null literal	
null reference	null
String literals	
String	"Hello, World" (sequence of characters and character escapes enclosed in double quotes)
Characters escapes in strings	
Unicodecharacter	\u3876 (\u followed by the hexadecimal unicode code point up to U+FFFF)
Octal escape	\352 (octal number not exceeding 377, preceded by backslash)
Line feed	\n
Carriage return	\r
Form feed	\f
Backslash	\\
Single quote	\'
Double quote	\"
Tab	\t
Backspace	\b

Integer literals are of int type by default unless long type is specified by appending L or l suffix to the literal, e.g. 367L. Since Java SE 7, it is possible to include underscores between the digits of a number to increase readability; for example, a number 145608987 can be written as 145_608_987.

Variables

Variables are identifiers associated with values. They are declared by writing the variable's type and name, and are optionally initialized in the same statement by assigning a value.

```
int count;      //Declaring an uninitialized variable called 'count',
of type 'int'
count = 35;     //Initializing the variable
```

```
int count = 35; //Declaring and initializing the variable at the same
time
```

Multiple variables of the same type can be declared and initialized in one statement using comma as a delimiter.

```
int a, b;              //Declaring multiple variables of the same type
int a = 2, b = 3; //Declaring and initializing multiple variables of
the same type
```

Code Blocks

The separators { and } signify a code block and a new scope. Class members and the body of a method are examples of what can live inside these braces in various contexts.

Inside of method bodies, braces may be used to create new scopes, as follows:

```
void doSomething() {
    int a;


    {
        int b;
        a = 1;
    }


    a = 2;
    b = 3; // Illegal because the variable b is declared in an inner scope.
}
```

Comments

Java has three kinds of comments: *traditional comments, end-of-line comments* and *documentation comments.*

Traditional comments, also known as block comments, start with /* and end with */, they may span across multiple lines. This type of comment was derived from C and C++.

```
/* This is a multi-line comment.
It may occupy more than one line. */
```

End-of-line comments start with // and extend to the end of the current line. This comment type is also present in C++ and in modern C.

```
// This is an end-of-line comment
```

Documentation comments in the source files are processed by the Javadoc tool to generate documentation. This type of comment is identical to traditional comments, except it starts with /** and follows conventions defined by the Javadoc tool. Technically, these comments are a special kind of traditional comment and they are not specifically defined in the language specification.

```
/**
 * This is a documentation comment.
 *
 * @author John Doe
 */
```

Program Structure

Java applications consist of collections of classes. Classes exist in packages but can also be nested inside other classes.

Main Method

Every Java application must have an entry point. This is true of both graphical interface applications and console applications. The entry point is the mainmethod. There can be more than one class with a main method, but the main class is always defined externally (for example, in a manifest file). The method must be static and is passed command-line arguments as an array of strings. Unlike C++ or C#, it never returns a value and must return void.

```
public static void main(String[] args) {

}
```

Packages

Packages are a part of a class name and they are used to group and/or distinguish named entities from other ones. Another purpose of packages is to govern code access together with access modifiers. For example, java.io.InputStream is a fully qualified class name for the class Input-Stream which is located in the package java.io.

A package is declared at the start of the file with the package declaration:

```
package myapplication.mylibrary;


public class MyClass {

}
```

Classes with the public modifier must be placed in the files with the same name and java extension and put into nested folders corresponding to the package name. The above class myapplication.mylibrary.MyClass will have the following path: myapplication/mylibrary/MyClass.java.

Import Declaration

Type Import Declaration

A type import declaration allows a named type to be referred to by a simple name rather than the full name that includes the package. Import declarations can be *single type import declarations* or *import-on-demand declarations*. Import declarations must be placed at the top of a code file after the package declaration.

```
package myPackage;


import java.util.Random; // Single type declaration


public class ImportsTest {
    public static void main(String[] args) {
        /* The following line is equivalent to
         * java.util.Random random = new java.util.Random();
         * It would've been incorrect without the import.
         */
        Random random = new Random();
    }
}
```

Import-on-demand declarations are mentioned in the code. A "type import" imports all the types of the package. A "static import" imports members of the package.

```
        import java.util.*;   /*This form of importing classes makes all
    classes in package java.util available by name, could be used instead
    of the import declaration in the previous example. */

        import java.*; /*This statement is legal, but does nothing, since
    there are no classes directly in package java. All of them are in pack-
    ages within package java. This does not import all available class-
    es.*/
```

Static Import Declaration

This type of declaration has been available since J2SE 5.0. Static importdeclarations allow access to static members defined in another class, interface, annotation, or enum; without specifying the class name:

```
import static java.lang.System.out; //'out' is a static field in java.
lang.System


public class HelloWorld {
```

```
    public static void main(String[] args) {
        /* The following line is equivalent to:
    System.out.println("Hi World!");

            and would have been incorrect without the import declara-
    tion. */
        out.println("Hello World!");
    }

}
```

Import-on-demand declarations allow to import all the fields of the type:

```
import static java.lang.System.*;
    /* This form of declaration makes all
        fields in the java.lang.System class available by name, and may be
used instead
        of the import declaration in the previous example. */
```

Enum constants may also be used with static import. For example, this enum is in the package called screen:

```
public enum ColorName {
    RED, BLUE, GREEN
};
```

It is possible to use static import declarations in another class to retrieve the enum constants:

```
    import screen.ColorName;
    import static screen.ColorName.*;

    public class Dots {
        /* The following line is equivalent to 'ColorName foo = ColorName.
    RED',
            and it would have been incorrect without the static import. */
        ColorName foo = RED;

        void shift() {
            /* The following line is equivalent to:

                if (foo == ColorName.RED) foo = ColorName.BLUE; */
            if (foo == RED) foo = BLUE;
```

```
    }

}
```

Operators

Operators in Java are similar to those in C++. However, there is no deleteoperator due to garbage collection mechanisms in Java, and there are no operations on pointers since Java does not support them. Another difference is that Java has an unsigned right shift operator (>>>), while C's right shift operator's signedness is type-dependent. Operators in Java cannot be overloaded.

Precedence	Operator	Description	Associativity
1	( )	Method invocation	Left-to-right
	[ ]	Array access	
	.	Class member selection	
2	++ --	Postfix increment and decrement	
3	++ --	Prefix increment and decrement	Right-to-left
	+ -	Unary plus and minus	
	! ~	Logical NOT and bitwise NOT	
	(*type*) val	Type cast	
	new	Class instance or array creation	
4	* / %	Multiplication, division, and modulus (remainder)	Left-to-right
5	+ -	Addition and subtraction	
	+	String concatenation	
6	<< >> >>>	Bitwise left shift, signed right shift and unsigned right shift	
7	< <=	Relational "less than" and "less than or equal to"	
	> >=	Relational "greater than" and "greater than or equal to"	
	instanceof	Type comparison	
8	== !=	Relational "equal to" and "not equal to"	
9	&	Bitwise and logical AND	
10	^	Bitwise and logical XOR (exclusive or)	
11	|	Bitwise and logical OR (inclusive or)	
12	&&	Logical conditional-AND	
13	||	Logical conditional-OR	
14	$c\,?\,t\,:f$	Ternary conditional	Right-to-left
15	=	Simple assignment	
	+= -=	Assignment by sum and difference	
	*= /= %=	Assignment by product, quotient, and remainder	
	<<= >>=>>>=	Assignment by bitwise left shift, signed right shift and unsigned right shift	
	&= ^= |=	Assignment by bitwise AND, XOR, and OR	

Control Structures

Conditional Statements

If Statement

if statements in Java are similar to those in C and use the same syntax:

```
if (i == 3) doSomething();
```

if statement may include optional else block, in which case it becomes an if-then-else statement:

```
if (i == 2) {
    doSomething();
} else {
    doSomethingElse();
}
```

Like C, else-if construction does not involve any special keywords, it is formed as a sequence of separate if-then-else statements:

```
if (i == 3) {
    doSomething();
} else if (i == 2) {
    doSomethingElse();
} else {
    doSomethingDifferent();
}
```

Also, note that the ?: operator can be used in place of simple if statement, for example

```
int a = 1;
int b = 2;
int minVal = (a < b) ? a : b;
```

Switch Statement

Switch statements in Java can use byte, short, char, and int (note: not long) primitive data types or their corresponding wrapper types. Starting with J2SE 5.0, it is possible to use enum types. Starting with Java SE 7, it is possible to use Strings. Other reference types cannot be used in switch statements.

Possible values are listed using case labels. These labels in Java may contain only constants (including enum constants and string constants). Execution will start after the label corresponding to the expression inside the brackets. An optional default label may be present to declare that the code following it will be executed if none of the case labels correspond to the expression.

Code for each label ends with the break keyword. It is possible to omit it causing the execution to proceed to the next label, however, a warning will usually be reported during compilation.

```
switch (ch) {
    case 'A':
        doSomething(); // Triggered if ch == 'A'
        break;
```

```
    case 'B':
    case 'C':
        doSomethingElse(); // Triggered if ch == 'B' or ch == 'C'
        break;
    default:
        doSomethingDifferent(); // Triggered in any other case
        break;
}
```

Iteration Statements

Iteration statements are statements that are repeatedly executed when a given condition is evaluated as true. Since J2SE 5.0, Java has four forms of such statements.

While Loop

In the while loop, the test is done before each iteration.

```
while (i < 10) {
    doSomething();
}
```

Do ... While Loop

In the do ... while loop, the test is done after each iteration. Consequently, the code is always executed at least once.

```
// doSomething() is called at least once
do {
    doSomething();
} while (i < 10);
```

For Loop

for loops in Java include an initializer, a condition and a counter expression. It is possible to include several expressions of the same kind using comma as delimiter (except in the condition). However, unlike C, the comma is just a delimiter and not an operator.

```
for (int i = 0; i < 10; i++) {
    doSomething();
}


// A more complex loop using two variables
```

```
for (int i = 0, j = 9; i < 10; i++, j -= 3) {
    doSomething();
}
```

Like C, all three expressions are optional. The following loop is infinite:

```
for (;;) {
    doSomething();
}
```

Enhanced for Loop

Enhanced for loops have been available since J2SE 5.0. This type of loop uses built-in iterators over arrays and collections to return each item in the given collection. Every element is returned and reachable in the context of the code block. When the block is executed, the next item is re-turned until there are no items remaining. Unlike C#, this kind of loop does not involve a special keyword, but instead uses a different notation style.

```
for (int i : intArray) {
    doSomething(i);
}
```

Jump Statements

Labels

Labels are given points in code used by break and continue statements. Note that the Java goto keyword cannot be used to jump to specific points in the code.

```
start:
someMethod();
```

Break Statement

The break statement breaks out of the closest loop or switch statement. Execution continues in the statement after the terminated statement, if any.

```
for (int i = 0; i < 10; i++) {
    while (true) {
        break;
    }
    // Will break to this point
}
```

It is possible to break out of the outer loop using labels:

```
outer:
for (int i = 0; i < 10; i++) {
    while (true) {
        break outer;
    }
}
// Will break to this point
```

Continue Statement

The continue statement discontinues the current iteration of the current control statement and begins the next iteration. The following while loop in the code below reads characters by calling getChar(), skipping the statements in the body of the loop if the characters are spaces:

```
int ch;
while (ch == getChar()) {
    if (ch == ' ') {
        continue; // Skips the rest of the while-loop
    }

    // Rest of the while-loop, will not be reached if ch == ' '
    doSomething();
}
```

Labels can be specified in continue statements and break statements:

```
outer:
for (String str : stringsArr) {
    char[] strChars = str.toCharArray();
    for (char ch : strChars) {
        if (ch == ' ') {
            /* Continues the outer cycle and the next
            string is retrieved from stringsArr */
            continue outer;
        }
        doSomething(ch);
    }
}
```

Return Statement

The return statement is used to end method execution and to return a value. A value returned by the method is written after the return keyword. If the method returns anything but void, it must use the return statement to return some value.

```java
void doSomething(boolean streamClosed) {
    // If streamClosed is true, execution is stopped
    if (streamClosed) {
        return;
    }
    readFromStream();
}


int calculateSum(int a, int b) {
    int result = a + b;
    return result;
}
```

return statement ends execution immediately, except for one case: if the statement is encountered within a try block and it is complemented by a finally, control is passed to the finally block.

```java
void doSomething(boolean streamClosed) {
    try {
        if (streamClosed) {
            return;
        }
        readFromStream();
    } finally {
        /* Will be called last even if
        readFromStream() was not called */
        freeResources();
    }
}
```

Exception Handling Statements

try-catch-finally Statements

Exceptions are managed within try ... catch blocks.

```
try {

    // Statements that may throw exceptions

    methodThrowingExceptions();

} catch (Exception ex) {

    // Exception caught and handled here

    reportException(ex);

} finally {

    // Statements always executed after the try/catch blocks

    freeResources();

}
```

The statements within the try block are executed, and if any of them throws an exception, execution of the block is discontinued and the exception is handled by the catch block. There may be multiple catch blocks, in which case the first block with an exception variable whose type matches the type of the thrown exception is executed.

Java SE 7 also introduced multi-catch clauses besides uni-catch clauses. This type of catch clauses allows Java to handle different types of exceptions in a single block provided they are not subclasses of each other.

```
try {

    methodThrowingExceptions();

} catch (IOException | IllegalArgumentException ex) {

    //Both IOException and IllegalArgumentException will be caught and
    handled here

    reportException(ex);

}
```

If no catch block matches the type of the thrown exception, the execution of the outer block (or method) containing the try ... catch statement is discontinued, and the exception is passed up and outside the containing block (or method). The exception is propagated upwards through the call stack until a matching catchblock is found within one of the currently active methods. If the exception propagates all the way up to the top-most main method without a matching catch block being found, a textual description of the exception is written to the standard output stream.

The statements within the finally block are always executed after the tryand catch blocks, whether or not an exception was thrown and even if a return statement was reached. Such blocks are useful for providing clean-up code that is guaranteed to always be executed.

The catch and finally blocks are optional, but at least one or the other must be present following the try block.

Try-with-resources Statements

try-with-resources statements are a special type of try-catch-finallystatements introduced as an implementation of the dispose pattern in Java SE 7. In a try-with-resources statement the try keyword is followed by initialization of one or more resources that are released automatically when the try block execution is finished. Resources must implement java.lang.AutoCloseable. try-with-resources statements are not required to have a catch or finallyblock unlike normal try-catch-finally statements.

```java
try (FileOutputStream fos = new FileOutputStream("filename");

    XMLEncoder xEnc = new XMLEncoder(fos))

{

    xEnc.writeObject(object);

} catch (IOException ex) {

        Logger.getLogger(Serializer.class.getName()).log(Level.SEVERE,
null, ex);

}
```

Throw Statement

The throw statement is used to throw an exception and end the execution of the block or method. The thrown exception instance is written after the throwstatement.

```java
void methodThrowingExceptions(Object obj) {

        if (obj == null) {

            // Throws exception of NullPointerException type

            throw new NullPointerException();

        }

        // Will not be called, if object is null

        doSomethingWithObject(obj);

}
```

Thread Concurrency Control

Java has built-in tools for multi-thread programming. For the purposes of thread synchronization the synchronized statement is included in Java language.

To make a code block synchronized, it is preceded by the synchronizedkeyword followed by the lock object inside the brackets. When the executing thread reaches the synchronized block, it acquires a mutual exclusion lock, executes the block, then releases the lock. No threads may enter this block until the lock is released. Any non-null reference type may be used as the lock.

```java
/* Acquires lock on someObject. It must be of

a reference type and must be non-null */
```

```
synchronized (someObject) {
    // Synchronized statements
}
```

Assert Statement

assert statements have been available since J2SE 1.4. These types of statements are used to make assertions in the source code, which can be turned on and off during execution for specific classes or packages. To declare an assertion the assert keyword is used followed by a conditional expression. If it evaluates to false when the statement is executed, an exception is thrown. This statement can include a colon followed by another expression, which will act as the exception's detail message.

```
// If n equals 0, AssertionError is thrown
assert n != 0;
/* If n equals 0, AssertionError will be thrown
with the message after the colon */
assert n != 0 : "n was equal to zero";
```

Primitive Types

Primitive types in Java include integer types, floating-point numbers, UTF-16 code units and a boolean type. There are no unsigned types in Java except char type, which is used to represent UTF-16 code units. The lack of unsigned types is offset by introducing unsigned right shift operation (>>>), which is not present in C++. Nevertheless, criticisms have been leveled about the lack of compatibility with C and C++ this causes.

Primitive Types					
Type Name	Wrapper class	Value	Range	Size	Default Value
byte	java.lang.Byte	integer	−128 through +127	8-bit (1-byte)	0
short	java.lang.Short	integer	−32,768 through +32,767	16-bit (2-byte)	0
int	java.lang.Integer	integer	−2,147,483,648 through +2,147,483,647	32-bit (4-byte)	0
long	java.lang.Long	integer	−9,223,372,036,854,775,808 through +9,223,372,036,854,775,807	64-bit (8-byte)	0
float	java.lang.Float	floating point number	±1.401298E−45 through ±3.402823E+38	32-bit (4-byte)	0.0f
double	java.lang.Double	floating point number	±4.94065645841246E−324 through ±1.79769313486232E+308	64-bit (8-byte)	0.0

boolean	java.lang.Boolean	Boolean	true or false	1-bit (1-bit)	false
char	java.lang.Character	UTF-16code unit (BMP-character or a part of a surrogate pair)	'\u0000' through '\uFFFF'	16-bit (2-byte)	'\u0000'

char does not necessarily correspond to a single character. It may represent a part of a surrogate pair, in which case Unicode code point is represented by a sequence of two char values.

Boxing and Unboxing

This language feature was introduced in J2SE 5.0. *Boxing* is the operation of converting a value of a primitive type into a value of a corresponding reference type, which serves as a wrapper for this particular primitive type. *Unboxing* is the reverse operation of converting a value of a reference type (previously boxed) into a value of a corresponding primitive type. Neither operation requires an explicit conversion.

Example:

```
int foo = 42; // Primitive type
Integer bar = foo; /* foo is boxed to bar, bar is of Integer type,
                      which serves as a wrapper for int */
int foo2 = bar; // Unboxed back to primitive type
```

Reference Types

Reference types include class types, interface types, and array types. When the constructor is called, an object is created on the heap and a reference is assigned to the variable. When a variable of an object gets out of scope, the reference is broken and when there are no references left, the object gets marked as garbage. The garbage collector then collects and destroys it some time afterwards.

A reference variable is null when it does not reference any object.

Arrays

Arrays in Java are created at runtime, just like class instances. Array length is defined at creation and cannot be changed.

```
int[] numbers = new int;
numbers = 2;
numbers = 5;
int x = numbers;
```

Initializers

```
// Long syntax
int[] numbers = new int[] {20, 1, 42, 15, 34};
```

```
// Short syntax
int[] numbers2 = {20, 1, 42, 15, 34};
```

Multi-dimensional Arrays

In Java, multi-dimensional arrays are represented as arrays of arrays. Technically, they are represented by arrays of references to other arrays.

```
int[][] numbers = new int;
numbers = 2;


int[][] numbers2 = {{2, 3, 2}, {1, 2, 6}, {2, 4, 5}};
```

Due to the nature of the multi-dimensional arrays, sub-arrays can vary in length, so multi-dimensional arrays are not bound to be rectangular unlike C:

```
int[][] numbers = new int[]; //Initialization of the first dimension
only


numbers = new int;
numbers = new int;
```

Classes

Classes are fundamentals of an object-oriented language such as Java. They contain members that store and manipulate data. Classes are divided into *top-level* and *nested*. Nested classes are classes placed inside another class that may access the private members of the enclosing class. Nested classes include *member classes* (which may be defined with the *static* modifier for simple nesting or without it for inner classes), *local classes* and *anonymous classes*.

Declaration

Top-level class	`class Foo {`
	`    // Class members`
	`}`

Inner class	`class Foo { // Top-level class`
	`    class Bar { // Inner class`
	`    }`
	`}`

Nested class	`class Foo { // Top-level class`
	`    static class Bar { // Nested class`
	`    }`
	`}`

| Local class | ```
class Foo {
    void bar() {
        class Foobar {// Local class within a method
        }
    }
}
``` |
| Anon-ymous class | ```
class Foo {
    void bar() {
        new Object() {// Creation of a new anonymous class extending Object
        };
    }
}
``` |

Instantiation

Non-static members of a class define the types of the instance variables and methods, which are related to the objects created from that class. To create these objects, the class must be instantiated by using the new operator and calling the class constructor.

```
Foo foo = new Foo();
```

Accessing Members

Members of both instances and static classes are accessed with the . (dot) operator.

Accessing an Instance Member

Instance members can be accessed through the name of a variable.

```
String foo = "Hello";
String bar = foo.toUpperCase();
```

Accessing a Static Class Member

Static members are accessed by using the name of the class or any other type. This does not require the creation of a class instance. Static members are declared using the static modifier.

```
public class Foo {
    public static void doSomething() {
    }
}


// Calling the static method
Foo.doSomething();
```

Modifiers

Modifiers are keywords used to modify declarations of types and type members. Most notably there is a sub-group containing the access modifiers.

- abstract - Specifies that a class only serves as a base class and cannot be instantiated.

- static - Used only for member classes, specifies that the member class does not belong to a specific instance of the containing class.

- final - Classes marked as final cannot be extended from and cannot have any subclasses.

- strictfp - Specifies that all floating-point operations must be carried out conforming to IEEE 754 and forbids using enhanced precision to store intermediate results.

Access Modifiers

The *access modifiers*, or *inheritance modifiers*, set the accessibility of classes, methods, and other members. Members marked as public can be reached from anywhere. If a class or its member does not have any modifiers, default access is assumed.

```
public class Foo {

    int go() {

        return 0;

    }


    private class Bar {

    }

}
```

The following table shows whether code within a class has access to the class or method depending on the accessing class location and the modifier for the accessed class or class member:

Modifier	Same class or nested class	Other class inside the same package	Extended Class inside another package	Non-extended inside another package
private	yes	no	no	no
default (package private)	yes	yes	no	no
protected	yes	yes	yes	no
public	yes	yes	yes	yes

Constructors and Initializers

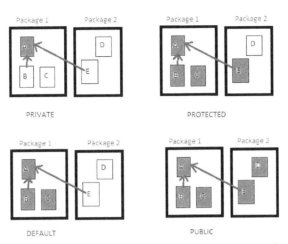

This image describes the class member scope within classes and packages.

A constructor is a special method called when an object is initialized. Its purpose is to initialize the members of the object. The main differences between constructors and ordinary methods are that constructors are called only when an instance of the class is created and never return anything. Constructors are declared as common methods, but they are named after the class and no return type is specified:

```java
class Foo {

    String str;


    Foo() { // Constructor with no arguments


        // Initialization

    }


    Foo(String str) { // Constructor with one argument
        this.str = str;

    }

}
```

Initializers are blocks of code that are executed when a class or an instance of a class is created. There are two kinds of initializers, *static initializers* and *instance initializers*.

Static initializers initialize static fields when the class is created. They are declared using the static keyword:

```java
class Foo {

    static {
```

```
        // Initialization

    }

}
```

A class is created only once. Therefore, static initializers are not called more than once. On the contrary, instance initializers are automatically called before the call to a constructor every time an instance of the class is created. Unlike constructors instance initializers cannot take any arguments and generally they cannot throw any checked exceptions (except in several special cases). Instance initializers are declared in a block without any keywords:

```
class Foo {

    {

        // Initialization

    }

}
```

Since Java has a garbage collection mechanism, there are no destructors. However, every object has a finalize() method called prior to garbage collection, which can be overridden to implement finalization.

Methods

All the statements in Java must reside within methods. Methods are similar to functions except they belong to classes. A method has a return value, a name and usually some parameters initialized when it is called with some arguments. Similar to C++, methods returning nothing have return type declared as void. Unlike in C++, methods in Java are not allowed to have default argument values and methods are usually overloaded instead.

```
class Foo {

    int bar(int a, int b) {

        return (a*2) + b;

    }


    /* Overloaded method with the same name but different set of ar-
guments */

    int bar(int a) {

        return a*2;

    }

}
```

A method is called using . notation on an object, or in the case of a static method, also on the name of a class.

```
Foo foo = new Foo();

int result = foo.bar(7, 2); // Non-static method is called on foo


int finalResult = Math.abs(result); // Static method call
```

The throws keyword indicates that a method throws an exception. All checked exceptions must be listed in a comma-separated list.

```
void openStream() throws IOException, myException { // Indicates that
IOException may be thrown

}
```

Lambda Expressions

```
(variables) -> {body}

variable -> body_with_one_statement

(type variable) -> {}
```

Modifiers

- abstract - Abstract methods can be present only in abstract classes, such methods have no body and must be overridden in a subclass unless it is abstract itself.

- static - Makes the method static and accessible without creation of a class instance. However static methods cannot access non-static members in the same class.

- final - Declares that the method cannot be overridden in a subclass.

- native - Indicates that this method is implemented through JNI in platform-dependent code. Actual implementation happens outside Java code, and such methods have no body.

- strictfp - Declares strict conformance to IEEE 754 in carrying out floating-point operations.

- synchronized - Declares that a thread executing this method must acquire monitor. For synchronized methods the monitor is the class instance or java.lang.Class if the method is static.

- Access modifiers - Identical to those used with classes.

Varargs

This language feature was introduced in J2SE 5.0. The last argument of the method may be declared as a variable arity parameter, in which case the method becomes a variable arity method (as opposed to fixed arity methods) or simply varargs method. This allows one to pass a variable number of values, of the declared type, to the method as parameters - including no parameters. These values will be available inside the method as an array.

```
void printReport(String header, int... numbers) { //numbers represents
varargs

    System.out.println(header);

    for (int num : numbers) {

        System.out.println(num);

    }

}
```

```
// Calling varargs method
printReport("Report data", 74, 83, 25, 96);
```

Fields

Fields, or class variables, can be declared inside the class body to store data.

```
class Foo {

    double bar;

}
```

Fields can be initialized directly when declared.

```
class Foo {

    double bar = 2.3;

}
```

Modifiers

- static - Makes the field a static member.

- final - Allows the field to be initialized only once in a constructor or inside initialization block or during its declaration, whichever is earlier.

- transient - Indicates that this field will not be stored during serialization.

- volatile - If a field is declared volatile, it is ensured that all threads a consistent value for the variable.

Inheritance

Classes in Java can only inherit from *one* class. A class can be derived from any class that is not marked as final. Inheritance is declared using the extendskeyword. A class can reference itself using the this keyword and its direct superclass using the super keyword.

```
class Foo {
```

```
}


class Foobar extends Foo {


}
```

If a class does not specify its superclass, it implicitly inherits from java.lang.Object class. Thus all classes in Java are subclasses of Objectclass.

If the superclass does not have a constructor without parameters the subclass must specify in its constructors what constructor of the superclass to use. For example:

```
class Foo {
    public Foo(int n) {
        // Do something with n
    }
}


class Foobar extends Foo {
    private int number;
    // Superclass does not have constructor without parameters
    // so we have to specify what constructor of our superclass to use
and how


    public Foobar(int number) {
        super(number);
        this.number = number;
    }
}
```

Overriding Methods

Unlike C++, all non-final methods in Java are virtual and can be overridden by the inheriting classes.

```
class Operation {
    public int doSomething() {
        return 0;
```

```
        }
}


class NewOperation extends Operation {
    @Override
    public int doSomething() {
        return 1;
    }
}
```

Abstract Classes

An Abstract Class is a class that is incomplete, or to be considered incomplete. Normal classes may have abstract methods, that is, methods that are declared but not yet implemented, only if they are abstract classes. A class C has abstract methods if any of the following is true:

- C explicitly contains a declaration of an abstract method.

- Any of C's superclasses has an abstract method and C neither declares nor inherits a method that implements it.

- A direct superinterface of C declares or inherits a method (which is therefore necessarily abstract) and C neither declares nor inherits a method that implements it.

- A subclass of an abstract class that is not itself abstract may be instantiated, resulting in the execution of a constructor for the abstract class and, therefore, the execution of the field initializers for instance variables of that class.

```
package org.dwwwp.test;


/**
 * @author jcrypto
 */
public class AbstractClass {
    private static final String hello;

    static {
        System.out.println(AbstractClass.class.getName() + ": static
block runtime");
        hello = "hello from " + AbstractClass.class.getName();
    }
```

```
    {
        System.out.println(AbstractClass.class.getName() + ": instance
block runtime");
    }


    public AbstractClass() {
            System.out.println(AbstractClass.class.getName() + ": con-
structor runtime");
    }


    public static void hello() {
        System.out.println(hello);
    }
}
package org.dwwwp.test;


/**
 * @author jcrypto
 */
public class CustomClass extends AbstractClass {

    static {
            System.out.println(CustomClass.class.getName() + ": static
block runtime");
    }


    {
        System.out.println(CustomClass.class.getName() + ": instance
block runtime");
    }


    public CustomClass() {
        System.out.println(CustomClass.class.getName() + ": construc-
tor runtime");
```

```
    }

    public static void main(String[] args) {
        CustomClass nc = new CustomClass();
        hello();
        //AbstractClass.hello();//also valid
    }
}
```

Output:

```
org.dwwwp.test.AbstractClass: static block runtime
org.dwwwp.test.CustomClass: static block runtime
org.dwwwp.test.AbstractClass: instance block runtime
org.dwwwp.test.AbstractClass: constructor runtime
org.dwwwp.test.CustomClass: instance block runtime
org.dwwwp.test.CustomClass: constructor runtime
hello from org.dwwwp.test.AbstractClass
```

Enumerations

This language feature was introduced in J2SE 5.0. Technically enumerations are a kind of class containing enum constants in its body. Each enum constant defines an instance of the enum type. Enumeration classes cannot be instantiated anywhere except in the enumeration class itself.

```
enum Season {
    WINTER, SPRING, SUMMER, AUTUMN
}
```

Enum constants are allowed to have constructors, which are called when the class is loaded:

```
public enum Season {
    WINTER("Cold"), SPRING("Warmer"), SUMMER("Hot"), AUTUMN("Cooler");

    Season(String description) {
        this.description = description;
    }
```

```
    private final String description;

    public String getDescription() {
        return description;
    }
}
```

Enumerations can have class bodies, in which case they are treated like anonymous classes extending the enum class:

```
public enum Season {
    WINTER {
        String getDescription() {return "cold";}
    },
    SPRING {
        String getDescription() {return "warmer";}
    },
    SUMMER {
        String getDescription() {return "hot";}
    },
    FALL {
        String getDescription() {return "cooler";}
    };
}
```

Interfaces

Interfaces are data structures that contain member definitions and not actual implementation. They are useful to define a contract between members in different types that have different implementations. Every interface is implicitly abstract. The only modifier allowed to use with interfaces apart from access modifiers is strictfp, which has the same effect as for classes.

```
interface ActionListener {
    int ACTION_ADD = 0;
    int ACTION_REMOVE = 1;

    void actionSelected(int action);
}
```

Implementing an Interface

An interface is implemented by a class using the implements keyword. It is allowed to implement more than one interface, in which case they are written after implements keyword in a comma-separated list. Class implementing an interface must override all its methods, otherwise it must be declared as abstract.

```
interface RequestListener {

        int requestReceived();

}


class ActionHandler implements ActionListener, RequestListener {
    public void actionSelected(int action) {

    }


    public int requestReceived() {

    }
}


//Calling method defined by interface
RequestListener listener = new ActionHandler(); /*ActionHandler can
be

                                represented as RequestListener...*/
listener.requestReceived(); /*...and thus is known to implement
                            requestReceived() method*/
```

Inheritance

Interfaces can inherit from other interfaces just like classes. Unlike classes it is allowed to inherit from multiple interfaces. However, it is possible that several interfaces have a field with the same name, in which case it becomes a single ambiguous member, which cannot be accessed.

```
/* Class implementing this interface must implement methods of both
ActionListener and RequestListener */
interface EventListener extends ActionListener, RequestListener {


}
```

Annotations

Annotations in Java are a way to embed metadata into code. This language feature was introduced in J2SE 5.0.

Annotation Types

Java has a set of predefined annotation types, but it is allowed to define new ones. An annotation type declaration is a special type of an interface declaration. They are declared in the same way as the interfaces, except the interface keyword is preceded by the @ sign. All annotations are implicitly extended from java.lang.annotation.Annotation and cannot be extended from anything else.

```
@interface BlockingOperations {

}
```

Annotations may have the same declarations in the body as the common interfaces, in addition they are allowed to include enums and annotations. The main difference is that abstract method declarations must not have any parameters or throw any exceptions. Also they may have a default value, which is declared using the default keyword after the method name:

```
@interface BlockingOperations {

    boolean fileSystemOperations();

    boolean networkOperations() default false;

}
```

Usage of Annotations

Annotations may be used in any kind of declaration, whether it is package, class (including enums), interface (including annotations), field, method, parameter, constructor, or local variable. Also they can be used with enum constants. Annotations are declared using the @ sign preceding annotation type name, after which element-value pairs are written inside brackets. All elements with no default value must be assigned a value.

```
@BlockingOperations(/*mandatory*/ fileSystemOperations,
/*optional*/ networkOperations = true)
void openOutputStream() { //Annotated method

}
```

Besides the generic form, there are two other forms to declare an annotation, which are shorthands. *Marker annotation* is a short form, it is used when no values are assigned to elements:

```
@Unused // Shorthand for @Unused()
void travelToJupiter() {

}
```

The other short form is called *single element annotation*. It is used with annotations types containing only one element or in the case when multiple elements are present, but only one elements lacks a default value. In single element annotation form the element name is omitted and only value is written instead:

```
/* Equivalent for @BlockingOperations(fileSystemOperations = true).
networkOperations has a default value and
does not have to be assigned a value */


@BlockingOperations(true)
void openOutputStream() {
}
```

Generics

Generics, or parameterized types, or parametric polymorphism is one of the major features introduced in J2SE 5.0. Before generics were introduced, it was required to declare all the types explicitly. With generics it became possible to work in a similar manner with different types without declaring the exact types. The main purpose of generics is to ensure type safety and to detect runtime errors during compilation. Unlike C#, information on the used parameters is not available at runtime due to type erasure.

Generic Classes

Classes can be parameterized by adding a type variable inside angle brackets (<and >) following the class name. It makes possible the use of this type variable in class members instead of actual types. There can be more than one type variable, in which case they are declared in a comma-separated list.

It is possible to limit a type variable to a subtype of some specific class or declare an interface that must be implemented by the type. In this case the type variable is appended by the extends keyword followed by a name of the class or the interface. If the variable is constrained by both class and interface or if there are several interfaces, the class name is written first, followed by interface names with & sign used as the delimiter.

```
/* This class has two type variables, T and V. T must be
a subtype of ArrayList and implement Formattable interface */
public class Mapper<T extends ArrayList & Formattable, V> {
    public void add(T array, V item) {
        // array has add method because it is an ArrayList subclass
        array.add(item);
    }
}
```

When a variable of a parameterized type is declared or an instance is created, its type is written exactly in the same format as in the class header, except the actual type is written in the place of the type variable declaration.

```
/* Mapper is created with CustomList as T and Integer as V.

CustomList must be a subclass of ArrayList and implement Formattable
*/

Mapper<CustomList, Integer> mapper = new Mapper<CustomList, Integer>();
```

Since Java SE 7, it is possible to use a diamond (<>) in place of type arguments, in which case the latter will be inferred. The following code in Java SE 7 is equivalent to the code in the previous example:

```
Mapper<CustomList, Integer> mapper = new Mapper<>();
```

When declaring a variable for a parameterized type, it is possible to use wildcards instead of explicit type names. Wildcards are expressed by writing ? sign instead of the actual type. It is possible to limit possible types to the subclasses or superclasses of some specific class by writing the extends keyword or the super keyword correspondingly followed by the class name.

```
/* Any Mapper instance with CustomList as the first parameter

may be used regardless of the second one.*/

Mapper<CustomList, ?> mapper;

mapper = new Mapper<CustomList, Boolean>();

mapper = new Mapper<CustomList, Integer>();


/* Will not accept types that use anything but

a subclass of Number as the second parameter */

void addMapper(Mapper<?, ? extends Number> mapper) {

}
```

Generic Methods and Constructors

Usage of generics may be limited to some particular methods, this concept applies to constructors as well. To declare a parameterized method, type variables are written before the return type of the method in the same format as for the generic classes. In the case of constructor, type variables are declared before the constructor name.

```
class Mapper {
        // The class itself is not generic, the constructor is
        <T, V> Mapper(T array, V item) {
```

```
        }
    }


    /* This method will accept only arrays of the same type as
    the searched item type or its subtype*/
    static <T, V extends T> boolean contains(T item, V[] arr) {
        for (T currentItem : arr) {
            if (item.equals(currentItem)) {
                return true;
            }
        }
        return false;
    }
```

Generic Interfaces

Interfaces can be parameterized in the similar manner as the classes.

```
    interface Expandable<T extends Number> {
        void addItem(T item);
    }


    // This class is parameterized
    class Array<T extends Number> implements Expandable<T> {
        void addItem(T item) {
        }
    }


    // And this is not and uses an explicit type instead
    class IntegerArray implements Expandable<Integer> {
        void addItem(Integer item) {
        }
    }
```

Java Concurrency

Back in the old days a computer had a single CPU, and was only capable of executing a single program at a time. Later came multitasking which meant that computers could execute multiple programs (AKA tasks or processes) at the same time. It wasn't really "at the same time" though. The single CPU was shared between the programs. The operating system would switch between the programs running, executing each of them for a little while before switching.

Along with multitasking came new challenges for software developers. Programs can no longer assume to have all the CPU time available, nor all memory or any other computer resources. A "good citizen" program should release all resources it is no longer using, so other programs can use them.

Later yet came multithreading which mean that you could have multiple threads of execution inside the same program. A thread of execution can be thought of as a CPU executing the program. When you have multiple threads executing the same program, it is like having multiple CPUs execute within the same program.

Multithreading can be a great way to increase the performance of some types of programs. However, mulithreading is even more challenging than multitasking. The threads are executing within the same program and are hence reading and writing the same memory simultanously. This can result in errors not seen in a singlethreaded program. Some of these errors may not be seen on single CPU machines, because two threads never really execute "simultanously". Modern computers, though, come with multi core CPUs, and even with multiple CPUs too. This means that separate threads can be executed by separate cores or CPUs simultanously.

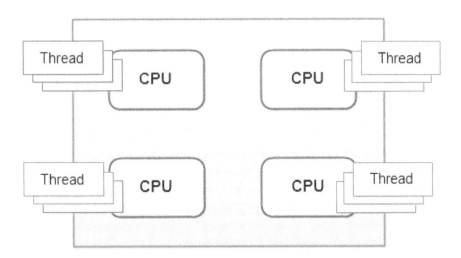

If a thread reads a memory location the second thread? Or a value that is a mix between the two? Or, if two threads are writing to the same memory location simultanously, what value will be left when they are done? The value written by the first thread? The value written by the second thread? Or a mix of the two values written?

Without proper precautions any of these outcomes are possible. The behaviour would not even be predictable. The outcome could change from time to time. Therefore it is important as a developer to know how to take the right precautions - meaning learning to control how threads access shared resources like memory, files, databases etc. That is one of the topics this Java concurrency tutorial addresses.

Java was one of the first languages to make multithreading easily available to developers. Java had multithreading capabilities from the very beginning. Therefore, Java developers often face the problems described above.

Concurrency

Computer users take it for granted that their systems can do more than one thing at a time. They assume that they can continue to work in a word processor, while other applications download files, manage the print queue, and stream audio. Even a single application is often expected to do more than one thing at a time. For example, that streaming audio application must simultaneously read the digital audio off the network, decompress it, manage playback, and update its display. Even the word processor should always be ready to respond to keyboard and mouse events, no matter how busy it is reformatting text or updating the display. Software that can do such things is known as concurrent software.

The Java platform is designed from the ground up to support concurrent programming, with basic concurrency support in the Java programming language and the Java class libraries. Since version 5.0, the Java platform has also included high-level concurrency APIs.

Processes and Threads

Most implementations of the Java virtual machine run as a single process and in the Java programming language, concurrent programming is mostly concerned with threads (also called lightweight processes). Multiple processes can only be realized with multiple JVMs.

Thread Objects

Threads share the process's resources, including memory and open files. This makes for efficient, but potentially problematic, communication. Every application has at least one thread called the main thread. The main thread has the ability to create additional threads as Runnable or Callable objects. (The Callableinterface is similar to Runnable, in that both are designed for classes whose instances are potentially executed by another thread. A Runnable, however, does not return a result and cannot throw a checked exception.)

Each thread can be scheduled on a different CPU core or use time-slicing on a single hardware processor, or time-slicing on many hardware processors. There is no generic solution to how Java threads are mapped to native OS threads. Every JVM implementation can do it in a different way.

Each thread is associated with an instance of the class Thread. Threads can be managed either directly using Thread objects or using abstract mechanisms such as Executors and java.util.concurrent collections.

Starting a Thread

Two ways to start a thread:

- Provide a Runnable Object

```java
public class HelloRunnable implements Runnable {

    @Override
    public void run() {

        System.out.println("Hello from thread!");

    }
    public static void main(String[] args) {

        (new Thread(new HelloRunnable())).start();

    }

}
```

- Subclass Thread

```java
public class HelloThread extends Thread {

    @Override
    public void run() {

        System.out.println("Hello from thread!");

    }
    public static void main(String[] args) {

        (new HelloThread()).start();

    }

}
```

Interrupts

An interrupt is an indication to a thread that it should stop what it is doing and do something else. A thread sends an interrupt by invoking interrupt on the Thread object for the thread to be interrupted. The interrupt mechanism is implemented using an internal flag known as the interrupt status. Invoking Thread.interruptsets this flag. By convention, any method that exits by throwing an InterruptedException clears interrupt status when it does so. However, it's always possible that interrupt status will immediately be set again, by another thread invoking interrupt.

Joins

The Thread.join methods allow one thread to wait for the completion of another.

Exceptions

Uncaught exceptions thrown by code will terminate the thread. The main thread prints exceptions to the console, but user-created threads need a handler registered to do so.

Memory Model

The Java memory model describes how threads in the Java programming language interact through memory. On modern platforms, code is frequently not executed in the order it was written. It is reordered by the compiler, the processorand the memory subsystem to achieve maximum performance. The Java programming language does not guarantee linearizability, or even sequential consistency, when reading or writing fields of shared objects, and this is to allow for compiler optimizations (such as register allocation, common subexpression elimination, and redundant read elimination) all of which work by reordering memory reads—writes.

Synchronization

Threads communicate primarily by sharing access to fields and the objects that reference fields refer to. This form of communication is extremely efficient, but makes two kinds of errors possible: thread interference and memory consistency errors. The tool needed to prevent these errors is synchronization.

Reorderings can come into play in incorrectly synchronized multithreadedprograms, where one thread is able to observe the effects of other threads, and may be able to detect that variable accesses become visible to other threads in a different order than executed or specified in the program. Most of the time, one thread doesn't care what the other is doing. But when it does, that's what synchronization is for.

To synchronize threads, Java uses monitors, which are a high-level mechanism for allowing only one thread at a time to execute a region of code protected by the monitor. The behavior of monitors is explained in terms of locks; there is a lock associated with each object.

Synchronization has several aspects. The most well-understood is mutual exclusion—only one thread can hold a monitor at once, so synchronizing on a monitor means that once one thread enters a synchronized block protected by a monitor, no other thread can enter a block protected by that monitor until the first thread exits the synchronized block.

But there is more to synchronization than mutual exclusion. Synchronization ensures that memory writes by a thread before or during a synchronized block are made visible in a predictable manner to other threads which synchronize on the same monitor. After we exit a synchronized block, we release the monitor, which has the effect of flushing the cache to main memory, so that writes made by this thread can be visible to other threads. Before we can enter a synchronized block, we acquire the monitor, which has the effect of invalidating the local processor cache so that variables will be reloaded from main memory. We will then be able to see all of the writes made visible by the previous release.

Reads—writes to fields are linearizable if either the field is volatile, or the field is protected by a unique lock which is acquired by all readers and writers.

Locks and Synchronized Blocks

A thread can achieve mutual exclusion either by entering a synchronized block or method, which acquires an implicit lock, or by acquiring an explicit lock (such as the ReentrantLock from the java. util.concurrent.locks package). Both approaches have the same implications for memory behavior. If all accesses to a particular field are protected by the same lock, then reads—writes to that field are linearizable (atomic).

Volatile Fields

When applied to a field, the Java volatile guarantees that:

1. *(In all versions of Java)* There is a global ordering on the reads and writes to a volatile variable. This implies that every thread accessing a volatile field will read its current value before continuing, instead of (potentially) using a cached value. (However, there is no guarantee about the relative ordering of volatile reads and writes with regular reads and writes, meaning that it's generally not a useful threading construct.)

2. *(In Java 5 or later)* Volatile reads and writes establish a happens-before relationship, much like acquiring and releasing a mutex. This relationship is simply a guarantee that memory writes by one specific statement are visible to another specific statement.

Volatile fields are linearizable. Reading a volatile field is like acquiring a lock: the working memory is invalidated and the volatile field's current value is reread from memory. Writing a volatile field is like releasing a lock: the volatile field is immediately written back to memory.

Final Fields

A field declared to be final cannot be modified once it has been initialized. An object's final fields are initialized in its constructor. If the constructor follows certain simple rules, then the correct value of any final fields will be visible to other threads without synchronization. The rule is simple: the this reference must not be released from the constructor before the constructor returns.

Real Time Java

Use of the Java language in real-time systems isn't widespread for a number of significant reasons. These include the nondeterministic performance effects inherent in the Java language's design, such as dynamic class loading, and in the Java Runtime Environment (JRE) itself, such as the garbage collector and native code compilation. The Real-time Specification for Java (RTSJ) is an open specification that augments the Java language to open the door more widely to using the language to build real-time systems . Implementing the RTSJ requires support in the operating system, the JRE, and the Java Class Library (JCL).

Real-time Requirements

Real-time (RT) is a broad term used to describe applications that have real-world timing requirements. For example, a sluggish user interface doesn't satisfy an average user's generic RT requirements. This type of application is often described as a *soft* RT application. The same requirement might be more explicitly phrased as "the application should not take more than 0.1 seconds to respond to a mouse click." If the requirement isn't met, it's a soft failure: the application can continue, and the user, though unhappy, can still use it. In contrast, applications that must strictly meet real-world timing requirements are typically called *hard* RT applications. An application controlling the rudder of an airplane, for example, must not be delayed for any reason because the result could be catastrophic. What it means to be an RT application depends in large part on how tolerant the application can be to faults in the form of missed timing requirements.

Another key aspect of RT requirements is response time. It's critical for programmers writing hard or soft RT applications to understand the response-time constraint. The techniques required to meet a hard 1-microsecond response are significantly different from those required to meet a hard 100-millisecond response. In practice, achieving response times below tens of microseconds requires a combination of custom hardware and software, possibly with no -- or a very thin -- operating-system layer.

Finally, designers of robust RT applications typically need some quantifiable level of deterministic performance characteristics in order to architect an application to meet the response-time requirements. Unpredictable performance effects large enough to impact a system's ability to meet an application's response-time requirements make it difficult and maybe even impossible to architect that application properly. The designers of most RT execution environments devote considerable effort to reducing nondeterministic performance effects to meet the response-time needs of the broadest possible spectrum of RT applications.

Challenges for RT Java Applications

Standard Java applications running on a general-purpose JVM on a general-purpose operating system can only hope to meet soft RT requirements at the level of hundreds of milliseconds. Several fundamental aspects of the language are responsible: thread management, class loading, Just-in-time (JIT) compiler activity, and garbage collection (GC). Some of these issues can be mitigated by application designers, but only with significant work.

Thread Management

Standard Java provides no guarantees for thread scheduling or thread priorities. An application that must respond to events in a well-defined time has no way to ensure that another low-priority thread won't get scheduled in front of a high-priority thread. To compensate, a programmer would need to partition an application into a set of applications that the operating system can then run at different priorities. This partitioning would increase the overhead of these events and make communication between the events far more challenging.

Class Loading

A Java-conformant JVM must delay loading a class until it's first referenced by a program. Loading a class can take a variable amount of time depending on the speed of the medium (disk or other) the class is loaded from, the class's size, and the overhead incurred by the class loaders themselves. The delay to load a class can commonly be as high as 10 milliseconds. If tens or hundreds of classes need to be loaded, the loading time itself can cause a significant and possibly unexpected delay. Careful application design can be used to load all classes at application start-up, but this must be done manually because the Java language specification doesn't let the JVM perform this step early.

Historically, garbage collections are performed while the application program is halted, a process coined Stop-the-world (STW). During a collection, the live objects are traced by starting from a set of "root" objects (those pointed to by static fields, objects that are currently live in some thread's stack, and so on) and then sweeping unused memory back onto a free list to be used for later allocation requests.

With a STW garbage collector, the application program experiences a GC as a pause in program operation. These STW pauses are unbounded in length and are typically quite intrusive, ranging from hundreds of milliseconds to several seconds. The length of a pause depends on the heap size, the amount of live data in the heap, and how aggressively the collector tries to reclaim free memory.

Many modern collectors use techniques, such as concurrent and incremental algorithms, to help reduce these pause times. But even with these techniques, GC pauses can still occur at indeterminate times with unbounded duration.

Garbage Collection

The benefits of GC to application development -- including pointer safety, leak avoidance, and freeing developers from needing to write custom memory-management tooling -- are well documented. However, GC is another source of frustration for hard RT programmers using the Java language. Garbage collects occur automatically when the Java heap has been exhausted to the point that an allocation request can't be satisfied. The application itself can also trigger a collection.

On the one hand, GC is a great thing for Java programmers. Errors introduced by the need to manage memory explicitly in languages such as C and C++ are some of the most difficult problems to diagnose. Proving the absence of such errors when an application is deployed is also a fundamental challenge. One of the Java programming model's major strengths is that the JVM, not the application, performs memory management, which eliminates this burden for the application programmer.

On the other hand, traditional garbage collectors can introduce long delays at times that are virtually impossible for the application programmer to predict. Delays of several hundred milliseconds are not unusual. The only way to solve this problem at the application level is to prevent GC by creating a set of objects that are reused, thereby ensuring that the Java heap memory is never exhausted. In other words, programmers solve this problem by throwing away the benefits of the managed memory by explicitly managing memory themselves. In practice, this approach generally fails because it prevents programmers from using many of the class libraries provided in the JDK and by other class vendors, which likely create many temporary objects that eventually fill up the heap.

Compilation

Compiling Java code to native code introduces a similar problem to class loading. Most modern JVMs initially interpret Java methods and, for only those methods that execute frequently, later compile to native code. Delayed compiling results in fast start-up and reduces the amount of compilation performed during an application's execution. But performing a task with interpreted code and performing it with compiled code can take significantly different amounts of time. For a hard RT application, the inability to predict when the compilation will occur introduces too much nondeterminism to make it possible to plan the application's activities effectively. As with class loading, this problem can be mitigated by using the Compiler class to compile methods programmatically at application start-up, but maintaining such a list of methods is tedious and error prone.

Real-Time Specification for Java

The Real-Time Specification for Java (RTSJ) is a set of interfaces and behavioral refinements that enable real-time computer programming in the Java programming language. RTSJ 1.0 was developed as JSR 1 under the Java Community Process, which approved the new standard in November, 2001. RTSJ 2.0 is being developed under JSR 282.

The RTSJ was created to address some of the limitations of the Java language that prevent its widespread use in RT execution environments. The RTSJ addresses several problematic areas, including scheduling, memory management, threading, synchronization, time, clocks, and asynchronous event handling.

Scheduling

RT systems need to control strictly how threads are scheduled and guarantee that they're scheduled deterministically: that is, that threads are scheduled the same way given the same set of conditions. Although the JCL defines the concept of thread priority, a traditional JVM is not required to enforce priorities. Also, non-RT Java implementations typically use a round-robin preemptive scheduling approach with unpredictable scheduling order. With the RTSJ, true priorities and a fixed-priority preemptive scheduler with priority-inheritance support is required for RT threads. This scheduling approach ensures that the highest-priority active thread will always be executing and it continues to execute until it voluntarily releases the CPU or is preempted by a higher-priority thread. Priority inheritance ensures that priority inversion is avoided when a higher-priority thread needs a resource held by a lower-priority thread. Priority inversion is a significant problem for RT systems, as we'll describe in more detail in RT Linux®.

Memory Management

Although some RT systems can tolerate delays resulting from the garbage collector, in many cases these delays are unacceptable. To support tasks that cannot tolerate GC interruptions, the RTSJ defines immortal and scoped memory areas to supplement the standard Java heap. These areas allow tasks to use memory without being required to block if the garbage collector needs to free memory in the heap. Objects allocated in the immortal memory area are accessible to all threads and are never collected. Because it is never collected, immortal memory is a limited resource that must be used carefully. Scope memory areas can be created and destroyed under programmer control. Each scope memory area is allocated with a maximum size and can be used for object allocation. To ensure the integrity of references between objects, the RTSJ defines rules that govern how objects in one memory area (heap, immortal, or scope) can refer to objects in other memory areas. More rules define when the objects in a scope memory are finalized and when the memory area can be reused. Because of these complexities, the recommended use of immortal and scoped memory is limited to components that cannot tolerate GC pauses.

Threads

The RTSJ adds support for two new thread classes that provide the basis for executing tasks with RT behaviour: RealtimeThread and NoHeapRealtimeThread (NHRT). These classes provide support for priorities, periodic behaviour, deadlines with handlers that can be triggered when the deadline is exceeded, and the use of memory areas other than the heap. NHRTs cannot access the heap and so, unlike other types of threads, NHRTs are mostly not interrupted or preempted by GC. RT systems typically use NHRTs with high priorities for tasks with the tightest latency requirements, RealtimeThreads for tasks with latency requirements that can be accommodated by a garbage collector, and regular Java threads for everything else. Because NHRTs cannot access the heap, using these threads requires a high degree of care. For example, even the use of container classes from the standard JCL must be carefully managed so that the container class doesn't unintentionally create temporary or internal objects on the heap.

Synchronization

Synchronization must be carefully managed within a RT system to prevent high-priority threads from waiting for lower-priority threads. The RTSJ includes priority-inheritance support to manage synchronization when it occurs, and it provides the ability for threads to communicate without synchronization via wait-free read and write queues.

Time and Clocks

RT systems need higher-resolution clocks than those provided by standard Java code. The new HighResolutionTime and Clock classes encapsulate these time services.

Asynchronous Event Handling

RT systems often manage and respond to asynchronous events. The RTSJ includes support for handling asynchronous events triggered by a number of sources including timers, operating-system signals, missed deadlines, and other application-defined events.

Deterministic Parallel Java

The advent of multicore processors demands parallel programming by mainstream programmers. The dominant model of concurrency today, multithreaded shared memory programming, is inherently complex due to the number of possible thread interleavings that can cause nondeterministic program behaviors. This nondeterminism causes subtle bugs: data races, atomicity violations, and deadlocks. The parallel programmer today prunes away the nondeterminism using constructs such as locks and semaphores, then debugs the program to eliminate the symptoms. This task is tedious, error prone, and extremely challenging even with good debugging tools.

The irony is that a vast number of computational algorithms (though not all) are in fact deterministic: a given input is always expected to produce the same output. Almost all scientific computing, encryption/decryption, sorting, compiler and program analysis, and processor simulation algorithms exhibit deterministic behavior. Today's parallel programming models force programmers to implement such algorithms in a nondeterministic notation and then convince themselves that the behavior will be deterministic. By contrast, a deterministic-by-default programming model can guarantee that any legal program produces the same externally visible results in all executions with a particular input unless nondeterministic behavior is explicitly requested by the programmer in disciplined ways. Such a model can make parallel application development and maintenance easier for several reasons. Programmers do not have to reason about notoriously subtle and difficult issues such as data races, deadlocks, and memory models. They can start with a sequential implementation and incrementally add parallelism, secure in the knowledge that the program behavior will remain unchanged. They can use familiar sequential tools for debugging and testing. Importantly, they can test an application only once for each input.

Ensuring that Java programmers aren't left out in the cold, parallel programming wise, computer scientists have developed Deterministic Parallel Java, a parallel programming language that guarantees deterministic semantics without run-time checks for general-purpose, object-oriented programs.

Researchers at the Universal Parallel Computing Research Center at the University of Illinois claim that Deterministic Parallel Java (DPJ) is the first language to use compile-time type checking for parallel operations on arrays of references ("pointers") to objects, and the first language to use regions and effects for flexible, nested data structures. On top of this, they claims that DPJ is the first language to guarantee deterministic use of object-oriented parallel frameworks, and the first language to allow safe mixing of deterministic and non-deterministic code.

DPJ is intended to simplify debugging and testing of parallel software as all potential data races are caught at compile-time. Because DPJ programs have obvious sequential semantics, all debugging and testing of DPJ code can happen essentially like that for sequential programs. Maintenance becomes easier as DPJ encodes the programmer's knowledge of parallel data sharing patterns in DPJ annotations — simplifying the tasks of understanding, modifying, and extending parallel DPJ software. Moreover, thanks to the same program annotations, each function or class can be understood and parallelized in a modular fashion, without knowing internal parallelism or synchronization details of other functions or classes.

Java Virtual Machine

JVM is short for Java Virtual Machine. JVM is an abstract computing machine, or virtual machine. It is a platform-independent execution environment that converts Java bytecode into machine language and executes it. Most programming languages compile source code directly into machine code that is designed to run on a specific microprocessor architecture or operating system, such as Windows or UNIX.

JVM -- a machine within a machine -- mimics a real Java processor, enabling Java bytecode to be executed as actions or operating system calls on any processor regardless of the operating system. For example, establishing a socket connection from a workstation to a remote machine involves an operating system call. Since different operating systems handle sockets in different ways, the JVM translates the programming code so that the two machines that may be on different platforms are able to connect.

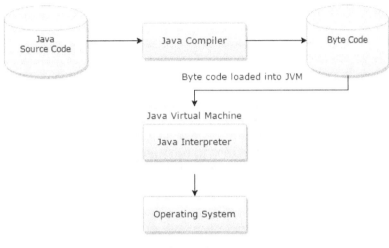

Diagram of JVM

JVM is:

1. A specification where working of Java Virtual Machine is specified. But implementation provider is independent to choose the algorithm. Its implementation has been provided by Sun and other companies.

2. Its implementation is known as JRE (Java Runtime Environment).

3. Runtime Instance Whenever you write java command on the command prompt to run the java class, an instance of JVM is created.

JVM Specification

The Java virtual machine is an abstract (virtual) computer defined by a specification. This specification omits implementation details that are not essential to ensure interoperability: the memory layout of run-time data areas, the garbage-collection algorithm used, and any internal optimization of the Java virtual machine instructions (their translation into machine code). The main reason for this omission is to not unnecessarily constrain implementers. Any Java application can be run only inside some concrete implementation of the abstract specification of the Java virtual machine.

Starting with Java Platform, Standard Edition (J2SE) 5.0, changes to the JVM specification have been developed under the Java Community Process as JSR 924. As of 2006, changes to specification to support changes proposed to the class file format (JSR 202) are being done as a maintenance release of JSR 924. The specification for the JVM was published as the *blue book*, The preface states:

> We intend that this specification should sufficiently document the Java Virtual Machine to make possible compatible clean-room implementations. Oracle provides tests that verify the proper operation of implementations of the Java Virtual Machine.

One of Oracle's JVMs is named HotSpot, the other, inherited from BEA Systems is JRockit. Clean-room Java implementations include Kaffe and IBM J9. Oracle owns the Java trademark and may allow its use to certify implementation suites as fully compatible with Oracle's specification.

Class Loader

One of the organizational units of JVM byte code is a class. A class loader implementation must be able to recognize and load anything that conforms to the Java class file format. Any implementation is free to recognize other binary forms besides *class* files, but it must recognize *class* files.

The class loader performs three basic activities in this strict order:

1. Loading: finds and imports the binary data for a type

2. Linking: performs verification, preparation, and (optionally) resolution

    o   Verification: ensures the correctness of the imported type

    o   Preparation: allocates memory for class variables and initializing the memory to default values

    o   Resolution: transforms symbolic references from the type into direct references.

3. Initialization: invokes Java code that initializes class variables to their proper starting values.

In general, there are two types of class loader: bootstrap class loader and user defined class loader.

Every Java virtual machine implementation must have a bootstrap class loader, capable of loading trusted classes. The Java virtual machine specification doesn't specify how a class loader should locate classes.

Virtual Machine Architecture

The JVM operates on primitive values (integers and floating-point numbers) and references. The JVM is fundamentally a 32-bit machine. long and doubletypes, which are 64-bits, are supported natively, but consume two units of storage in a frame's local variables or operand stack, since each unit is 32 bits. boolean, byte, short, and char types are all sign-extended (except char which is zero-extended) and operated on as 32-bit integers, the same as int types. The smaller types only have a few type-specific instructions for loading, storing, and type conversion. boolean is not known at all to the JVM; booleans are operated on as 8-bit byte values, with 0 representing false and 1 representing true.

The JVM has a garbage-collected heap for storing objects and arrays. Code, constants, and other class data are stored in the "method area". The method area is logically part of the heap, but implementations may treat the method area separately from the heap, and for example might not garbage collect it. Each JVM thread also has its own call stack (called a "Java Virtual Machine stack" for clarity), which stores frames. A new frame is created each time a method is called, and the frame is destroyed when that method exits.

Each frame provides an "operand stack" and an array of "local variables". The operand stack is used for operands to computations and for receiving the return value of a called method, while local variables serve the same purpose as registers and are also used to pass method arguments. Thus, the JVM is both a stack machine and a register machine.

64-bit "Data Model" JVM

A 64-bit version of Java is available, but while the "word" is still 32-bit, memory "addressing" is 64-bit; however array indexes are still 32-bit, so each array can't be bigger, but cumulatively the heap can be bigger.

Bytecode Instructions

The JVM has instructions for the following groups of tasks:

- Load and store
- Arithmetic
- Type conversion
- Object creation and manipulation
- Operand stack management (push / pop)
- Control transfer (branching)
- Method invocation and return
- Throwing exceptions
- Monitor-based concurrency

The aim is binary compatibility. Each particular host operating system needs its own implementation of the JVM and runtime. These JVMs interpret the bytecode semantically the same way, but the actual implementation may be different. More complex than just emulating bytecode is compatibly and efficiently implementing the Java core API that must be mapped to each host operating system.

These instructions operate on a set of common abstracted data types rather the native data types of any specific instruction set architecture.

JVM Languages

A JVM language is any language with functionality that can be expressed in terms of a valid class file which can be hosted by the Java Virtual Machine. A class file contains Java Virtual Machine instructions (Java byte code) and a symbol table, as well as other ancillary information. The class file format is the hardware- and operating system-independent binary format used to represent compiled classes and interfaces.

There are several JVM languages, both old languages ported to JVM and completely new languages. JRuby and Jython are perhaps the most well-known ports of existing languages, i.e. Ruby and Python respectively. Of the new languages that have been created from scratch to compile to Java bytecode, Clojure, Apache Groovy, Scala and Kotlin may be the most popular ones. A notable feature with the JVM languages is that they are compatible with each other, so that, for example, Scala libraries can be used with Java programs and vice versa.

Java 7 JVM implements *JSR 292: Supporting Dynamically Typed Languages* on the Java Platform, a new feature which supports dynamically typed languages in the JVM. This feature is developed within the Da Vinci Machine project whose mission is to extend the JVM so that it supports languages other than Java.

Bytecode Verifier

A basic philosophy of Java is that it is inherently safe from the standpoint that no user program can crash the host machine or otherwise interfere inappropriately with other operations on the host machine, and that it is possible to protect certain methods and data structures belonging to trusted code from access or corruption by untrusted code executing within the same JVM. Furthermore, common programmer errors that often led to data corruption or unpredictable behavior such as accessing off the end of an array or using an uninitialized pointer are not allowed to occur. Several features of Java combine to provide this safety, including the class model, the garbage-collected heap, and the verifier.

The JVM verifies all bytecode before it is executed. This verification consists primarily of three types of checks:

- Branches are always to valid locations

- Data is always initialized and references are always type-safe

- Access to private or package private data and methods is rigidly controlled

The first two of these checks take place primarily during the verification step that occurs when a class is loaded and made eligible for use. The third is primarily performed dynamically, when data items or methods of a class are first accessed by another class.

The verifier permits only some bytecode sequences in valid programs, e.g. a jump (branch) instruction can only target an instruction within the same method. Furthermore, the verifier ensures that any given instruction operates on a fixed stack location, allowing the JIT compiler to transform stack accesses into fixed register accesses. Because of this, that the JVM is a stack architecture does not imply a speed penalty for emulation on register-based architectures when using a JIT compiler. In the face of the code-verified JVM architecture, it makes no difference to a JIT compiler whether it gets named imaginary registers or imaginary stack positions that must be allocated to the target architecture's registers. In fact, code verification makes the JVM different from a classic stack architecture, of which efficient emulation with a JIT compiler is more complicated and typically carried out by a slower interpreter.

The original specification for the bytecode verifier used natural language that was incomplete or incorrect in some respects. A number of attempts have been made to specify the JVM as a formal system. By doing this, the security of current JVM implementations can more thoroughly be analyzed, and potential security exploits prevented. It will also be possible to optimize the JVM by skipping unnecessary safety checks, if the application being run is proven to be safe.

Secure Execution of Remote Code

A virtual machine architecture allows very fine-grained control over the actions that code within the machine is permitted to take. It assumes the code is "semantically" correct, that is, it successfully passed the (formal) bytecode verifier process, materialized by a tool, possibly off-board the virtual machine. This is designed to allow safe execution of untrusted code from remote sources, a model used by Java applets, and other secure code downloads. Once bytecode-verified, the downloaded code runs in a restricted "sandbox", which is designed to protect the user from misbehaving or malicious code. As an addition to the bytecode verification process, publishers can purchase a certificate with which to digitally sign applets as safe, giving them permission to ask the user to break out of the sandbox and access the local file system, clipboard, execute external pieces of software, or network.

Bytecode Interpreter and Just-in-time Compiler

For each hardware architecture a different Java bytecode interpreter is needed. When a computer has a Java bytecode interpreter, it can run any Java bytecode program, and the same program can be run on any computer that has such an interpreter.

When Java bytecode is executed by an interpreter, the execution will always be slower than the execution of the same program compiled into native machine language. This problem is mitigated by just-in-time (JIT) compilers for executing Java bytecode. A JIT compiler may translate Java bytecode into native machine language while executing the program. The translated parts of the program can then be executed much more quickly than they could be interpreted. This technique gets applied to those parts of a program frequently executed. This way a JIT compiler can significantly speed up the overall execution time.

There is no necessary connection between the Java programming language and Java bytecode. A program written in Java can be compiled directly into the machine language of a real computer and programs written in other languages than Java can be compiled into Java bytecode.

Java bytecode is intended to be platform-independent and secure. Some JVM implementations do not include an interpreter, but consist only of a just-in-time compiler.

JVM in the Web Browser

At the start of the Java platform's lifetime, the JVM was marketed as a web technology for creating Rich Internet Applications. As of 2018, most web browsers and operating systems bundling web browsers do not ship with a Java plug-in, nor do they permit side-loading any non-Flash plug-in. The Java browser plugin was deprecated in JDK 9.

The NPAPI Java browser plug-in was designed to allow the JVM to execute so-called Java applets embedded into HTML pages. For browsers with the plug-in installed, the applet is allowed to draw into a rectangular region on the page assigned to it. Because the plug-in includes a JVM, Java applets are not restricted to the Java programming language; any language targeting the JVM may run in the plug-in. A restricted set of APIs allow applets access to the user's microphone or 3D acceleration, although applets are not able to modify the page outside its rectangular region. Adobe Flash Player, the main competing technology, works in the same way in this respect.

As of June 2015 according to W3Techs, Java applet and Silverlight use had fallen to 0.1% each for all web sites, while Flash had fallen to 10.8%.

JavaScript JVMs and Interpreters

As of May 2016, JavaPoly allows users to import unmodified Java libraries, and invoke them directly from JavaScript. JavaPoly allows websites to use run unmodified Java libraries, even if the user does not have Java installed on their computer.

Compilation to JavaScript

With the continuing improvements in JavaScript execution speed, combined with the increased use of mobile devices whose web browsers do not implement support for plugins, there are efforts to target those users through compilation to JavaScript. It is possible to either compile the source code or JVM bytecode to JavaScript.

Compiling the JVM bytecode, which is universal across JVM languages, allows building upon the language's existing compiler to bytecode. The main JVM bytecode to JavaScript compilers are TeaVM, the compiler contained in Dragome Web SDK, Bck2Brwsr, and j2js-compiler.

Leading compilers from JVM languages to JavaScript include the Java-to-JavaScript compiler contained in Google Web Toolkit, Clojurescript (Clojure), GrooScript (Apache Groovy), Scala.js (Scala) and others.

Java Runtime Environment

The Java Runtime Environment (JRE) released by Oracle is a freely available software distribution containing a stand-alone JVM (HotSpot), the Java standard library (Java Class Library), a configuration tool, and—until its discontinuation in JDK 9—a browser plug-in. It is the most common Java environment installed on personal computers in the laptop and desktop form factor. Mobile phonesincluding feature phones and early smartphones that ship with a JVM are most likely to include a JVM meant to run applications targeting Micro Edition of the Java platform. Meanwhile, most modern smartphones, tablet computers, and other handheld PCs that run Java apps are most likely to do so through support of the Android operating system, which includes an open source virtual machine incompatible with the JVM specification. (Instead, Google's Android development tools take Java programs as input and output Dalvik bytecode, which is the native input format for the virtual machine on Android devices.)

Performance

The JVM specification gives a lot of leeway to implementors regarding the implementation details. Since Java 1.3, JRE from Oracle contains a JVM called HotSpot. It has been designed to be a high-performance JVM.

To speed-up code execution, HotSpot relies on just-in-time compilation. To speed-up object allocation and garbage collection, HotSpot uses generational heap.

Generational Heap

The *Java virtual machine heap* is the area of memory used by the JVM for dynamic memory allocation.

In HotSpot the heap is divided into *generations*:

- The *young generation* stores short-lived objects that are created and immediately garbage collected.

- Objects that persist longer are moved to the *old generation* (also called the *tenured generation*). This memory is subdivided into (two) Survivors spaces where the objects that survived the first and next garbage collections are stored.

The *permanent generation* (or *permgen*) was used for class definitions and associated metadata prior to Java 8. Permanent generation was not part of the heap. The *permanent generation* was removed from Java 8.

Originally there was no permanent generation, and objects and classes were stored together in the same area. But as class unloading occurs much more rarely than objects are collected, moving class structures to a specific area allowed significant performance improvements.

Security

Oracle's JRE is installed on a large number of computers. End users with an out-of-date version of JRE therefore are vulnerable to many known attacks. This led to the widely shared belief that Java is inherently insecure. Since Java 1.7, Oracle's JRE for Windows includes automatic update functionality.

Before the discontinuation of the Java browser plug-in, any web page might have potentially run a Java applet, which provided an easily accessible attack surface to malicious web sites. In 2013 Kaspersky Labs reported that the Java plug-in was the method of choice for computer criminals. Java exploits are included in many exploit packs that hackers deploy onto hacked web sites.

Classpath (Java)

We'll all need direction at some point. Java is no different. The CLASSPATH variable lets Java know where to find class libraries.

CLASSPATH is actually an environment variable in Java, and tells Java applications and the Java Virtual Machine (JVM) where to find the libraries of classes. These include any that you have developed on your own.

An environment variable is a global system variable, accessible by the computer's operating system (e.g., Windows). Other variables include COMPUTERNAME, USERNAME (computer's name and user name).

In Java, CLASSPATH holds the list of Java class file directories, and the JAR file, which is Java's delivered class library file.

If you are trying to run a stand-alone Java program, you may find it necessary to change the CLASSPATH variable. When the program runs, Java's run-time system, called the interpreter, is working through your code. If it comes across a class name, it will look at each directory listed in the CLASSPATH variable. If it does not find the class name, it will error out.

We can set the value of CLASSPATH in DOS.

Setting the Path to Execute Java Programs

Supplying as Application Argument

Suppose we have a package called *org.mypackage* containing the classes:

- *HelloWorld* (main class)
- *SupportClass*
- *UtilClass*

and the files defining this package are stored physically under the directory *D:\myprogram* (on Windows) or */home/user/myprogram* (on Linux).

The file structure looks like this:

Microsoft Windows	Linux
| ```
D:\myprogram\
   |
   ---> org\
      |
      ---> mypackage\
         |
         ---> HelloWorld.class
         ---> SupportClass.class
         ---> UtilClass.class
``` | ```
/home/user/myprogram/
   |
   ---> org/
      |
      ---> mypackage/
         |
         ---> HelloWorld.class
         ---> SupportClass.class
         ---> UtilClass.class
``` |

When we invoke Java, we specify the name of the application to run: org.mypackage.HelloWorld. However we must also tell Java where to look for the files and directories defining our package. So to launch the program, we use the following command:

Microsoft Windows	Linux
`java -classpath D:\myprogram org.` `mypackage.HelloWorld`	`java -cp /home/user/myprogram org.` `mypackage.HelloWorld`

where:

- java is a java application launcher, a type of sdkTool(A command-line tool, such as javac, javadoc, or apt)

- *-classpath D:\myprogram* sets the path to the packages used in the program (on Linux, *-cp /home/user/myprogram*) and

- *org.mypackage.HelloWorld* is the name of the main class

Setting the Path Through an Environment Variable

The environment variable named CLASSPATH may be alternatively used to set the classpath. For the above example, we could also use on Windows:

```
set CLASSPATH=D:\myprogram

java org.mypackage.HelloWorld
```

The rule is that -classpath option, when used to start the java application, overrides the CLASSPATH environment variable. If none are specified, the current working directory is used as classpath. This means that when our working directory is D:\myprogram\ (on Linux, /home/user/myprogram/), we would not need to specify the classpath explicitly. When overriding however, it is advised to include current folder "." into the classpath in the case when loading classes from current folder is desired.

The same applies not only to java launcher but also to javac, the java compiler.

Setting the Path of a Jar File

If a program uses a supporting library enclosed in a Jar file called *supportLib.jar*, physically in the directory *D:\myprogram\lib* and the corresponding physical file structure is:

```
D:\myprogram\
      |
      ---> lib\
            |
            ---> supportLib.jar
      |
      ---> org\
            |
```

```
--> mypackage\
            |
            ---> HelloWorld.class
            ---> SupportClass.class
            ---> UtilClass.class
```

the following command-line option is needed:

```
java  -classpath  D:\myprogram;D:\myprogram\lib\supportLib.jar  org.
mypackage.HelloWorld
```

or alternatively:

```
set CLASSPATH=D:\myprogram;D:\myprogram\lib\supportLib.jar
```

```
java org.mypackage.HelloWorld
```

Adding all JAR Files in a Directory

In Java 6 and higher, one can add all jar-files in a specific directory to the classpath using wildcard notation.

Windows example:

```
java -classpath ".;c:\mylib\*" MyApp
```

Linux example:

```
java -classpath '.:/mylib/*' MyApp
```

This works for both -classpath options and environment classpaths.

Setting the Path in a Manifest file

If a program has been enclosed in a Jar file called *helloWorld.jar,* located directly in the directory *D:\myprogram,* the directory structure is as follows:

```
D:\myprogram\
       |
   ---> helloWorld.jar
       |
   ---> lib\
           |
           ---> supportLib.jar
```

The manifest file defined in *helloWorld.jar* has this definition:

```
Main-Class: org.mypackage.HelloWorld
Class-Path: lib/supportLib.jar
```

The manifest file should end with either a new line or carriage return.

```
The program is launched with the following command:
java -jar D:\myprogram\helloWorld.jar [app arguments]
```

This automatically starts *org.mypackage.HelloWorld* specified in class *Main-Class* with the arguments. The user cannot replace this class name using the invocation java -jar. *Class-Path* describes the location of *supportLib.jar* relative to the location of the library *helloWorld.jar*. Neither absolute file path, which is permitted in -classpath parameter on the command line, nor jar-internal paths are supported. This means that if the main class file is contained in a jar, *org/mypackage/HelloWorld.class* must be a valid path on the root within the jar.

Multiple classpath entries are separated with spaces:

```
Class-Path: lib/supportLib.jar lib/supportLib2.jar
```

OS Specific Notes

Being closely associated with the file system, the command-line Classpath syntax depends on the operating system. For example:

- on all Unix-like operating systems (such as Linux and Mac OS X), the directory structure has a Unix syntax, with separate file paths separated by a colon (":").

- on Windows, the directory structure has a Windows syntax, and each file path must be separated by a semicolon (";").

This does not apply when the Classpath is defined in manifest files, where each file path must be separated by a space (" "), regardless of the operating system.

Java Bytecode

Java bytecode is the result of the compilation of a Java program, an intermediate representation of that program which is machine independent.

The Java bytecode gets processed by the Java virtual machine (JVM) instead of the processor. It is the job of the JVM to make the necessary resource calls to the processor in order to run the bytecode.

Java bytecode is the resulting compiled object code of a Java program. This bytecode can be run in any platform which has a Java installation in it.

This machine independence is because of the Java virtual machine that runs the bytecode in proxy of the processor which means that a Java programmer does not have to be knowledgeable about the quirks and nuances about specific operating systems and processors that the program will be run on because the virtual machine takes care of those specifics.

The Java bytecode is not completely compiled, but rather just an intermediate code sitting in the middle because it still has to be interpreted and executed by the JVM installed on the specific platform such as Windows, Mac or Linux.

Upon compile, the Java source code is converted into the .class bytecode.

Most developers although have never seen byte code. One way to view the byte code is to compile your class and then open the .class file in a hex editor and translate the bytecodes by referring to the virtual machine specification. A much easier way is to utilize the command-line utility javap. The Java SDK from Sun includes the javap disassembler, that will convert the byte codes into human-readable mnemonics.

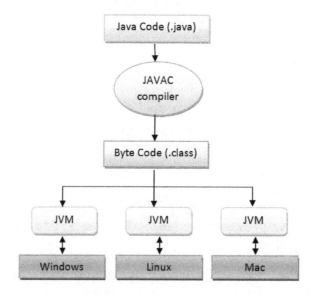

An example of bytecode is shown below:

Let us take a sample program. A Main class is created with login function.

Source Code:

```
1    import java.io.*;
2    class Main
3    {
4            public static void main(String args[])
5      {
6        new Login();
7      }
8    }
```

In command prompt compile it by typing "javac Main.java".

After that type "javap -c Main". You will get the byte code as follows

Byte Code:

```
1    Compiled from "Main.java"
2    class Main extends java.lang.Object{
3    Main();
4      Code:
5      0:    aload_0
6      1:    invokespecial   #1; //Method java/lang/Object.''<init>'':()V
7      4:    return
8
9    public static void main(java.lang.String[]);
10     Code:
11     0:    new       #2; //class Login
12     3:    dup
13     4:    invokespecial   #3; //Method Login.''<init>'':()V
14     7:    pop
15     8:    return
16
17   }
18   </init></init>
```

Instruction Set Architecture

The JVM is both a stack machine and a register machine. Each frame for a method call has an "operand stack" and an array of "local variables". The operand stack is used for operands to computations and for receiving the return value of a called method, while local variables serve the same purpose as registers and are also used to pass method arguments. The maximum size of the operand stack and local variable array, computed by the compiler, is part of the attributes of each method. Each can be independently sized from 0 to 65535 values, where each value is 32 bits. long and double types, which are 64 bits, take up two consecutive local variables (which need not be 64-bit aligned in the local variables array) or one value in the operand stack (but are counted as two units in the depth of the stack).

Instruction Set

Each bytecode is composed of one byte that represents the opcode, along with zero or more bytes for operands.

Of the 256 possible byte-long opcodes, as of 2015, 202 are in use (~79%), 51 are reserved for future use (~20%), and 3 instructions (~1%) are permanently reserved for JVM implementations to use. Two of these (impdep1 and impdep2) are to provide traps for implementation-specific software and hardware, respectively. The third is used for debuggers to implement breakpoints.

Instructions fall into a number of broad groups:

- Load and store (e.g. aload_0, istore)
- Arithmetic and logic (e.g. ladd, fcmpl)

- Type conversion (e.g. `i2b`, `d2i`)

- Object creation and manipulation (`new`, `putfield`)

- Operand stack management (e.g. `swap`, `dup2`)

- Control transfer (e.g. `ifeq`, `goto`)

- Method invocation and return (e.g. `invokespecial`, `areturn`)

There are also a few instructions for a number of more specialized tasks such as exception throwing, synchronization, etc.

Many instructions have prefixes and/or suffixes referring to the types of operands they operate on. These are as follows:

Prefix/suffix	Operand type
i	integer
l	long
s	short
b	byte
c	character
f	float
d	double
a	reference

For example, `iadd` will add two integers, while dadd will add two doubles. The `const`, `load`, and `store` instructions may also take a suffix of the form _n, where n is a number from 0–3 for loadand store. The maximum n for const differs by type.

The `const` instructions push a value of the specified type onto the stack. For example, `iconst_5` will push an integer (32 bit value) with the value 5 onto the stack, while `dconst_1` will push a double (64 bit floating point value) with the value 1 onto the stack. There is also an `aconst_null`, which pushes a `null` reference. The n for the load and store instructions specifies the index in the local variable array to load from or store to. The `aload_0` instruction pushes the object in local variable 0 onto the stack (this is usually the this object). `istore_1` stores the integer on the top of the stack into local variable 1. For local variables beyond 3 the suffix is dropped and operands must be used.

Example

Consider the following Java code:

```
outer:
for (int i = 2; i < 1000; i++) {
    for (int j = 2; j < i; j++) {
        if (i % j == 0)
            continue outer;
    }
```

```
       System.out.println (i);

}
```

A Java compiler might translate the Java code above into byte code as follows, assuming the above was put in a method:

```
0:     iconst_2
1:     istore_1
2:     iload_1
3:     sipush  1000
6:     if_icmpge        44
9:     iconst_2
10:    istore_2
11:    iload_2
12:    iload_1
13:    if_icmpge        31
16:    iload_1
17:    iload_2
18:    irem
19:    ifne      25
22:    goto      38
25:    iinc      2, 1
28:    goto      11
31:    getstatic      #84; // Field java/lang/System.out:Ljava/io/Print-
Stream;
34:    iload_1
35:    invokevirtual    #85; // Method java/io/PrintStream.println:(I)V
38:    iinc      1, 1
41:    goto      2
44:    return
```

Generation

The most common language targeting Java virtual machine by producing Java bytecode is Java. Originally only one compiler existed, the javac compiler from Sun Microsystems, which compiles Java source code to Java bytecode; but because all the specifications for Java bytecode are now available, other parties have supplied compilers that produce Java bytecode. Examples of other compilers include:

- Jikes, compiles from Java to Java bytecode (developed by IBM, implemented in C++).

- Espresso, compiles from Java to Java bytecode (Java 1.0 only).

- GNU Compiler for Java (GCJ), compiles from Java to Java bytecode; it can also compile to native machine code and was part of the GNU Compiler Collection (GCC) up until version 6.

Some projects provide Java assemblers to enable writing Java bytecode by hand. Assembly code may be also generated by machine, for example by a compiler targeting a Java virtual machine. Notable Java assemblers include:

- Jasmin, takes text descriptions for Java classes, written in a simple assembly-like syntax using Java virtual machine instruction set and generates a Java class file.

- Jamaica, a macro assembly language for the Java virtual machine. Java syntax is used for class or interface definition. Method bodies are specified using bytecode instructions.

- Krakatau Bytecode Tools, currently contains three tools: a decompiler and disassembler for Java classfiles and an assembler to create classfiles.

- Lilac, an assembler and disassembler for the Java virtual machine.

Others have developed compilers, for different programming languages, to target the Java virtual machine, such as:

- ColdFusion

- JRuby and Jython, two scripting languages based on Ruby and Python.

- Apache Groovy, a scripting language based on Java.

- Scala, a type-safe general-purpose programming language supporting object-oriented and functional programming.

- JGNAT and AppletMagic, compile from the language Ada to Java bytecode.

- C to Java byte-code compilers.

- Clojure, a functional, immutable, general-purpose programming language in the Lisp family with a strong emphasis on concurrency.

- MIDletPascal.

- JavaFX Script code is compiled to Java bytecode.

- Kotlin.

- Object Pascal source code is compiled to Java bytecode using the Free Pascal 3.0+ compiler.

Execution

There are several machines available today, both free and commercial products.

If executing Java bytecode in a Java virtual machine is undesirable, a developer can also compile

Java source code or bytecode directly to native machine code with tools such as the GNU Compiler for Java (GCJ). Some processors can execute Java bytecode natively. Such processors are termed *Java processors*.

Support for Dynamic Languages

The Java virtual machine provides some support for dynamically typed languages. Most of the extant JVM instruction set is statically typed - in the sense that method calls have their signatures type-checked at compile time, without a mechanism to defer this decision to run time, or to choose the method dispatch by an alternative approach.

JSR 292 (*Supporting Dynamically Typed Languages on the Java™ Platform*) added a new invokedynamic instruction at the JVM level, to allow method invocation relying on dynamic type checking(instead of the extant statically type-checked invokevirtual instruction). The Da Vinci Machine is a prototype virtual machine implementation that hosts JVM extensions aimed at supporting dynamic languages. All JVMs supporting JSE 7 also include the invokedynamic opcode.

Java Class File

A Java class file is a file containing Java bytecode and having .class extension that can be executed by JVM. A Java class file is created by a Java compiler from *.java*files as a result of successful compilation. As we know that a single Java programming language source file (*or we can say .java file*) may contain one class or more than one class. So if a *.java* file has more than one class then each class will compile into a separate class files.

For Example: Save this below code as Test.java on your system.

```
// Compiling this Java program would
// result in multiple class files.


class Sample
{


}


// Class Declaration
class Student
{


}
// Class Declaration
class Test
```

```
{
        public static void main (String[] args)
        {
            System.out.println(``Class File Structure'');
        }
}
```

For Compiling:

After compilation there will be 3 class files in corresponding folder named as:

- Sample.class
- Student.class
- Test.class

In general every class file in java contains definition of a single class or interface in stream of 8 bit bytes. Every .class file follows a predefined class file format, failing which .class file will be deemed invalid and not run on any JVM or JRE. class file is generated by Java compilers and executed by Java virtual machine and its byte code is verified during class loading process, which address possibility of altering .class file externally. One of the reason Java is considered relatively safe and secure language is its ability to verify class file byte codes before executing it. class file contains 10 basic sections which specifies all data and meta data like magic numbers, major and minor version of class file etc.

File Layout and Structure

Sections

There are 10 basic sections to the Java Class File structure:

- Magic Number: 0xCAFEBABE
- Version of Class File Format: the minor and major versions of the class file
- Constant Pool: Pool of constants for the class
- Access Flags: for example whether the class is abstract, static, etc.
- This Class: The name of the current class
- Super Class: The name of the super class
- Interfaces: Any interfaces in the class
- Fields: Any fields in the class
- Methods: Any methods in the class
- Attributes: Any attributes of the class (for example the name of the sourcefile, etc.)

Magic Number

Class files are identified by the following 4 byte header (in hexadecimal): CA FE BA BE. The history of this magic numberwas explained by James Gosling referring to a restaurant in Palo Alto:

> "We used to go to lunch at a place called St Michael's Alley. According to local legend, in the deep dark past, the Grateful Deadused to perform there before they made it big. It was a pretty funky place that was definitely a Grateful Dead Kinda Place. When Jerrydied, they even put up a little Buddhist-esque shrine. When we used to go there, we referred to the place as Cafe Dead. Somewhere along the line it was noticed that this was a HEX number. I was re-vamping some file format code and needed a couple of magic numbers: one for the persistent object file, and one for classes. I used CAFEDEAD for the object file format, and in grepping for 4 character hex words that fit after "CAFE" (it seemed to be a good theme) I hit on BABE and decided to use it. At that time, it didn't seem terribly important or destined to go anywhere but the trash-can of history. So CAFEBABE became the class file format, and CAFEDEAD was the persistent object format. But the persistent object facility went away, and along with it went the use of CAFEDEAD - it was eventually replaced by RMI.

General Layout

Because the class file contains variable-sized items and does not also contain embedded file offsets (or pointers), it is typically parsed sequentially, from the first byte toward the end. At the lowest level the file format is described in terms of a few fundamental data types:

- u1: an unsigned 8-bit integer

- u2: an unsigned 16-bit integer in big-endian byte order

- u4: an unsigned 32-bit integer in big-endian byte order

- table: an array of variable-length items of some type. The number of items in the table is identified by a preceding count number, but the size in bytes of the table can only be determined by examining each of its items.

Some of these fundamental types are then re-interpreted as higher-level values (such as strings or floating-point numbers), depending on context. There is no enforcement of word alignment, and so no padding bytes are ever used. The overall layout of the class file is as shown in the following table.

byte offset	size	type or value	description
0		u1 = 0xCA hex	
1		u1 = 0xFE hex	magic number (CAFEBABE) used to identify file as conforming to the class file format
2	4 bytes	u1 = 0xBA hex	
3		u1 = 0xBE hex	

4			minor version number of the class file format being used
5	2 bytes	u2	
6			major version number of the class file format being used.
			Java SE 10 = 54 (0x36 hex),
			Java SE 9 = 53 (0x35 hex),
			Java SE 8 = 52 (0x34 hex),
	2 bytes	u2	Java SE 7 = 51 (0x33 hex),
7			Java SE 6.0 = 50 (0x32 hex),
			Java SE 5.0 = 49 (0x31 hex),
			JDK 1.4 = 48 (0x30 hex),
			JDK 1.3 = 47 (0x2F hex),
			JDK 1.2 = 46 (0x2E hex),
			JDK 1.1 = 45 (0x2D hex).
8			constant pool count, number of entries in the following constant pool table. This count is at least one greater than the actual number of entries.
9	2 bytes	u2	
10			constant pool table, an array of variable-sized constant pool entries, containing items such as literal numbers, strings, and references to classes or methods. Indexed starting at 1, containing (*constant pool count* - 1) number of entries in total.
...	*cpsize* (variable)	table	
...			
...			
10+*cpsize*	2 bytes	u2	access flags, a bitmask
11+*cpsize*			
12+*cpsize*	2 bytes	u2	identifies *this* class, index into the constant pool to a "Class"-type entry
13+*cpsize*			
14+*cpsize*	2 bytes	u2	identifies *super* class, index into the constant pool to a "Class"-type entry
15+*cpsize*			
16+*cpsize*	2 bytes	u2	interface count, number of entries in the following interface table
17+*cpsize*			
18+*cpsize*			
...	*isize* (variable)	table	interface table, an array of variable-sized interfaces
...			
...			
18+*cpsize*+*isize*	2 bytes	u2	field count, number of entries in the following field table
19+*cpsize*+*isize*			
20+*cpsize*+*isize*			
...	*fsize*(-variable)	table	field table, variable length array of fields
...			
...			
20+*cpsize*+*isize*+*fsize*	2 bytes	u2	method count, number of entries in the following method table
21+*cpsize*+*isize*+*fsize*			
22+*cpsize*+*isize*+*fsize*			
...	*msize*(-variable)	table	method table, variable length array of methods
...			
...			
22+*cpsize*+*isize*+*fsize*+*msize*	2 bytes	u2	attribute count, number of entries in the following attribute table
23+*cpsize*+*isize*+*fsize*+*msize*			
24+*cpsize*+*isize*+*fsize*+*msize*			
...	*asize*(-variable)	table	attribute table, variable length array of attributes
...			
...			

Representation in a C-like Programming Language

Since C doesn't support multiple variable length arrays within a struct, the code below won't compile and only serves as a demonstration.

```
struct Class_File_Format {
    u4 magic_number;

    u2 minor_version;
    u2 major_version;

    u2 constant_pool_count;

    cp_info constant_pool[constant_pool_count - 1];

    u2 access_flags;

    u2 this_class;
    u2 super_class;

    u2 interfaces_count;

    u2 interfaces[interfaces_count];

    u2 fields_count;
    field_info fields[fields_count];

    u2 methods_count;
    method_info methods[methods_count];

    u2 attributes_count;
    attribute_info attributes[attributes_count];
}
```

The Constant Pool

The constant pool table is where most of the literal constant values are stored. This includes values such as numbers of all sorts, strings, identifier names, references to classes and methods, and type descriptors. All indexes, or references, to specific constants in the constant pool table are given by 16-bit (type u2) numbers, where index value 1 refers to the first constant in the table (index value 0 is invalid).

Due to historic choices made during the file format development, the number of constants in the constant pool table is not actually the same as the constant pool count which precedes the table. First, the table is indexed starting at 1 (rather than 0), but the count should actually be interpreted as the maximum index plus one. Additionally, two types of constants (longs and doubles) take up two consecutive slots in the table, although the second such slot is a phantom index that is never directly used.

The type of each item (constant) in the constant pool is identified by an initial byte *tag*. The number of bytes following this tag and their interpretation are then dependent upon the tag value. The valid constant types and their tag values are:

Tag byte	Additional bytes	Description of constant
1	2+x bytes (variable)	UTF-8 (Unicode) string: a character string prefixed by a 16-bit number (type u2) indicating the number of bytes in the encoded string which immediately follows (which may be different than the number of characters). Note that the encoding used is not actually UTF-8, but involves a slight modification of the Unicode standard encoding form.
3	4 bytes	Integer: a signed 32-bit two's complement number in big-endian format
4	4 bytes	Float: a 32-bit single-precision IEEE 754 floating-point number
5	8 bytes	Long: a signed 64-bit two's complement number in big-endian format (takes two slots in the constant pool table)
6	8 bytes	Double: a 64-bit double-precision IEEE 754 floating-point number (takes two slots in the constant pool table)
7	2 bytes	Class reference: an index within the constant pool to a UTF-8 string containing the fully qualified class name (in *internal format*) (big-endian)
8	2 bytes	String reference: an index within the constant pool to a UTF-8 string (big-endian too)
9	4 bytes	Field reference: two indexes within the constant pool, the first pointing to a Class reference, the second to a Name and Type descriptor. (big-endian)
10	4 bytes	Method reference: two indexes within the constant pool, the first pointing to a Class reference, the second to a Name and Type descriptor. (big-endian)
11	4 bytes	Interface method reference: two indexes within the constant pool, the first pointing to a Class reference, the second to a Name and Type descriptor. (big-endian)
12	4 bytes	Name and type descriptor: two indexes to UTF-8 strings within the constant pool, the first representing a name (identifier) and the second a specially encoded type descriptor.
15	3 bytes	Method handle: this structure is used to represent a method handle and consists of one byte of type descriptor, followed by an index within the constant pool.
16	2 bytes	Method type: this structure is used to represent a method type, and consists of an index within the constant pool.
18	4 bytes	InvokeDynamic: this is used by an *invokedynamic* instruction to specify a bootstrap method, the dynamic invocation name, the argument and return types of the call, and optionally, a sequence of additional constants called static arguments to the bootstrap method.

There are only two integral constant types, integer and long. Other integral types appearing in the high-level language, such as boolean, byte, and short must be represented as an integer constant.

Class names in Java, when fully qualified, are traditionally dot-separated, such as "java.lang.Object". However within the low-level Class reference constants, an internal form appears which uses slashes instead, such as "java/lang/Object".

The Unicode strings, despite the moniker "UTF-8 string", are not actually encoded according to the Unicode standard, although it is similar. There are two differences. The first is that the codepoint U+0000 is encoded as the two-byte sequence C0 80 (in hex) instead of the standard single-byte encoding 00. The second difference is that supplementary characters (those outside the BMP at U+10000 and above) are encoded using a surrogate-pair construction similar to UTF-16 rather than being directly encoded using UTF-8. In this case each of the two surrogates is encoded separately in UTF-8. For example, U+1D11E is encoded as the 6-byte sequence ED A0 B4 ED B4 9E, rather than the correct 4-byte UTF-8 encoding of F0 9D 84 9E.

Verification of Class Files

Even though a compiler for the Java programming language must only produce class files that satisfy all the static and structural constraints in the previous sections, the Java Virtual Machine has no guarantee that any file it is asked to load was generated by that compiler or is properly formed. Applications such as web browsers do not download source code, which they then compile; these applications download already-compiled class files. The browser needs to determine whether the class file was produced by a trustworthy compiler or by an adversary attempting to exploit the Java Virtual Machine.

Because of these potential problems, the Java Virtual Machine needs to verify for itself that the desired constraints are satisfied by the classfiles it attempts to incorporate. A Java Virtual Machine implementation verifies that each classfile satisfies the necessary constraints at linking time.

Linking-time verification enhances the performance of the interpreter. Expensive checks that would otherwise have to be performed to verify constraints at run time for each interpreted instruction can be eliminated. The Java Virtual Machine can assume that these checks have already been performed. For example, the Java Virtual Machine will already know the following:

- There are no operand stack overflows or underflows.
- All local variable uses and stores are valid.
- The arguments to all the Java Virtual Machine instructions are of valid types.

The verifier also performs verification that can be done without looking at the code array of the Code attribute. The checks performed include the following:

- Ensuring that final classes are not subclassed and that final methods are not overridden.
- Checking that every class (except Object) has a direct superclass.
- Ensuring that the constant pool satisfies the documented static constraints; for example, that each CONSTANT_Class_info structure in the constant pool contains in its name_indexitem a valid constant pool index for a CONSTANT_Utf8_info structure.
- Checking that all field references and method references in the constant pool have valid names, valid classes, and a valid type descriptor.

Note that these checks do not ensure that the given field or method actually exists in the given class, nor do they check that the type descriptors given refer to real classes. They ensure only that these items are well formed. More detailed checking is performed when the bytecodes themselves are verified, and during resolution.

There are two strategies that Java Virtual Machine implementations may use for verification:

- Verification by type checking must be used to verify class files whose version number is greater than or equal to 50.0.

- Verification by type inference must be supported by all Java Virtual Machine implementations, except those conforming to the Java ME CLDC and Java Card profiles, in order to verify class files whose version number is less than 50.0.

Verification on Java Virtual Machine implementations supporting the Java ME CLDC and Java Card profiles is governed by their respective specifications.

Java Performance

For a long time in SO and in other places Java has the reputation of being slow. From jokes to many comments in questions and answers, people still believe Java is slow based solely on experience with it in the 90s.

Java, like most new languages, suffered from immature implementations and very weak performance in the early days. The unprecedented success of early Java, though, should teach us the first important lesson about performance – it's not always critical. The Web was expanding like the Big Bang, the world demanded features like secure, portable, Internet-friendly code. Even at that time, (then-) interpreted languages like Visual Basic or PERL were highly popular. Moreover, implementations always improve and Moore's Law is always doing its magic.

Java was not born to handle tiny web page embellishments forever, so it had to evolve to support everything from smart card applets to scalable enterprise applications. Moore's Law barely compensates the distance from the "Nervous Text" applet to any current J2EE server. More than size, change in applicability imposes more and more efficiency constraints. Java debuted as a "glue" language, and as a front-end language; in these cases, most time is spend waiting user input or invoking external (fast) code, like GUI toolkits or network stacks. As soon as the language becomes successful, it must be intrinsically fast, not only look fast in easy scenarios (like servers that don't care for large loading time or runtime footprint). Successful languages are always forced into domains their creators didn't dream of (and didn't design for), and the initial trade-offs are either removed or replaced by new ones as implementers strive to make developers happy.

Portable code and Virtual Machines exist since the sixties, so by 1996 the field was already mature with superb pervious art in interpreters, Just In Time compilers, Garbage Collectors, and more general items such as threading or multiplatform frameworks. Java introduced at least one significant performance challenge, security; but in retrospect, the costs of security only appeared important due to the overall bad performance of early implementations. Right now, only in the

J2ME space the security features cause concern and drive new optimizations like pre-verification. Therefore, most of the exciting history of JVM optimisation resembles a Hollywood-style remake of an old movie by a famous director with lots of money: the result is a blockbuster loved by the public, even if some self-defined elite prefers the original black-and-white production.

Not all is remaking, though. The big news in Java history, of course, is becoming a mainstream platform. Even acknowledging that many successful real-world applications were built with pre-cursor technologies, there is no comparison with Java, remarkably in the economics – very relevant if we consider that top performance costs huge investments from commercial implementers (even though most JVM performance tricks are rooted on academic research). Thanks to all previous work, the formula for the first wave of JVM improvements (the "JDK 1.1.x generation") could be summarized as: implement the techniques that worked before for the other guys.

- High Performance Interpretation. The classloader can perform a few easy optimisations as bytecode-to-bytecode transformations, like devirtualizing calls to final methods. An optimal interpreter is typically generated at loading time with the best Assembly code for the machine.

- Direct References. The Classic VMs implemented references as indirect handles, making GC very simple but code slower. This was fixed in Sun's EVM (aka "Solaris Production"), IBM JDK 1.1.6 and finally, Sun's Java2 releases.

- Just-In-Time Compilation and Generational GC. The first generation of JIT compilers could do local optimisations and offered enough speed for applets. Late in the JDK1.1 cycle, the Sun EVM and the IBM JDK introduced stronger JITs and also the first decent GCs for Java. These were times of fast research and poor stability, so most JITs were disabled by default.

- Library Optimisations. Sun proceeded with many general enhancements during the 1.1 series, while Microsoft improved low-level libraries like the AWT to extract better performance in the Windows OS.

This set of improvements delivered a Java that was usable for many desktop applications and even some servers – mostly I/O-bound apps, like two-tier Servlet-based apps that are a thin bridge between a relational database and a web browser – provided that one didn't need to serve more than a handful of simultaneous users.

Virtual Machine Optimization Methods

Many optimizations have improved the performance of the JVM over time. However, although Java was often the first Virtual machine to implement them successfully, they have often been used in other similar platforms as well.

Just-in-time Compiling

Early JVMs always interpreted Java bytecodes. This had a large performance penalty of between a factor 10 and 20 for Java versus C in average applications.To combat this, a just-in-time (JIT) compiler was introduced into Java 1.1. Due to the high cost of compiling, an added system called HotSpot was introduced in Java 1.2 and was made the default in Java 1.3. Using this framework, the Java virtual machine continually analyses program performance for *hot spots* which are executed frequently or repeatedly. These are then targeted for optimizing, leading to high performance execution with a minimum of overhead for less performance-critical code. Some benchmarks show a 10-fold speed gain by this means.However, due to time constraints, the compiler cannot fully optimize the program, and thus the resulting program is slower than native code alternatives.

Adaptive Optimizing

Adaptive optimizing is a method in computer science that performs dynamic recompilation of parts of a program based on the current execution profile. With a simple implementation, an adaptive optimizer may simply make a trade-off between just-in-time compiling and interpreting instructions. At another level, adaptive optimizing may exploit local data conditions to optimize away branches and use inline expansion.

A Java virtual machine like HotSpot can also deoptimize code formerly JITed. This allows performing aggressive (and potentially unsafe) optimizations, while still being able to later deoptimize the code and fall back to a safe path.

Garbage Collection

The 1.0 and 1.1 Java virtual machines (JVMs) used a mark-sweep collector, which could fragment the heap after a garbage collection. Starting with Java 1.2, the JVMs changed to a generational collector, which has a much better defragmentation behaviour. Modern JVMs use a variety of methods that have further improved garbage collection performance.

Other Optimizing Methods

Compressed Oops

Compressed Oops allow Java 5.0+ to address up to 32 GB of heap with 32-bit references. Java does not support access to individual bytes, only objects which are 8-byte aligned by default. Because of this, the lowest 3 bits of a heap reference will always be 0. By lowering the resolution of 32-bit references to 8 byte blocks, the addressable space can be increased to 32 GB. This significantly reduces memory use compared to using 64-bit references as Java uses references much more than some languages like C++. Java 8 supports larger alignments such as 16-byte alignment to support up to 64 GB with 32-bit references.

Split Bytecode Verification

Before executing a class, the Sun JVM verifies its Java bytecodes. This verification is performed lazily: classes' bytecodes are only loaded and verified when the specific class is loaded and prepared for use, and not at the beginning of the program. (Note that other verifiers, such as the Java/400 verifier for IBM iSeries (System i), can perform most verification in advance and cache verification information from one use of a class to the next.) However, as the Java class libraries are also regular Java classes, they must also be loaded when they are used, which means that the start-up time of a Java program is often longer than for C++ programs, for example.

A method named *split-time verification*, first introduced in the Java Platform, Micro Edition (J2ME), is used in the JVM since Java version 6. It splits the verification of Java bytecode in two phases:

- Design-time – when compiling a class from source to bytecode

- Runtime – when loading a class.

In practice this method works by capturing knowledge that the Java compiler has of class flow and annotating the compiled method bytecodes with a synopsis of the class flow information. This does not make runtime verification appreciably less complex, but does allow some shortcuts.

Escape Analysis and Lock Coarsening

Java is able to manage multithreading at the language level. Multithreading is a method allowing programs to perform multiple processes concurrently, thus producing faster programs on computer systems with multiple processors or cores. Also, a multithreaded application can remain responsive to input, even while performing long running tasks.

However, programs that use multithreading need to take extra care of objectsshared between threads, locking access to shared methods or blocks when they are used by one of the threads. Locking a block or an object is a time-consuming operation due to the nature of the underlying operating system-level operation involved (see concurrency control and lock granularity).

As the Java library does not know which methods will be used by more than one thread, the standard library always locks blocks when needed in a multithreaded environment.

Before Java 6, the virtual machine always locked objects and blocks when asked to by the program, even if there was no risk of an object being modified by two different threads at once. For example, in this case, a local `vector` was locked before each of the *add* operations to ensure that it would not be modified by other threads (vector is synchronized), but because it is strictly local to the method this is needless:

```
public String getNames() {
    Vector v = new Vector();
    v.add("Me");
    v.add("You");
    v.add("Her");
    return v.toString();
}
```

Starting with Java 6, code blocks and objects are locked only when needed, so in the above case, the virtual machine would not lock the Vector object at all.

Since version 6u23, Java includes support for escape analysis.

Register Allocation Improvements

Before Java 6, allocation of registers was very primitive in the *client* virtual machine (they did not live across blocks), which was a problem in CPU designswhich had fewer processor registers available, as in x86s. If there are no more registers available for an operation, the compiler must copy from register to memory (or memory to register), which takes time (registers are significantly faster to access). However, the *server* virtual machine used a color-graph allocator and did not have this problem.

An optimization of register allocation was introduced in Sun's JDK 6; it was then possible to use the same registers across blocks (when applicable), reducing accesses to the memory. This led to a reported performance gain of about 60% in some benchmarks.

Class Data Sharing

Class data sharing (called CDS by Sun) is a mechanism which reduces the startup time for Java applications, and also reduces memory footprint. When the JRE is installed, the installer loads a set of classes from the system JAR file (the JAR file holding all the Java class library, called rt.jar) into a private internal representation, and dumps that representation to a file, called a "shared archive". During subsequent JVM invocations, this shared archive is memory-mapped in, saving the cost of loading those classes and allowing much of the JVM's metadata for these classes to be shared among multiple JVM processes.

The corresponding improvement in start-up time is more obvious for small programs.

Performance Improvements

Apart from the improvements listed here, each release of Java introduced many performance improvements in the JVM and Java application programming interface (API).

JDK 1.1.6: First just-in-time compilation (Symantec's JIT-compiler)

J2SE 1.2: Use of a generational collector.

J2SE 1.3: Just-in-time compiling by HotSpot.

J2SE 1.4: For a Sun overview of performance improvements between 1.3 and 1.4 versions.

Java SE 5.0: Class data sharing

Java SE 6:

- Split bytecode verification

- Escape analysis and lock coarsening

- Register allocation improvements

Other improvements:

- Java OpenGL Java 2D pipeline speed improvements

- Java 2D performance also improved significantly in Java 6

Java SE 6 Update 10

- Java Quick Starter reduces application start-up time by preloading part of JRE data at OS startup on disk cache.

- Parts of the platform needed to execute an application accessed from the web when JRE is not installed are now downloaded first. The full JRE is 12 MB, a typical Swing application only needs to download 4 MB to start. The remaining parts are then downloaded in the background.

- Graphics performance on Windows improved by extensively using Direct3D by default, and use shaders on graphics processing unit (GPU) to accelerate complex Java 2D operations.

Java 7

Several performance improvements have been released for Java 7: Future performance improvements are planned for an update of Java 6 or Java 7:

- Provide JVM support for dynamic programming languages, following the prototyping work currently done on the Da Vinci Machine (Multi Language Virtual Machine),

- Enhance the existing concurrency library by managing parallel computing on multi-core processors,

- Allow the JVM to use both the *client* and *server* JIT compilers in the same session with a method called tiered compiling:

  o The *client* would be used at startup (because it is good at startup and for small applications),

  o The *server* would be used for long-term running of the application (because it outperforms the *client* compiler for this).

- Replace the existing concurrent low-pause garbage collector (also called concurrent mark-sweep (CMS) collector) by a new collector called Garbage First (G1) to ensure consistent pauses over time.

Comparison to other Languages

Objectively comparing the performance of a Java program and an equivalent one written in another language such as C++ needs a carefully and thoughtfully constructed benchmark which compares programs completing identical tasks. The target platform of Java's bytecode compiler is the Java platform, and the bytecode is either interpreted or compiled into machine code by the JVM. Other compilers almost always target a specific hardware and software platform, producing machine code that will stay virtually unchanged during execution. Very different and hard-to-compare scenarios arise from these two different approaches: static vs. dynamic compilations and re-compilations, the availability of precise information about the runtime environment and others.

Java is often compiled just-in-time at runtime by the Java virtual machine, but may also be compiled ahead-of-time, as is C++. When compiled just-in-time, the micro-benchmarks of The Computer Language Benchmarks Game indicate the following about its performance:

- slower than or similar to compiled languages such as C or C++,

- similar to other just-in-time compiled languages such as C#,

- much faster than languages without an effective native-code compiler (JIT or AOT), such as Perl, Ruby, PHP and Python.

Program Speed

Benchmarks often measure performance for small numerically intensive programs. In some rare real-life programs, Java out-performs C. One example is the benchmark of Jake2 (a clone of Quake II written in Java by translating the original GPL C code). The Java 5.0 version performs better in some hardware configurations than its C counterpart. While it is not specified how the data was measured (for example if the original Quake II executable compiled in 1997 was used, which may be considered bad as current C compilers may achieve better optimizations for Quake), it notes how the same Java source code can have a huge speed boost just by updating the VM, something impossible to achieve with a 100% static approach.

For other programs, the C++ counterpart can, and usually does, run significantly faster than the Java equivalent. A benchmark performed by Google in 2011 showed a factor 10 between C++ and Java. At the other extreme, an academic benchmark performed in 2012 with a 3D modelling algorithm showed the Java 6JVM being from 1.09 to 1.91 times slower than C++ under Windows.

Some optimizations that are possible in Java and similar languages may not be possible in certain circumstances in C++:

- C-style pointer use can hinder optimizing in languages that support pointers,

- The use of escape analysis methods is limited in C++, for example, because a C++ compiler does not always know if an object will be modified in a given block of code due to pointers,

- Java can access derived instance methods faster than C++ can access derived virtual methods due to C++'s extra virtual-table look-up. However, non-virtual methods in C++ do not suffer from v-table performance bottlenecks, and thus exhibit performance similar to Java.

The JVM is also able to perform processor specific optimizations or inline expansion. And, the ability to deoptimize code already compiled or inlined sometimes allows it to perform more aggressive optimizations than those performed by statically typed languages when external library functions are involved.

Results for microbenchmarks between Java and C++ highly depend on which operations are compared. For example, when comparing with Java 5.0:

- 32 and 64 bit arithmetic operations, File I/O and Exception handling, have a similar performance to comparable C++ programs

- Arrays operations performance are better in C.

- Trigonometric functions performance is much better in C.

Multi-core Performance

The scalability and performance of Java applications on multi-core systems is limited by the object allocation rate. This effect is sometimes called an "allocation wall". However, in practice, modern garbage collector algorithms use multiple cores to perform garbage collection, which to some degree alleviates this problem. Some garbage collectors are reported to sustain allocation rates of over a gigabyte per second, and there exist Java-based systems that have no problems scaling to several hundreds of CPU cores and heaps sized several hundreds of GB.

Automatic memory management in Java allows for efficient use of lockless and immutable data structures that are extremely hard or sometimes impossible to implement without some kind of a garbage collection. Java offers a number of such high-level structures in its standard library in the java.util.concurrent package, while many languages historically used for high performance systems like C or C++ are still lacking them.

Startup Time

Java startup time is often much slower than many languages, including C, C++, Perl or Python, because many classes (and first of all classes from the platform Class libraries) must be loaded before being used.

When compared against similar popular runtimes, for small programs running on a Windows machine, the startup time appears to be similar to Mono's and a little slower than .NET's.

It seems that much of the startup time is due to input-output (IO) bound operations rather than JVM initialization or class loading (the *rt.jar* class data file alone is 40 MB and the JVM must seek much data in this big file). Some tests showed that although the new split bytecode verification method improved class loading by roughly 40%, it only realized about 5% startup improvement for large programs.

Albeit a small improvement, it is more visible in small programs that perform a simple operation and then exit, because the Java platform data loading can represent many times the load of the actual program's operation.

Starting with Java SE 6 Update 10, the Sun JRE comes with a Quick Starter that preloads class data at OS startup to get data from the disk cache rather than from the disk.

Excelsior JET approaches the problem from the other side. Its Startup Optimizer reduces the amount of data that must be read from the disk on application startup, and makes the reads more sequential.

In November 2004, Nailgun, a "client, protocol, and server for running Java programs from the command line without incurring the JVM startup overhead" was publicly released. introducing for the first time an option for scripts to use a JVM as a daemon, for running one or more Java applications with no JVM startup overhead. The Nailgun daemon is insecure: "all programs are run with the same permissions as the server". Where multi-user security is needed, Nailgun is inappropriate without special precautions. Scripts where per-application JVM startup dominates resource use, see one to two order of magnitude runtime performance improvements.

Memory use

Java memory use is much higher than C++'s memory use because:

- There is an overhead of 8 bytes for each object and 12 bytes for each array in Java. If the size of an object is not a multiple of 8 bytes, it is rounded up to next multiple of 8. This means an object holding one byte field occupies 16 bytes and needs a 4-byte reference. C++ also allocates a pointer (usually 4 or 8 bytes) for every object which class directly or indirectly declares virtual functions.

- Lack of address arithmetic makes creating memory-efficient containers, such as tightly spaced structures and XOR linked lists, currently impossible (the OpenJDK Valhalla project aims to mitigate these issues, though it does not aim to introduce pointer arithmetic; this cannot be done in a garbage collected environment).

- Contrary to malloc and new, the average performance overhead of garbage collection asymptotically nears zero (more accurately, one CPU cycle) as the heap size increases.

- Parts of the Java Class Library must load before program execution (at least the classes used within a program). This leads to a significant memory overhead for small applications.

- Both the Java binary and native recompilations will typically be in memory.

- The virtual machine uses substantial memory.

- In Java, a composite object (class A which uses instances of B and C) is created using references to allocated instances of B and C. In C++ the memory and performance cost of these types of references can be avoided when the instance of B and/or C exists within A.

In most cases a C++ application will consume less memory than an equivalent Java application due to the large overhead of Java's virtual machine, class loading and automatic memory resizing. For programs in which memory is a critical factor for choosing between languages and runtime environments, a cost/benefit analysis is needed.

Trigonometric Functions

Performance of trigonometric functions is bad compared to C, because Java has strict specifications for the results of mathematical operations, which may not correspond to the underlying hardware implementation. On the x87 floating point subset, Java since 1.4 does argument reduction for sin and cos in software, causing a big performance hit for values outside the range.

Java Native Interface

The Java Native Interface invokes a high overhead, making it costly to cross the boundary between code running on the JVM and native code. Java Native Access (JNA) provides Java programs easy access to native shared libraries(dynamic-link library (DLLs) on Windows) via Java code only, with no JNI or native code. This functionality is comparable to Windows' Platform/Invoke and Python'sctypes. Access is dynamic at runtime without code generation. But it has a cost, and JNA is usually slower than JNI.

User Interface

Swing has been perceived as slower than native widget toolkits, because it delegates the rendering of widgets to the pure Java 2D API. However, benchmarks comparing the performance of Swing versus the Standard Widget Toolkit, which delegates the rendering to the native GUI libraries of the operating system, show no clear winner, and the results greatly depend on the context and the environments. Additionally, the newer JavaFX framework, intended to replace Swing, addresses many of Swing's inherent issues.

Use for High Performance Computing

Some people believe that Java performance for high performance computing(HPC) is similar to Fortran on compute-intensive benchmarks, but that JVMs still have scalability issues for performing intensive communication on a grid computing network.

However, high performance computing applications written in Java have won benchmark competitions. In 2008, and 2009, an Apache Hadoop (an open-source high performance computing project written in Java) based cluster was able to sort a terabyte and petabyte of integers the fastest. The hardware setup of the competing systems was not fixed, however.

In Programming Contests

Programs in Java start slower than those in other compiled languages.Thus, some online judge systems, notably those hosted by Chinese universities, use longer time limits for Java programs to be fair to contestants using Java.

In conclusion, the Java VM has come a long way approaching maximum performance, first with better implementations, and more recently, with more specialised implementations. The very competitive market, with multiple implementers including licensees and clean-room, advanced the state of the art in a pace that no single company could do alone; competition played a major role in the "better implementations" stage but that's certainly not enough. As evidenced by the evolution of J2ME, specialisation is very important in scenarios where Java's usual trade-offs are not acceptable. Part of the solution here is making the VM work more like a traditional environment, removing as much hard work as possible from the application's closed system: either moving work to development time (pre-verification, pre-optimisation, or install-time code generation) or even better, removing work completely (e.g., fixing the overweight memory model so optimised code uses less resources, or adding language features that reduce allocation in the heap so the garbage collector is triggered less often).

A few issues depend on fixes or enhancements in the current Java specs; now the trade-off is not against bytes or cycles, it's a matter of politics and strategy: major VM or language changes impact the investment of all Sun licensees, and may force complexity and compatibility issues into developers. The evolution of Java standards is historically much faster in the APIs: licensees redistribute most libraries without change, and developers face a smoother learning curve for features encapsulated by class libraries.

The JVM's use of profiling to only optimize the commonly-used codepaths, but to optimize those heavily has paid off. JIT-compiled Java code is now as fast as C++ in a large (and growing) number of cases.

Despite this, the perception of Java as a slow platform persists, perhaps due to a negative historical bias from people who had experiences with early versions of the Java platform.

References

- Gosling, James; Joy, Bill; Steele, Guy L., Jr.; Bracha, Gilad (2005). The Java Language Specification (3rd ed.). Addison-Wesley. ISBN 0-321-24678-0

- "Chapter 4. Types, Values, and Variables". The Java® Language Specification (Java SE 8 Edition). Oracle America, Inc. 2015. Retrieved 23 Feb 2015

- Stephen N. Freund and John C. Mitchell. 1999. A formal framework for the Java bytecode language and verifier. In Proceedings of the 14th ACM SIGPLAN conference on Object-oriented programming, systems, languages, and applications (OOPSLA '99), A. Michael Berman (Ed.) Association for Computing Machinery, New York, pp.147–166. doi:10.1145/320384.320397

- "Microbenchmarking C++, C#, and Java: 32-bit integer arithmetic". Dr. Dobb›s Journal. 1 July 2005. Retrieved 18 January 2011

- Flanagan, David (May 1997). "Chapter 5 Inner Classes and Other New Language Features:5.6 Other New Features of Java 1.1". Java in a Nutshell (2nd ed.). O'Reilly. ISBN 1-56592-262-X

- Coward, Danny (2006-11-02). "JSR 175: A Metadata Facility for the JavaTM Programming Language". Java Community Process. Retrieved 2008-03-05

- Bloch, Joshua (2008). Effective Java: A Programming Language Guide. The Java Series (2nd ed.). Addison-Wesley. ISBN 0-321-35668-3

- Jelovic, Dejan. "Why Java will always be slower than C++". Archived from the original on February 11, 2008. Retrieved February 15, 2008

Java Programming

Java derives its syntax from C and C++ mostly. It is an object-oriented language. This chapter elucidates the programming basics of Java such as leap year program, binary program, bouncing ball program, factors program, etc. to develop an easy understanding of Java programming.

Java Programming Basics

When we consider a Java program, it can be defined as a collection of objects that communicate via invoking each other's methods. Let us now briefly look into what do class, object, methods, and instance variables mean.

- Object – Objects have states and behaviors. Example: A dog has states - color, name, breed as well as behavior such as wagging their tail, barking, eating. An object is an instance of a class.

- Class – A class can be defined as a template/blueprint that describes the behavior/state that the object of its type supports.

- Methods – A method is basically a behavior. A class can contain many methods. It is in methods where the logics are written, data is manipulated and all the actions are executed.

- Instance Variables – Each object has its unique set of instance variables. An object's state is created by the values assigned to these instance variables.

Basic Syntax

About Java programs, it is very important to keep in mind the following points.

- Case Sensitivity – Java is case sensitive, which means identifier Hello and hello would have different meaning in Java.

- Class Names – For all class names the first letter should be in Upper Case. If several words are used to form a name of the class, each inner word's first letter should be in Upper Case.

- Example: *class MyFirstJavaClass*

- Method Names – All method names should start with a Lower Case letter. If several words are used to form the name of the method, then each inner word›s first letter should be in Upper Case.

- Example: *public void myMethodName()*

- Program File Name – Name of the program file should exactly match the class name.

- When saving the file, you should save it using the class name (Remember Java is case sensitive) and append '.java' to the end of the name (if the file name and the class name do not match, your program will not compile).

- Example: Assume 'MyFirstJavaProgram' is the class name. Then the file should be saved as *'MyFirstJavaProgram.java'*

- public static void main(String args[]) – Java program processing starts from the main() method which is a mandatory part of every Java program.

Java Identifiers

All Java components require names. Names used for classes, variables, and methods are called identifiers.

In Java, there are several points to remember about identifiers. They are as follows –

- All identifiers should begin with a letter (A to Z or a to z), currency character ($) or an underscore (_).

- After the first character, identifiers can have any combination of characters.

- A key word cannot be used as an identifier.

- Most importantly, identifiers are case sensitive.

- Examples of legal identifiers: age, $salary, _value, __1_value.

- Examples of illegal identifiers: 123abc, -salary.

Java Modifiers

Like other languages, it is possible to modify classes, methods, etc., by using modifiers. There are two categories of modifiers –

- Access Modifiers – default, public, protected, private

- Non-access Modifiers – final, abstract, strictfp

Java Variables

Following are the types of variables in Java –

- Local Variables

- Class Variables (Static Variables)

- Instance Variables (Non-static Variables)

Java Arrays

Arrays are objects that store multiple variables of the same type. However, an array itself is an object on the heap.

Java Enums

Enums were introduced in Java 5.0. Enums restrict a variable to have one of only a few predefined values. The values in this enumerated list are called enums.

With the use of enums it is possible to reduce the number of bugs in your code.

For example, if we consider an application for a fresh juice shop, it would be possible to restrict the glass size to small, medium, and large. This would make sure that it would not allow anyone to order any size other than small, medium, or large.

Example

```
class FreshJuice {

      enum FreshJuiceSize{ SMALL, MEDIUM, LARGE }

      FreshJuiceSize size;

}
public class FreshJuiceTest {

      public static void main(String args[]) {

      FreshJuice juice = new FreshJuice();

      juice.size = FreshJuice.FreshJuiceSize.MEDIUM ;

      System.out.println("Size: " + juice.size);

      }

}
```

The above example will produce the following result –

Output:

Size: MEDIUM

Note – Enums can be declared as their own or inside a class. Methods, variables, constructors can be defined inside enums as well.

Java Keywords

The following list shows the reserved words in Java. These reserved words may not be used as constant or variable or any other identifier names.

abstract	assert	boolean	break
byte	case	catch	char
class	const	continue	default
do	double	else	enum
extends	final	finally	float
for	goto	if	implements
import	instanceof	int	interface
long	native	new	package
private	protected	public	return
short	static	strictfp	super
switch	synchronized	this	throw
throws	transient	try	void
volatile	while		

Comments in Java

Java supports single-line and multi-line comments very similar to C and C++. All characters available inside any comment are ignored by Java compiler.

Example

```java
public class MyFirstJavaProgram {

  /* This is my first java program.

   * This will print 'Hello World' as the output

   * This is an example of multi-line comments.

   */


  public static void main(String []args) {

    // This is an example of single line comment

    /* This is also an example of single line comment. */

    System.out.println("Hello World");

  }

}
```

```
Hello World
```

Using Blank Lines

A line containing only white space, possibly with a comment, is known as a blank line, and Java totally ignores it.

Inheritance

In Java, classes can be derived from classes. Basically, if you need to create a new class and here is already a class that has some of the code you require, then it is possible to derive your new class from the already existing code.

This concept allows you to reuse the fields and methods of the existing class without having to rewrite the code in a new class. In this scenario, the existing class is called the superclass and the derived class is called the subclass.

Interfaces

In Java language, an interface can be defined as a contract between objects on how to communicate with each other. Interfaces play a vital role when it comes to the concept of inheritance.

An interface defines the methods, a deriving class (subclass) should use. But the implementation of the methods is totally up to the subclass.

First Java Program

Step 1: Write the Source Code: Enter the following source codes, which defines a *class* called "Hello", using a programming text editor (such as TextPad or NotePad++ for Windows; jEdit or gedit for Mac OS X; gedit for Ubuntu). Do not enter the line numbers (on the left panel), which were added to aid in the explanation.

Save the source file as "Hello.java". A Java source file should be saved with a file extension of ".java". The filename shall be the same as the classname - in this case "Hello". Filename and classname are case-sensitive.

```
1  /*
2   * First Java program, which says "Hello, world!"
3   */
4  public class Hello { // Save as "Hello.java"
5    public static void main(String[] args) { // program entry point
6      System.out.println("Hello, world!"); // print message
```

```
7    }

8  }
```

Step 2: Compile the Source Code: Compile the source code "Hello.java" into Java bytecode "Hello.class" using the JDK Compiler "javac". Start a CMD Shell (Windows) or Terminal (UNIX/Linux/Mac OS X) and issue these commands:

```
// Change directory (cd) to the directory containing the source code
"Hello.java"

javac Hello.java
```

Step 3: Run the Program: Run the program using Java Runtime "java", by issuing this command:

```
java Hello

Hello, world!
```

Brief Explanation of the Program

```
/*...... */

//... until the end of the line
```

These are called *comments*. Comments are NOT executable and are ignored by the compiler. But they provide useful explanation and documentation to your readers (and to yourself three days later). There are two kinds of comments:

1. *Multi-Line Comment*: begins with /* and ends with */, and may span more than one lines (as in Lines 1-3).

2. *End-of-Line (Single-Line) Comment*: begins with // and lasts until the end of the current line (as in Lines 4, 5, and 6).

```
public class Hello {

   ......

}
```

The basic unit of a Java program is a *class*. A class called "Hello" is defined via the keyword "class" in Lines 4-8. The braces {......} encloses the *body* of the class.

In Java, the name of the source file must be the same as the name of the class with a mandatory file extension of ".java". Hence, this file MUST be saved as "Hello.java", case-sensitive.

```
public static void main(String[] args) {

   ......

}
```

Lines 5-7 defines the so-called main() *method*, which is the *entry point* for program execution. Again, the braces {......} encloses the *body* of the method, which contains programming statements.

```
System.out.println("Hello, world!");
```

In Line 6, the programming statement System.out.println("Hello, world!") is used to print the string "Hello, world!" to the display console. A *string* is surrounded by a pair of double quotes and contain texts. The text will be printed as it is, without the double quotes. A programming statement ends with a semi-colon (;).

Java Program Template

You can use the following *template* to write your Java programs. Choose a meaningful *"Classname"* that reflects the *purpose* of your program, and write your programming statements inside the body of the main() method.

```
1  /*
2  * Comment to state the purpose of the program
3  */
4  public class Classname { // Choose a meaningful Classname. Save as
   "Classname.java"
5   public static void main(String[] args) { // Entry point of the program
6     // Your programming statements here!
7   }
8  }
```

Output Via System.out.println() and System.out.print()

You can use System.out.println() (print-line) or System.out.print() to print message to the display console:

- System.out.println(*aString*) (print-line) prints the given *aString*, and advances the *cursor* to the beginning of the next line.
- System.out.print(*aString*) prints *aString* but places the cursor after the printed string.

Try the following program and explain the output produced:

```
1  /*
2   * Test System.out.println() (print-line) and System.out.print()
3   */
4  public class PrintTest { // Save as "PrintTest.java"
```

```
5   public static void main(String[] args) {

6   System.out.println("Hello, world!"); // Advance the cursor to the
    beginning of next line after printing

7   System.out.println(); // Print a empty line

8   System.out.print("Hello, world!"); // Cursor stayed after the print-
    ed string

9   System.out.println("Hello,");

10   System.out.print(" "); // Print a space

11   System.out.print("world!");

12   System.out.println("Hello, world!");

13   }

14   }
```

The expected outputs are:

```
Hello, world!
Hello, world!Hello,
world!Hello, world!
```

A Program to Add a Few Numbers

Let us write a program to add five integers and display their sum, as follows:

```
1   /*

2   * Add five integers and display their sum

3   */

4   public class FiveNumberSum { // Save as "FiveNumberSum.java"

5   public static void main(String[] args) {

6   int number1 = 11; // Declare 5 integer variables and assign a value

7   int number2 = 22;

8   int number3 = 33;

9   int number4 = 44;

10   int number5 = 55;
```

```
11    int sum; // Declare an int variable called sum to hold the sum

12    sum = number1 + number2 + number3 + number4 + number5; // Compute
      sum

13    System.out.print("The sum is "); // Print a descriptive string

14    System.out.println(sum); // Print the value stored in variable sum

15  }

16  }
```

The expected output is:

```
The sum is 165
```

Working

```
int number1 = 11;

int number2 = 22;

int number3 = 33;

int number4 = 44;

int number5 = 55;
```

These five statements declare five int (integer) variables called number1, number2, number3, number4, and number5; and assign values of 11, 22, 33, 44 and 55 to the variables, respectively, via the so-called assignment operator '='. You could also declare many variables in one statement separated by commas, e.g.,

```
int number1 = 11, number2 = 22, number3 = 33, number4 = 44, number5 = 55;

int sum;
```

declares an int (integer) variable called sum, without assigning an initial value.

```
sum = number1 + number2 + number3 + number4 + number5;
```

computes the sum of number1 to number 5 and assign the result to the variable sum. The symbol '+' denotes *arithmetic addition*, just like Mathematics.

```
System.out.print("The sum is ");

System.out.println(sum);
```

Line 13 prints a descriptive string. A String is surrounded by double quotes, and will be printed *as it is* (without the double quotes). Line 14 prints the *value* stored in the variable sum (in this case, the sum of the five numbers). You should not surround a variable to be printed by double quotes; otherwise, the text will get printed instead of the value stored in the variable.

Program

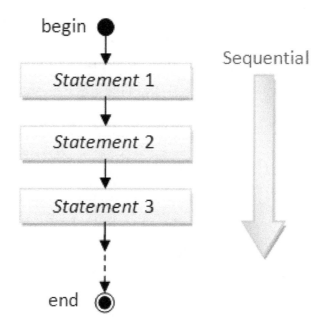

A *program* is *a sequence of instructions* (called *programming statements*), executing one after another in a *predictable* manner. *Sequential* flow is the most common and straight-forward, where programming statements are executed in the order that they are written - from top to bottom in a sequential manner, as illustrated in the following flow chart.

Example

The following program prints the area and circumference of a circle, given its radius. Take note that the programming statements are executed sequentially - one after another in the order that they were written.

```
1  /*
2   * Print the area and circumference of a circle, given its radius.
3   */
4  public class CircleComputation { // Saved as "CircleComputation.java"
5    public static void main(String[] args) {
6      // Declare double (real-number) variables to hold radius, area and
         circumference
7      double radius, area, circumference;
8      // Declare a constant for PI
9      final double PI = 3.14159265;
```

```
10
11      // Assign a value to radius
12      radius = 1.2;
13      // Compute area and circumference
14      area = radius * radius * PI;
15      circumference = 2.0 * radius * PI;
16
17      // Print results
18      System.out.print("The radius is "); // Print description
19      System.out.println(radius); // Print the value stored in the vari-
        able
20      System.out.print("The area is ");
21      System.out.println(area);
22      System.out.print("The circumference is ");
23      System.out.println(circumference);
24  }
25  }
```

The expected outputs are:

```
The radius is 1.2
The area is 4.523893416
The circumference is 7.5398223600000005
```

Working

```
double radius, area, circumference;
```

declare three double variables radius, area and circumference. A double variable can hold a real number (or floating-point number, with an optional fractional part).

```
final double PI = 3.14159265;
```

declare a double variables called PI and assign a value. PI is declared final, i.e., its value cannot be changed.

```
radius = 1.2;
```

assigns a value (real number) to the double variable radius.

```
area = radius * radius * PI;

circumference = 2.0 * radius * PI;
```

compute the area and circumference, based on the value of radius and PI.

```
System.out.print("The radius is ");

System.out.println(radius);

System.out.print("The area is ");

System.out.println(area);

System.out.print("The circumference is ");

System.out.println(circumference);
```

print the results with proper descriptions.

Take note that the programming statements inside the main() method are executed one after another, in a *sequential* manner.

Variable

Computer programs manipulate (or process) data. A *variable* is a storage location (like a house, a pigeon hole, a letter box) that stores a piece of data for processing. It is called *variable* because you can change the value stored inside.

More precisely, a *variable* is a *named* storage location, that stores a *value* of a particular data *type*. In other words, a *variable* has a *name*, a *type* and stores a *value* of that type.

- A variable has a *name* (aka *identifier*), e.g., radius, area, age, height. The name is needed to uniquely identify each variable, so as to assign a value to the variable (e.g., radius = 1.2), as well as to retrieve the value stored (e.g., radius * radius * 3.14159265).

- A variable has a *type*. Examples of *type* are:

  o int: meant for integers (or whole numbers or fixed-point numbers), such as 123 and -456;

  o double: meant for floating-point numbers or real numbers, such as 3.1416, -55.66, having an optional decimal point and fractional part.

  o String: meant for texts such as "Hello", "Good Morning!". Strings shall be enclosed with a pair of double quotes.

- A variable can store a *value* of the declared *type*. It is important to take note that a variable in most programming languages is associated with a *type*, and can only store value of that particular type. For example, a int variable can store an integer value such as 123, but NOT a real number such as 12.34, nor texts such as "Hello". The concept of *type* was introduced into the early programming languages to simplify interpretation of data.

The following diagram illustrates three types of variables: int, double and String. An int variable stores an integer (whole number); a double variable stores a real number (which includes integer as a special form of real number); a String variable stores texts.

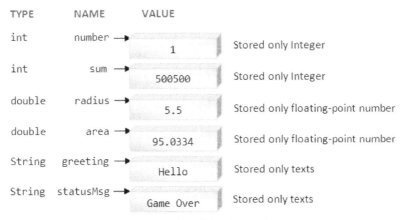

A *variable* has a **name**, stores a **value** of the declared **type**.

Declaring and using Variables

To use a variable, you need to first *declare* its *name* and *type*, in one of the following syntaxes:

```
type varName; // Declare a variable of a type

type varName1, varName2,...; // Declare multiple variables of the same
type

type varName = initialValue; // Declare a variable of a type, and assign
an initial value

type varName1 = initialValue1, varName2 = initialValue2,... ; // Declare
variables with initial values
```

For examples,

```
int sum; // Declare a variable named "sum" of the type "int" for storing
an integer.

 // Terminate the statement with a semi-colon.

double average; // Declare a variable named "average" of the type "dou-
ble" for storing a real number.

int number1, number2; // Declare 2 "int" variables named "number1" and
"number2", separated by a comma.
```

```
int height = 20; // Declare an "int" variable, and assign an initial val-
ue.
```

```
String msg = "Hello"; // Declare a "String" variable, and assign an ini-
tial value.
```

Take note that:

- Each *variable declaration statement* begins with a *type* name, and works for only that type. That is, you cannot mix 2 types in one variable declaration statement.

- Each *statement* is terminated with a semi-colon (;).

- In multiple-variable declaration, the names are separated by commas (,).

- The symbol '=', known as the *assignment operator*, can be used to assign an initial value to a variable.

More examples,

```
int number; // Declare a variable named "number" of the type "int" (in-
teger).
```

```
number = 99; // Assign an integer value of 99 to the variable "number".
```

```
number = 88; // Re-assign a value of 88 to "number".
```

```
number = number + 1; // Evaluate "number + 1", and assign the result back
to "number".
```

```
int sum = 0; // Declare an int variable named "sum" and assign an initial
value of 0.
```

```
sum = sum + number; // Evaluate "sum + number", and assign the result
back to "sum", i.e. add number into sum.
```

```
int num1 = 5, num2 = 6; // Declare and initialize 2 int variables in one
statement, separated by a comma.
```

```
double radius = 1.5; // Declare a variable named "radius", and initialize
to 1.5.
```

```
String msg; // Declare a variable named msg of the type "String"
```

```
msg = "Hello"; // Assign a double-quoted text string to the String vari-
able.
```

```
int number; // ERROR: A variable named "number" has already been declared.
```

```
sum = 55.66; // ERROR: The variable "sum" is an int. It cannot be assigned
a double.
```

```
sum = "Hello"; // ERROR: The variable "sum" is an int. It cannot be as-
signed a string.
```

Take note that:

- Each variable can only be declared once. (You cannot have two houses with the same address.)

- In Java, you can declare a variable anywhere inside your program, as long as it is declared before it is being used.

- Once a variable is declared, you can *assign* and *re-assign* a value to that variable, via the *assignment operator* '='.

- Once the *type* of a variable is declared, it can only store a value of that particular *type*. For example, an int variable can hold only integer such as 123, and NOT floating-point number such as -2.17 or text string such as "Hello".

- Once declared, the *type* of a variable CANNOT be changed.

x=x+1?

Assignment in programming (denoted as '=') is different from equality in Mathematics (also denoted as '='). E.g., "x=x+1" is invalid in Mathematics. However, in programming, it means compute the value of x plus 1, and *assign* the result back to variable x.

"x+y=1" is valid in Mathematics, but is invalid in programming. In programming, the RHS (Right-Hand Side) of '=' has to be evaluated to a value; while the LHS (Left-Hand Side) shall be a variable. That is, evaluate the RHS first, then assign the result to LHS.

Some languages uses := as the assignment operator to avoid confusion with equality.

Basic Arithmetic Operations

The basic *arithmetic operations* are:

Operator	Meaning	Example
+	Addition	x + y
-	Subtraction	x - y
*	Multiplication	x * y
/	Division	x / y
%	Modulus (Remainder)	x % y
++	Increment by 1 (Unary)	++x or x++
--	Decrement by 1 (Unary)	--x or x--

Addition, subtraction, multiplication, division and remainder are *binary operators* that take two operands (e.g., x + y); while negation (e.g., -x), increment and decrement (e.g., ++x, --x) are *unary operators* that take only one operand.

Example

The following program illustrates these arithmetic operations:

```
1   /*
2   * Test Arithmetic Operations
3   */
4   public class ArithmeticTest { // Save as "ArithmeticTest.java"
5    public static void main(String[] args) {
6     int number1 = 98; // Declare an int variable number1 and initialize
      it to 98
7     int number2 = 5; // Declare an int variable number2 and initialize
      it to 5
8     int sum, difference, product, quotient, remainder; // Declare 5 int
      variables to hold results
9
10    // Perform arithmetic Operations
11    sum = number1 + number2;
12    difference = number1 - number2;
13    product = number1 * number2;
14    quotient = number1 / number2;
15    remainder = number1 % number2;
16
17    // Print results
18    System.out.print("The sum, difference, product, quotient and re-
      mainder of "); // Print description
19    System.out.print(number1); // Print the value of the variable
20    System.out.print(" and ");
21    System.out.print(number2);
22    System.out.print(" are ");
23    System.out.print(sum);
```

```
24      System.out.print(", ");

25      System.out.print(difference);

26      System.out.print(", ");

27      System.out.print(product);

28      System.out.print(", ");

29      System.out.print(quotient);

30      System.out.print(", and ");

31      System.out.println(remainder);

32

33      ++number1; // Increment the value stored in the variable "number1"
        by 1

34      // Same as "number1 = number1 + 1"

35      --number2; // Decrement the value stored in the variable "number2"
        by 1

36      // Same as "number2 = number2 - 1"

37      System.out.println("number1 after increment is " + number1); //
        Print description and variable

38      System.out.println("number2 after decrement is " + number2);

39      quotient = number1 / number2;

40      System.out.println("The new quotient of " + number1 + " and " +
        number2

41      + " is " + quotient);

42      }

43  }
```

The expected outputs are:

```
The sum, difference, product, quotient and remainder of 98 and 5 are 103,
93, 490, 19, and 3

number1 after increment is 99

number2 after decrement is 4

The new quotient of 99 and 4 is 24
```

Working

```
int number1 = 98;

int number2 = 5;

int sum, difference, product, quotient, remainder;
```

Declare all the variables number1, number2, sum, difference, product, quotient and remainder needed in this program. All variables are of the type int (integer).

```
sum = number1 + number2;

difference = number1 - number2;

product = number1 * number2;

quotient = number1 / number2;

remainder = number1 % number2;
```

Carry out the arithmetic operations on number1 and number2. Take note that division of two integers produces a *truncated* integer, e.g., $98/5 \rightarrow 19$, $99/4 \rightarrow 24$, and $1/2 \rightarrow 0$.

```
System.out.print("The sum, difference, product, quotient and remainder
of ");
```

......

Prints the results of the arithmetic operations, with the appropriate string descriptions in between. Take note that text strings are enclosed within double-quotes, and will get printed as they are, including the white spaces but without the double quotes. To print the *value* stored in a variable, no double quotes should be used. For example,

```
System.out.println("sum"); // Print text string "sum" - as it is

System.out.println(sum); // Print the value stored in variable sum, e.g.,
98

++number1;

--number2;
```

Illustrate the increment and decrement operations. Unlike '+', '-', '*', '/' and '%', which work on two operands (*binary operators*), '++' and '--' operate on only one operand (*unary operators*). ++x is equivalent to x = x + 1, i.e., increment x by 1.

```
System.out.println("number1 after increment is " + number1);

System.out.println("number2 after decrement is " + number2);
```

Print the new values stored after the increment/decrement operations. Take note that instead of using many print() statements as in Lines 18-31, we could simply place all the items (text strings and variables) into one println(), with the items separated by '+'. In this case, '+' does not perform *addition*. Instead, it *concatenates* or *joins* all the items together.

If your Need to Add a Thousand Numbers - Use a Loop

Suppose that you want to add all the integers from 1 to 1000. If you follow the previous example, you would require a thousand-line program! Instead, you could use a so-called *loop* in your program to perform a *repetitive* task, that is what the computer is good at.

Example

Try the following program, which sums all the integers from a lowerbound (=1) to an upperbound (=1000) using a so-called *while-loop*.

```
1  /*
2  * Sum from a lowerbound to an upperbound using a while-loop
3  */
4  public class RunningNumberSum { // Save as "RunningNumberSum.java"
5   public static void main(String[] args) {
6    int lowerbound = 1; // Store the lowerbound
7    int upperbound = 1000; // Store the upperbound
8    int sum = 0; // Declare an int variable "sum" to accumulate the numbers
9            // Set the initial sum to 0
10   // Use a while-loop to repeatedly sum from the lowerbound to the upperbound
11   int number = lowerbound;
12   while (number <= upperbound) {
13     sum = sum + number; // Accumulate number into sum
14     ++number; // Next number
15   }
16   // Print the result
17   System.out.println("The sum from " + lowerbound + " to " + upperbound + " is " + sum);
18  }
19 }
```

The expected output is:

```
The sum from 1 to 1000 is 500500
```

Working

```
int lowerbound = 1;

int upperbound = 1000;
```

declare two int variables to hold the upperbound and lowerbound, respectively.

```
int sum = 0;
```

declares an int variable to hold the sum. This variable will be used to *accumulate* over the steps in the repetitive loop, and thus initialized to 0.

```
int number = lowerbound;

while (number <= upperbound) {

  sum = sum + number;

  ++number;

}
```

This is the so-called *while-loop*. A *while-loop* takes the following syntax:

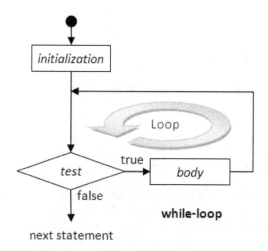

```
initialization-statement;

while (test) {

 loop-body;

}

next-statement;
```

As illustrated in the flow chart, the *initialization* statement is first executed. The *test* is then checked. If *test* is true, the *body* is executed. The *test* is checked again and the process repeats until the *test* is false. When the *test* is false, the loop completes and program execution continues to the *next statement* after the loop.

In our program, the *initialization* statement declares an int variable named number and initializes it to lowerbound. The *test* checks if number is equal to or less than the upperbound. If it is true, the current value of number is added into the sum, and the statement ++number increases the value of number by 1. The *test* is then checked again and the process repeats until the *test* is false (i.e., numberincreases to upperbound+1), which causes the loop to terminate. Execution then continues to the next statement (in Line 17).

In this example, the loop repeats upperbound-lowerbound+1 times. After the loop is completed, Line 17 prints the result with a proper description.

```
System.out.println("The sum from " + lowerbound + " to " + upperbound +
" is " + sum);
```

prints the results.

Conditional (or Decision)

What if you want to sum all the odd numbers and also all the even numbers between 1 and 1000? There are many ways to do this. You could declare two variables: sumOdd and sumEven. You can then use a *conditional* statement to check whether the number is odd or even, and accumulate the number into the respective sums. The program is as follows:

```
1  /*
2  * Sum the odd numbers and the even numbers from a lowerbound to an
   upperbound
3  */
4  public class OddEvenSum { // Save as "OddEvenSum.java"
5   public static void main(String[] args) {
6    int lowerbound = 1, upperbound = 1000; // lowerbound and upperbound
7    int sumOdd = 0; // For accumulating odd numbers, init to 0
8    int sumEven = 0; // For accumulating even numbers, init to 0
9    int number = lowerbound;
10    while (number <= upperbound) {
11      if (number % 2 == 0) { // Even
12        sumEven += number; // Same as sumEven = sumEven + number
```

```
13      } else { // Odd

14         sumOdd += number; // Same as sumOdd = sumOdd + number

15      }

16      ++number; // Next number

17    }

18    // Print the result

19    System.out.println("The sum of odd numbers from " + lowerbound + "
       to " + upperbound + " is " + sumOdd);

20    System.out.println("The sum of even numbers from " + lowerbound + "
       to " + upperbound + " is " + sumEven);

21    System.out.println("The difference between the two sums is " + (su-
       mOdd - sumEven));

22    }

23    }
```

The expected outputs are:

```
The sum of odd numbers from 1 to 1000 is 250000

The sum of even numbers from 1 to 1000 is 250500

The difference between the two sums is -500
```

Working

```
int lowerbound = 1, upperbound = 1000;
```

declares and initializes the upperbound and lowerbound.

```
int sumOdd = 0;

int sumEven = 0;
```

declare two int variables named sumOdd and sumEven and initialize them to 0, for accumulating the odd and even numbers, respectively.

```
if (number % 2 == 0) {

  sumEven += number;

} else {

  sumOdd += number;

}
```

This is a *conditional* statement. The conditional statement can take one these forms: *if-then* or *if-then-else*.

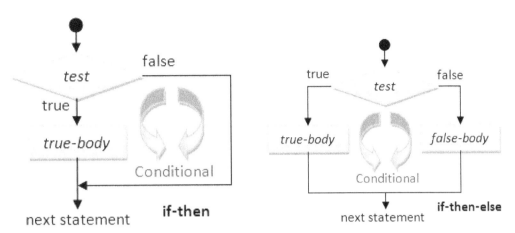

```
// if-then

if ( test ) {

   true-body;

}
// if-then-else

if ( test ) {

   true-body;

} else {

   false-body;

}
```

For a *if-then* statement, the *true-body* is executed if the *test* is true. Otherwise, nothing is done and the execution continues to the next statement. For a *if-then-else* statement, the *true-body* is executed if the *test* is true; otherwise, the *false-body* is executed. Execution is then continued to the next statement.

In our program, we use the *remainder* or *modulus* operator (%) to compute the remainder of number divides by 2. We then compare the remainder with 0 to test for even number.

Furthermore, sumEven += number is a *shorthand* for sumEven = sumEven + number.

Comparison Operators

There are six comparison (or relational) operators:

Operator	Meaning	Example
==	Equal to	x == y
!=	Not equal to	x != y
>	Greater than	x > y
>=	Greater than or equal to	x >= y
<	Less than	x < y
<=	Less than or equal to	x <= y

Take note that the comparison operator for equality is a double-equal sign (==); whereas a single-equal sign (=) is the assignment operator.

Combining Simple Conditions

Suppose that you want to check whether a number x is between 1 and 100 (inclusive), i.e., 1 <= x <= 100. There are two *simple conditions* here, (x >= 1) AND (x <= 100). In Java, you cannot write 1 <= x <= 100, but need to write (x >= 1) && (x <= 100), where "&&" denotes the "AND" operator. Similarly, suppose that you want to check whether a number x is divisible by 2 OR by 3, you have to write (x % 2 == 0) || (x % 3 == 0) where "||" denotes the "OR" operator.

There are three so-called *logical operators* that operate on the *boolean* conditions:

Operator	Meaning	Example
&&	Logical AND	(x >= 1) && (x <= 100)
||	Logical OR	(x < 1) || (x > 100)
!	Logical NOT	!(x == 8)

For examples:

```
// Return true if x is between 0 and 100 (inclusive)

(x >= 0) && (x <= 100) // AND (&&)

// Incorrect to use 0 <= x <= 100

// Return true if x is outside 0 and 100 (inclusive)

(x < 0) || (x > 100) // OR (||)

!((x >= 0) && (x <= 100)) // NOT (!), AND (&&)

// Return true if "year" is a leap year

// A year is a leap year if it is divisible by 4 but not by 100, or it
is divisible by 400.

((year % 4 == 0) && (year % 100 != 0)) || (year % 400 == 0)
```

More on Type Double and Floating-Point Numbers

Recall that a variable in Java has a name and a type, and can hold a value of only that particular type. We have so far used a type called int. A int variable holds an integer, such as 123 and -456; it cannot hold a real number, such as 12.34.

In programming, real numbers such as 3.1416 and -55.66 are called floating-point numbers, and belong to a type called double. You can express floating-point numbers in fixed notation (e.g., 1.23, -4.5) or scientific notation (e.g., 1.2e3, -4E-5) where e or E denote the exponent of base 10.

Example

```
1  /*
2   * Convert temperature between Celsius and Fahrenheit
3   */
4 public class ConvertTemperature { // Save as "ConvertTemperature.java"
5   public static void main(String[] args) {
6      double celsius, fahrenheit;
7
8      celsius = 37.5;
9      fahrenheit = celsius * 9.0 / 5.0 + 32.0;
10     System.out.println(celsius + " degree C is " + fahrenheit + " degree F.");
11
12     fahrenheit = 100.0;
13     celsius = (fahrenheit - 32.0) * 5.0 / 9.0;
14     System.out.println(fahrenheit + " degree F is " + celsius + " degree C.");
15
16   }
17 }
```

The expected outputs are:

```
37.5 degree C is 99.5 degree F.
100.0 degree F is 37.77777777777778 degree C.
```

Mixing int and Double, and Type Casting

Although you can use a double to keep an integer value (e.g., double count = 5.0, as floating-point numbers includes integers as special case), you should use an int for integer, as int is far more efficient than double, in terms of running time, accuracy and storage requirement.

At times, you may need both int and double in your program. For example, keeping the *sum* from 1 to 1000 as int, and their *average* as double. You need to be *extremely careful* when different types are mixed.

It is important to note that:

- Arithmetic operations ('+', '-', '*', '/') of two int's produce an int; while arithmetic operations of two double's produce a double. Hence, 1/2 → 0 (take that this is truncated to 0, not 0.5) and 1.0/2.0 → 0.5.

- Arithmetic operations of an int and a double produce a double. Hence, 1.0/2 → 0.5 and 1/2.0 → 0.5.

You can assign an integer value to a double variable. The integer value will be converted to a double value automatically, e.g., 3 → 3.0. For examples,

```
int i = 3;

double d;

d = i; // 3 → 3.0, d = 3.0

d = 88; // 88 → 88.0, d = 88.0

double nought = 0; // 0 → 0.0; there is a subtle difference between int
0 and double 0.0
```

However, you CANNOT assign a double value directly to an int variable. This is because the *fractional* part could be lost, and the Java compiler signals an error in case that you were not aware. For example,

```
double d = 5.5;

int i;

i = d; // error: possible loss of precision

i = 6.6; // error: possible loss of precision
```

Type Casting Operators

To assign an double value to an int variable, you need to explicitly invoke a *type-casting operation* to *truncate the fractional part*, as follows:

```
(new-type) expression;
```

For example,

```
double d = 5.5;

int i;

i = (int) d; // Type-cast the value of double d, which returns an int value,

 // assign the resultant int value to int i.

 // The value stored in d is not affected.

i = (int) 3.1416; // i = 3
```

Take note that type-casting operator, in the form of (int) or (double), applies to one operand immediately after the operator (i.e., unary operator).

Type-casting is an operation, like increment or addition, which operates on a operand and return a value (in the specified type), e.g., (int)3.1416 takes a double value of 3.1416 and returns 3 (of type int); (double)5 takes an int value of 5 and returns 5.0 (of type double).

Example

Try the following program and explain the outputs produced:

```
1 /*

2  * Find the sum and average from a lowerbound to an upperbound

3  */

4 public class TypeCastingTest { // Save as "TypeCastingTest.java"

5   public static void main(String[] args) {

6     int lowerbound = 1, upperbound = 1000;

7     int sum = 0; // sum is "int"

8     double average; // average is "double"

9

10    // Compute the sum (in "int")

11    int number = lowerbound;

12    while (number <= upperbound) {

13      sum = sum + number;

14      ++number;
```

```
15    }

16    System.out.println("The sum from " + lowerbound + " to " + upper-
      bound + " is " + sum);

17

18    // Compute the average (in "double")

19    average = sum / (upperbound - lowerbound + 1);

20    System.out.println("Average 1 is " + average);

21    average = (double)sum / (upperbound - lowerbound + 1);

22    System.out.println("Average 2 is " + average);

23    average = sum / 1000;

24    System.out.println("Average 3 is " + average);

25    average = sum / 1000.0;

26    System.out.println("Average 4 is " + average);

27    average = (double)(sum / 1000);

28    System.out.println("Average 5 is " + average);

29  }

30 }
```

The expected output are:

```
The sum from 1 to 1000 is 500500

Average 1 is 500.0 <== incorrect

Average 2 is 500.5

Average 3 is 500.0 <== incorrect

Average 4 is 500.5

Average 5 is 500.0 <== incorrect
```

The first average is incorrect, as int/int produces an int (of 500), which is converted to double (of 500.0) to be stored in average (of double).

For the second average, the value of sum (of int) is first converted to double. Subsequently, double/int produces a double.

For the fifth average, int/int produces an int (of 500), which is casted to double (of 500.0) and assigned to average (of double).

Leap Year Program

```
/*********************************************************************
********
 * Compilation: javac LeapYear.java
 * Execution: java LeapYear n
 *
 * Prints true if n corresponds to a leap year, and false otherwise.
 * Assumes n >= 1582, corresponding to a year in the Gregorian calendar.
 *
 * % java LeapYear 2004
 * true
 *
 * % java LeapYear 1900
 * false
 *
 * % java LeapYear 2000
 * true
 *
 *********************************************************************
********/
public class LeapYear {
    public static void main(String[] args) {
        int year = Integer.parseInt(args[0]);
        boolean isLeapYear;
        // divisible by 4
        isLeapYear = (year % 4 == 0);
        // divisible by 4 and not 100
        isLeapYear = isLeapYear && (year % 100 != 0);
```

```java
            // divisible by 4 and not 100 unless divisible by 400
            isLeapYear = isLeapYear || (year % 400 == 0);
        System.out.println(isLeapYear);
    }
}
```

10 Hellos Program

```java
/***************************************************************************
 * Compilation: javac TenHellos.java
 * Execution: java TenHellos
 *
 * Prints ith Hello for i = 1 to 10. Illlustrates using a while loop
 * for a repetitive task.
 *
 * % java TenHellos
 * 1st Hello
 * 2nd Hello
 * 3rd Hello
 * 4th Hello
 * 5th Hello
 * 6th Hello
 * 7th Hello
 * 8th Hello
 * 9th Hello
 * 10th Hello
 *
 ***************************************************************************/
```

```java
public class TenHellos {
    public static void main(String[] args) {
        // print out special cases whose ordinal doesn't end in th
        System.out.println("1st Hello");
        System.out.println("2nd Hello");
        System.out.println("3rd Hello");
        // count from i = 4 to 10
        int i = 4;
        while (i <= 10) {
            System.out.println(i + "th Hello");
            i = i + 1;
        }
    }
}
```

Binary Program

```
/***************************************************************************
 ********
 * Compilation: javac Binary.java
 * Execution: java Binary n
 *
 * Prints out n in binary.
 *
 * % java Binary 5
 * 101
 *
 * % java Binary 106
 * 1101010
 *
```

```
 *  % java Binary 0

 *  0

 *

 *  % java Binary 16

 *  10000

 *

 *  Limitations

 *  -----------

 *  Does not handle negative integers.

 *

 *  Remarks

 *  -------

 *  could use Integer.toBinaryString(N) instead.

 *

 ************************************************************************
 ********/

public class Binary {

    public static void main(String[] args) {

        // read in the command-line argument

        int n = Integer.parseInt(args[0]);

        // set power to the largest power of 2 that is <= n

        int power = 1;

        while (power <= n/2) {

            power *= 2;

        }

        // check for presence of powers of 2 in n, from largest to
        smallest

        while (power > 0) {

            // power is not present in n
```

```
                    if (n < power) {

                        System.out.print(0);

            }

            // power is present in n, so subtract power from n

            else {

                System.out.print(1);

                n -= power;

            }

            // next smallest power of 2

            power /= 2;

        }

        System.out.println();

    }

}
```

Twenty Questions Program

```
/***************************************************************************
********

 * Compilation: javac TwentyQuestions.java

 * Execution: java TwentyQuestions

 * Dependencies StdIn.java

 *

 * % java TwentyQuestions

 * I'm thinking of a number between 1 and 1,000,000

 * What's your guess? 500000

 * Too high

 * What's your guess? 250000

 * Too low

 * What's your guess? 375000
```

```
 * Too high

 * What's your guess? 312500

 * Too high

 * What's your guess? 300500

 * Too low

 *...

 *

 *********************************************************************
 ******/

public class TwentyQuestions {

    public static void main(String[] args) {

    // Generate a number and answer questions

    // while the user tries to guess the value.

    int secret = 1 + (int) (Math.random() * 1000000);

    StdOut.print("I'm thinking of a number ");

    StdOut.println("between 1 and 1,000,000");

    int guess = 0;

    while (guess != secret) {

        // Solicit one guess and provide one answer

        StdOut.print("What's your guess? ");

        guess = StdIn.readInt();

        if (guess == secret) StdOut.println("You win!");

        else if (guess < secret) StdOut.println("Too low ");

        else if (guess > secret) StdOut.println("Too high");

        }

    }

}
```

Self-avoiding Walks Program

```
/*********************************************************************
********

* Compilation: javac SelfAvoidingWalk.java

* Execution: java SelfAvoidingWalk n trials

*

* Generate trials self-avoiding walks of length n.

* Report the fraction of time the random walk is non self-intersecting.

*

*********************************************************************
*******/

public class SelfAvoidingWalk {

    public static void main(String[] args) {

        int n = Integer.parseInt(args[0]); // lattice size

        int trials = Integer.parseInt(args[1]); // number of trials

        int deadEnds = 0; // trials resulting in a dead end

        // simulate trials self-avoiding walks

        for (int t = 0; t < trials; t++) {

            boolean[][] a = new boolean[n][n]; // intersections vis-
            ited

        int x = n/2, y = n/2; // current position

        // repeatedly take a random step, unless you've already es-
        caped

            while (x > 0 && x < n-1 && y > 0 && y < n-1) {

            // dead-end, so break out of loop

            if (a[x-1][y] && a[x+1][y] && a[x][y-1] && a[x][y+1]) {

                deadEnds++;

                break;

            }
```

```
                // mark (x, y) as visited
                a[x][y] = true;
                // take a random step to unvisited neighbor
                double r = Math.random();
                if (r < 0.25) {
                    if (!a[x+1][y])
                      x++;
                }
                else if (r < 0.50) {
                    if (!a[x-1][y])
                      x--;
                }
                else if (r < 0.75) {
                    if (!a[x][y+1])
                      y++;
                }
                else if (r < 1.00) {
                    if (!a[x][y-1])
                        y--;
                }
            }
        }
        System.out.println(100*deadEnds/trials + "% dead ends");
    }
}
```

Bouncing Ball Program

```
/**************************************************************************
********

* Compilation: javac BouncingBall.java
* Execution: java BouncingBall
```

```
 * Dependencies: StdDraw.java
 *
 * Implementation of a 2-d bouncing ball in the box from (-1, -1) to (1, 1).
 *
 * % java BouncingBall
 *
 *************************************************************************
 *******/
public class BouncingBall {
    public static void main(String[] args) {
        // set the scale of the coordinate system
        StdDraw.setXscale(-1.0, 1.0);
        StdDraw.setYscale(-1.0, 1.0);
        StdDraw.enableDoubleBuffering();
        // initial values
        double rx = 0.480, ry = 0.860; // position
        double vx = 0.015, vy = 0.023; // velocity
        double radius = 0.05; // radius
        // main animation loop
        while (true) {
            // bounce off wall according to law of elastic collision
            if (Math.abs(rx + vx) > 1.0 - radius) vx = -vx;
            if (Math.abs(ry + vy) > 1.0 - radius) vy = -vy;
            // update position
            rx = rx + vx;
            ry = ry + vy;
            // clear the background
            StdDraw.clear(StdDraw.LIGHT_GRAY);
            // draw ball on the screen
            StdDraw.setPenColor(StdDraw.BLACK);
```

```
            StdDraw.filledCircle(rx, ry, radius);
            // copy offscreen buffer to onscreen
            StdDraw.show();
            // pause for 20 ms
            StdDraw.pause(20);
        }
    }
}
```

Sample Program

```
/****************************************************************************
********
* Compilation: javac Sample.java
* Execution: java Sample m n
*
* This program takes two command-line arguments m and n and produces
* a random sample of m of the integers from 0 to n-1.
*
* % java Sample 6 49
* 10 20 0 46 40 6
*
* % java Sample 10 1000
* 656 488 298 534 811 97 813 156 424 109
*
****************************************************************************
*******/
public class Sample {
    public static void main(String[] args) {
        int m = Integer.parseInt(args[0]); // choose this many ele-
        ments
        int n = Integer.parseInt(args[1]); // from 0, 1,..., n-1
        // create permutation 0, 1,..., n-1
```

```
            int[] perm = new int[n];
            for (int i = 0; i < n; i++)
                perm[i] = i;
            // create random sample in perm[0], perm[1],..., perm[m-1]
            for (int i = 0; i < m; i++) {
                // random integer between i and n-1
                int r = i + (int) (Math.random() * (n-i));
                // swap elements at indices i and r
                int t = perm[r];
                perm[r] = perm[i];
                perm[i] = t;
            }
            // print results
            for (int i = 0; i < m; i++)
                System.out.print(perm[i] + " ");
            System.out.println();
        }
}
```

Factors Program

```
/***********************************************************************
********
* Compilation: javac Factors.java
* Execution: java Factors n
*
* Computes the prime factorization of n using brute force.
*
* % java Factors 81
* The prime factorization of 81 is: 3 3 3 3
*
* % java Factors 168
```

```
* The prime factorization of 168 is: 2 2 2 3 7
*
* % java Factors 4444444444
* The prime factorization of 4444444444 is: 2 2 11 41 271 9091
*
* % java Factors 4444444444444463
* The prime factorization of 4444444444444463 is: 4444444444444463
*
* % java Factors 10000001400000049
* The prime factorization of 10000001400000049 is: 100000007 100000007
*
* % java Factors 1000000014000000049
* The prime factorization of 1000000014000000049 is: 1000000007 1000000007
*
* % java Factors 9201111169755555649
* The prime factorization of 9201111169755555649 is: 3033333343 3033333343
*
* Can use these for timing tests - biggest 3, 6, 9, 12, 15, and 18 digit
*   primes
* % java Factors 997
* % java Factors 999983
* % java Factors 999999937
* % java Factors 999999999989
* % java Factors 999999999999989
* % java Factors 999999999999999989
*
* Remarks
* -------
* - Tests factor*factor <= n instead of factor <= n for efficiency.
*
* - The last two examples still take a few minutes.
```

```
*

****************************************************************************
*******/
public class Factors {
    public static void main(String[] args) {


        // command-line argument
        long n = Long.parseLong(args[0]);
        System.out.print("The prime factorization of " + n + " is: ");
        // for each potential factor
        for (long factor = 2; factor*factor <= n; factor++) {
            // if factor is a factor of n, repeatedly divide it out
            while (n % factor == 0) {
                System.out.print(factor + " ");
                n = n / factor;
            }
        }
        // if biggest factor occurs only once, n > 1
        if (n > 1) System.out.println(n);
        else System.out.println();
    }
}
```

Transition Program

```
/****************************************************************************
********

* Compilation: javac Transition.java

* Execution: java Transition < input.txt

* Data files: https://introcs.cs.princeton.edu/16pagerank/tiny.txt

* https://introcs.cs.princeton.edu/16pagerank/medium.txt

*
```

```
 * This program is a filter that reads links from standard input and
 * produces the corresponding transition matrix on standard output.
 * First, it processes the input to count the outlinks from each page.
 * Then it applies the 90-10 rule to compute the transition matrix.
 * It assumes that there are no pages that have no outlinks in the
 * input.
 *
 * % more tiny.txt
 * 5
 * 0 1
 * 1 2 1 2
 * 1 3 1 3 1 4
 * 2 3
 * 3 0
 * 4 0 4 2
 *
 * % java Transition < tiny.txt
 * 5 5
 * 0.02 0.92 0.02 0.02 0.02
 * 0.02 0.02 0.38 0.38 0.20
 * 0.02 0.02 0.02 0.92 0.02
 * 0.92 0.02 0.02 0.02 0.02
 * 0.47 0.02 0.47 0.02 0.02
 *
 *******************************************************************
 *******/

public class Transition {
    public static void main(String[] args) {
```

```
        int n = StdIn.readInt(); // number of pages

        int[][] counts = new int[n][n]; // counts[i][j] = #
links from page i to page j

        int[] outDegree = new int[n]; // outDegree[i] = # links
from page i to anywhere

        // Accumulate link counts.

        while (!StdIn.isEmpty()) {

          int i = StdIn.readInt();

          int j = StdIn.readInt();

          outDegree[i]++;

          counts[i][j]++;

        }

        StdOut.println(n + " " + n);

        // Print probability distribution for row i.

        for (int i = 0; i < n; i++) {

          // Print probability for column j.

          for (int j = 0; j < n; j++) {

              double p = 0.90*counts[i][j]/outDegree[i] + 0.10/n;

              StdOut.printf("%7.5f ", p);

          }

          StdOut.println();

        }

    }

}
```

Java Pattern Programs

Pattern 1 : Printing Floyd's triangle pattern

Floyd's triangle is a right-angled triangular array of natural numbers.

It is named after Robert Floyd.

It is defined by filling the rows of the triangle with consecutive numbers, starting with a 1 in the top left corner.

```
1

2 3

4 5 6

7 8 9 10

11 12 13 14 15
```

```java
package com.topjavatutorial;

public class FloydTriangle {

    public static void main(String[] args) {

        int i, j, k = 1;

        for (i = 1; i <= 5; i++) {

            for (j = 1; j < i + 1; j++) {

                System.out.print(k++ + " ");

            }

            System.out.println();

        }

    }

}
```

Pattern 2 : Printing Pascal's triangle Pattern

Pascal's triangle is a triangular array of the binomial coefficients.

It is named after Blaise Pascal.

The triangle may be constructed in the following manner: In row 0 (the topmost row), there is a unique nonzero entry 1. Each entry of each subsequent row is constructed by adding the number above and to the left with the number above and to the right, treating blank entries as 0.

```
            1
         1     1
      1     2     1
   1     3     3     1
1     4     6     4     1
```

```java
package com.topjavatutorial;
public class PascalTriangle {
    public static void main(String[] args) {
    int n = 5;
    for (int i = 0; i < n; i++) {
        int number = 1;
        System.out.printf("%" + (n - i) * 2 + "s", "");
        for (int j = 0; j <= i; j++) {
            System.out.printf("%4d", number);
            number = number * (i - j) / (j + 1);
        }
        System.out.println();
    }
    }
}
```

Pattern 3 : Diamond shape composed of Star(*)

```
    *
   * * *
  * * * * *
 * * * * * * *
* * * * * * * * *
 * * * * * * *
  * * * * *
   * * *
    *
```

```java
package com.topjavatutorial;
public class DiamondPattern {
    public static void main(String[] args) {
        int number, i, k, count = 1;
        number = 5;
```

```
count = number - 1;
for (k = 1; k <= number; k++)
    {
            for (i = 1; i <= count; i++)
              System.out.print(" ");
            count--;
            for (i = 1; i <= 2 * k - 1; i++)
              System.out.print("*");
            System.out.println();
    }
count = 1;
for (k = 1; k <= number - 1; k++)
{
for (i = 1; i <= count; i++)
        System.out.print(" ");
count++;
for (i = 1; i <= 2 * (number - k) - 1; i++)
        System.out.print("*");
System.out.println();
    }
    }
}
```

Pattern 4 : Diamond Shape Composed of Numbers

```
   1
  212
 32123
4321234
 32123
  212
   1
```

```java
package com.topjavatutorial;
public class DiamondPattern {
    public static void main(String[] args) {
        for (int i = 1; i <= 4; i++)
        {
            int n = 4;
            for (int j = 1; j <= n - i; j++)
            {
                System.out.print(" ");
            }
            for (int k = i; k >= 1; k--)
            {
                System.out.print(k);
            }
            for (int l = 2; l <= i; l++)
            {
                System.out.print(l);
            }
            System.out.println();
        }
        for (int i = 3; i >= 1; i--)
        {
            int n = 3;
            for (int j = 0; j <= n - i; j++)
            {
                System.out.print(" ");
            }
            for (int k = i; k >= 1; k--)
            {
                System.out.print(k);
```

```
                    }
                    for (int l = 2; l <= i; l++)
                    {
                      System.out.print(l);
                    }
                      System.out.println();
                }
            }
}
```

Pattern 5 : Diamond shape composed of Alphabets

Enter a Char between A to Z : G

```
          A
         B B
        C   C
       D     D
      E       E
     F         F
    G           G
     F         F
      E       E
       D     D
        C   C
         B B
          A
```

```
package com.topjavatutorial;

import java.util.Scanner;

public class DiamondPattern {

    public static void main(String[] args) {

        char[] letter = { 'A', 'B', 'C', 'D', 'E', 'F', 'G', 'H', 'I',
        'J',

                'K', 'L', 'M', 'N', 'O', 'P', 'Q', 'R', 'S', 'T', 'U',
                'V',

                'W', 'X', 'Y', 'Z' };

        int letter_number = 0;
```

```java
// array of strings
String[] diamond = new String[26];
// get the letter
System.out.print("Enter a Char between A to Z : ");
Scanner reader = new Scanner(System.in);
try {
    char user_letter = reader.next("[A-Z]").charAt(0);
    // search for letter number in the array letter
    for (int i = 0; i < letter.length; i++) {
    if (letter[i] == user_letter) {
        letter_number = i;
        break;
    }
}
}
// construct diamond
for (int i = 0; i <= letter_number; i++) {
    diamond[i] = "";
    // add initial spaces
    for (int j = 0; j < letter_number - i; j++) {
        diamond[i] += " ";
    }
    // add letter (first time)
        diamond[i] += letter[i];
    // add space between letters
    if (letter[i] != 'A') {
        for (int j = 0; j < 2 * i - 1; j++) {
            diamond[i] += " ";
        }
        // add letter (second time)
        diamond[i] += letter[i];
```

```
                    }
                    // Draw the first part of the diamond as it's composing.
                    System.out.println(diamond[i]);
                }
                for (int i = letter_number - 1; i >= 0; i--) {
                    // Draw the second part of the diamond
                    // Writing the diamondArray in reverse order.
                    System.out.println(diamond[i]);
                }
            } catch (Exception e) {
                // TODO Auto-generated catch block
                e.printStackTrace();
            } finally {
                reader.close();
            }
        }
    }
```

Pattern 6

Enter a number between 1 to 9 : 4

```
      1
    121
  12321
1234321
```

```
package com.topjavatutorial;
import java.util.Scanner;
public class NumberPattern {
    public static void main(String[] args) {
        int num, space;
        System.out.print("Enter a number between 1 to 9 : ");
        Scanner reader = new Scanner(System.in);
```

```java
        try {

                num = reader.nextInt();

                space = num - 1;

                for (int i = 1; i <= num; i++) {

                   for (space = 1; space <= (num - i); space++) {

                        System.out.print(" ");

                   }

                   for (int j = 1; j <= i; j++) {

                        System.out.print(j);

                   }

                   for (int k = (i - 1); k >= 1; k--) {

                        System.out.print(k);

                   }

                   System.out.println();

                }

        } finally {

                reader.close();

        }

    }

}
```

Pattern 7

```
1
22
333
4444
55555
```

```java
package com.topjavatutorial;

public class NumberPattern {

        public static void main(String[] args) {

                int count = 5;
```

```
        for (int i = 1; i <= count; i++) {
                for (int j = 1; j <= i; j++) {
                        System.out.print(i);
                }
                System.out.println();
        }
    }
}
```

Pattern 8

```
1
12
123
1234
12345
1234
123
12
1
```

```
package com.topjavatutorial;
public class NumberPattern {
    public static void main(String[] args) {
        int n = 5;
        for (int i = 1; i < n; i++) {
            for (int j = 1; j <= i; j++)
                System.out.print(j);
            System.out.println();
        }
        for (int i = n; i >= 0; i--) {
            for (int j = 1; j <= i; j++)
                System.out.print(j);
```

```
                System.out.println();
            }
            System.out.println();
        }
    }
```

Pattern 9

```
12345
1234
123
12
1
1
12
123
1234
12345
```

```
package com.topjavatutorial;
public class NumberPattern {
    public static void main(String[] args) {
        int n = 5;
        for (int i = n; i >= 0; i--) {
            for (int j = 1; j <= i; j++)
                System.out.print(j);
            System.out.println();
        }
        for (int i = 1; i <= n; i++) {
            for (int j = 1; j <= i; j++)
                System.out.print(j);
            System.out.println();
        }
```

```
            System.out.println();
        }
}
```

Pattern 10

```
1
01
101
0101
10101
```

```java
package com.topjavatutorial;
public class NumberPattern {
    public static void main(String[] args) {
        int n, p, q;
        n = 5;
        for (int i = 1; i <= n; i++)
        {
            if (i % 2 == 0)
            { p = 1; q = 0; }
            else
            { p = 0; q = 1; }
            for (int j = 1; j <= i; j++)
                if (j % 2 == 0)
                    System.out.print(p);
                else
                    System.out.print(q);
            System.out.println();
        }
    }
}
```

Pattern 11

```
A
BB
CCC
DDDD
EEEEE
```

```java
package com.topjavatutorial;

public class CharPattern{

    public static void main(String []args){

        char ch = 'A';

        for (int i = 1; i <= 5; i++) {

            for (int j = 1; j <= i; j++) {

                System.out.print(ch);

            }

            ch++;

            System.out.println();

        }

    }

}
```

Pattern 12

```
    1
   1 2
  1 2 3
 1 2 3 4
1 2 3 4 5
```

```java
package com.topjavatutorial;

public class NumberPattern {

    public static void main(String[] args) {

        int n= 5;

        for (int i = 1; i <= n; i++) {

            for (int j = 1; j <= n - i; j++) {
```

```
                    System.out.print(" ");
                }
                for (int k = 1; k <= i; k++) {
                    System.out.print(k + " ");
                }
                System.out.println("");
            }
        }
    }
```

Pattern 13

```
5
54
543
5432
54321
```

```java
package com.topjavatutorial;
public class NumberPattern {
    public static void main(String[] args) {
        int i = 5;
        while (i >= 1) {
            int j = 5;
            while (j >= i) {
                System.out.print(j);
                j--;
            }
            i--;
            System.out.println();
        }
    }
}
```

Pattern 14

```
1****
12***
123**
1234*
12345
```

```java
package com.topjavatutorial;
public class NumberPattern {
    public static void main(String[] args) {
        int i, j, k;
        int n = 5;
        for (i = 1; i <= n; i++) {
            for (j = 1; j <= i; ++j)
                System.out.print(j);
            for (k = n - i; k >= 1; k--)
                System.out.print("*");
            System.out.println();
        }
    }
}
```

Pattern 15

```
    1
   1 2
  1 2 3
 1 2 3 4
1 2 3 4 5
 1 2 3 4
  1 2 3
   1 2
    1
```

```java
package com.topjavatutorial;
public class NumberPattern {
```

```java
public static void main(String[] args) {
    int i, j, k;
        for (i = 1; i <= 5; i++) {
            for (j = 1; j <= 5 - i; j++)
                System.out.print(" ");
            for (k = 1; k <= i; k++)
                System.out.print(k + " ");
            System.out.println();
        }
        for (i = 1; i <= 4; i++) {
            for (j = 1; j <= i; j++)
                System.out.print(" ");
            for (k = 1; k <= 5 - i; k++)
                System.out.print(k + " ");
        System.out.println();
        }
    }
}
```

Pattern 16

```
* * * * * * * *
* * * * * * *
* * * * * *
* * * * *
* * * *
* * *
* *
*
```

```java
package com.topjavatutorial;
```

```java
public class JavaStarPattern {
    public static void main(String[] args) {
        for (int row = 8; row >= 1; --row) {
            for (int col = 1; col <= row; ++col) {
                System.out.print("*");
            }
            System.out.println();
        }
    }
}
```

Pattern 17

```
*
**
***
****
*****
******
*******
********
```

```java
package com.topjavatutorial;
public class JavaStarPattern {
    public static void main(String[] args) {
        for (int row = 1; row <= 8; ++row) {
            for (int col = 1; col <= row; ++col) {
                System.out.print("*");
            }
            System.out.println();
        }
    }
}
```

Pattern 18

```
      *
     ***
    *****
   *******
  *********
 ***********
*************
```

```java
package com.topjavatutorial;
public class JavaStarPattern {
    public static void main(String[] args) {
        int number = 7;
        int count = number - 1;
        for (int k = 1; k <= number; k++) {
            for (int i = 1; i <= count; i++)
              System.out.print(" ");
            count--;
            for (int i = 1; i <= 2 * k - 1; i++)
              System.out.print("*");
            System.out.println();
        }
    }
}
```

Pattern 19: Diamond Pattern

```
      *
     ***
    *****
   *******
  *********
   *******
    *****
     ***
      *
```

```java
package com.topjavatutorial;
```

```java
public class JavaStarPattern {
    public static void main(String[] args) {
        int number = 5;
        int count = number - 1;
        for (int k = 1; k <= number; k++) {
            for (int i = 1; i <= count; i++)
                System.out.print(" ");
            count--;
            for (int i = 1; i <= 2 * k - 1; i++)
                System.out.print("*");
            System.out.println();
        }
        count = 1;
        for (int k = 1; k <= number - 1; k++) {
            for (int i = 1; i <= count; i++)
                System.out.print(" ");
            count++;
            for (int i = 1; i <= 2 * (number - k) - 1; i++)
                System.out.print("*");
            System.out.println();
        }
    }
}
```

Pattern 20

```
      *
     **
    ***
   ****
  *****
 ******
*******
********
```

```java
package com.topjavatutorial;
public class JavaStarPattern {

    public static void main(String[] args) {
        int val = 8;
        for (int i = 1; i <= val; i++) {
            for (int j = 1; j <= val - i; j++) {
                System.out.print(" ");
            }
            for (int k = 1; k <= i; k++) {
                System.out.print("*");
            }
            System.out.println("");
        }
    }
}
```

Pattern 21

```
* *
** **
*** ***
**** ****
***** *****
****** ******
******* *******
******** ********
```

```java
package com.topjavatutorial;
public class JavaStarPattern {

    public static void main(String[] args) {
        int number = 8;
        for (int i = 0; i < number; ++i) {
            for (int j = 0; j <= i; ++j) {
```

```
                    System.out.print("*");
                }
                if (i != number - 1) {
                  System.out.print(" ");
                } else {
                  System.out.print(" *");
                }
                for (int j = 0; j <= i; ++j) {
                  System.out.print("*");
                }
                System.out.println();
            }
        }
}
```

Pattern 22

```
*******
*     *
*     *
*     *
*     *
*     *
*******
```

```
package com.topjavatutorial;
public class JavaStarPattern {
    public static void main(String[] args) {
        int number = 7;
        for (int i = 0; i < number; i++) {
            if (i == 0 || i == 6) {
                for (int j = 0; j < number; j++) {
                    System.out.print("*");
```

```
                    }
                    System.out.println();
                }
                if (i >= 1 && i <= 5) {
                    for (int j = 0; j < number; j++) {
                    if (j == 0 || j == 6) {
                      System.out.print("*");
                    } else if (j >= 1 && j <= 5) {
                      System.out.print(" ");
                    }
                }
                System.out.println();
            }
        }
    }
}
```

Pattern 23

```
*               * * * * * * * * * * * * * * *            *
* *             * * * * * * *  * * * * * *            * *
* * *           * * * * * *    * * * * *            * * *
* * * *         * * * * *      * * * *        * * * *
* * * * *       * * * * *        * * * *    * * * * *
* * * * * *     * * * *          * * *   * * * * * *
* * * * * * *   * * *              * *  * * * * * * *
* * * * * * * * *                    * * * * * * * *
```

```
package com.topjavatutorial;
public class JavaStarPattern {
    private static void stars(int count) {
        for (int i = 0; i < count; ++i)
```

```
            System.out.print("*");
    }
    private static void spaces(int count) {
        for (int i = 0; i < count; ++i)
            System.out.print(" ");
    }
    public static void main(String[] args) {
        int n = 8;
        for (int i = 0; i < n; ++i) {
            stars(i + 1);
            spaces(n - i - 1);
            stars(n - i + 1);
            spaces(2 * i);
            stars(n - i);
            spaces(n - i - 1);
            stars(i + 1);
            System.out.println();
        }
    }
}
```

Pattern 24

```
1 2 3 4 5

2 3 4 5

3 4 5

4 5

5

4 5

3 4 5

2 3 4 5

1 2 3 4 5
```

```
class PrintPattern
{
    public static void main(String[] args)
    {
        int n = 5;
        for (int i = 1; i <= n; i++)
        {
            for (int j = i; j <= n; j++)
            {
                System.out.print(j+" ");
            }
            System.out.println();
        }
        for (int i = n-1; i >= 1; i--)
        {
            for (int j = i; j <= n; j++)
            {
                System.out.print(j+" ");
            }
            System.out.println();
        }
    }
}
```

Pattern 25

```
1 2 3 4 5
  2 3 4 5
    3 4 5
      4 5
        5
      4 5
    3 4 5
  2 3 4 5
1 2 3 4 5
```

```
class PrintPattern
{
    public static void main(String[] args)
    {
        int n = 5;
        for (int i = 1; i <= n; i++)
        {
            for (int j = 1; j < i; j++)
            {
              System.out.print(" ");
            }
            for (int k = i; k <= n; k++)
            {
              System.out.print(k+" ");
            }
              System.out.println();
        }
          for (int i = n-1; i >= 1; i--)
          {
            for (int j = 1; j < i; j++)
            {
              System.out.print(" ");
            }
            for (int k = i; k <= n; k++)
            {
              System.out.print(k+" ");
            }
```

```
            System.out.println();

        }

    }

}
```

Pattern 26

A

BC

DEF

GHIJ

KLMNO

```java
class CharPattern {

    public static void main(String[] args) {

        char ch = 'A';

        for (int i = 1; i <= 5; i++) {

            for (int j = 1; j <= i; j++) {

                System.out.print(ch);

                ch++;

            }

            System.out.println();

        }

    }

}
```

Divisor Pattern

```
/*******************************************************************
********
 * Compilation: javac DivisorPattern.java
 * Execution: java DivisorPattern n
 *
```

```
 * Prints a table where entry (i, j) is a '* ' if i divides j
 * or j divides i and '. ' otherwise.
 *
 *
 * % java DivisorPattern 20
 * * * * * * * * * * * * * * * * * * * * 1
 * * * * * * * * * * * 2
 * * * * * * * * 3
 * * * * * * * * 4
 * * * * * * 5
 * * * * * * * 6
 * * * * 7
 * * * * * * 8
 * * * * * 9
 * * * * * * 10
 * * * 11
 * * * * * * * 12
 * * * 13
 * * * * * 14
 * * * * * 15
 * * * * * * * 16
 * * * 17
 * * * * * * * 18
 * * * 19
 * * * * * * * 20
 *

**********************************************************************
*******/

public class DivisorPattern {
    public static void main(String[] args) {
        int n = Integer.parseInt(args[0]);
        for (int i = 1; i <= n; i++) {
            for (int j = 1; j <= n; j++) {
                if (i % j == 0 || j % i == 0) {
```

```java
                System.out.print("* ");
            }
            else {
              System.out.print(" ");
            }
        }
        System.out.println(i);
      }
    }
}
```

Java Computing Platforms

The Java platform is a set of programs that enables the development and operation of programs using the Java programming language. Such platforms include an execution engine, a compiler and a set of libraries. This chapter discusses in detail all the varied types of Java computing platforms along with important aspects such as Java card, java development kit, etc.

Java Software Platform

Java (with a capital J) is a platform for application development. A platform is a loosely defined computer industry buzzword that typically means some combination of hardware and system software that will mostly run all the same software. For instance PowerMacs running Mac OS 9.2 would be one platform. DEC Alphas running Windows NT would be another.

There's another problem with distributing executable programs from web pages. Computer programs are very closely tied to the specific hardware and operating system they run. A Windows program will not run on a computer that only runs DOS. A Mac application can't run on a Unix workstation. VMS code can't be executed on an IBM mainframe, and so on. Therefore major commercial applications like Microsoft Word or Netscape have to be written almost independently for all the different platforms they run on. Netscape is one of the most cross-platform of major applications, and it still only runs on a minority of platforms.

Java solves the problem of platform-independence by using byte code. The Java compiler does not produce native executable code for a particular machine like a C compiler would. Instead it produces a special format called *byte code*. Java byte code written in hexadecimal, byte by byte, looks like this:

CA FE BA BE 00 03 00 2D 00 3E 08 00 3B 08 00 01 08 00 20 08

This looks a lot like machine language, but unlike machine language Java byte code is exactly the same on every platform. This byte code fragment means the same thing on a Solaris workstation as it does on a Macintosh PowerBook. Java programs that have been compiled into byte code still need an interpreter to execute them on any given platform. The interpreter reads the byte code and translates it into the native language of the host machine on the fly. The most common such interpreter is Sun's program java (with a little j). Since the byte code is completely platform independent, only the interpreter and a few native libraries need to be ported to get Java to run on a new computer or operating system. The rest of the runtime environment including the compiler and most of the class libraries are written in Java.

All these pieces, the javac compiler, the java interpreter, the Java programming language, and more are collectively referred to as Java.

Java Platform

Java platform is a collection of programs that help to develop and run programs written in the Java programming language. Java platform includes an execution engine, a compiler, and a set of libraries. JAVA is platform-independent language. It is not specific to any processor or operating system.

The Garbage Collector

Rather than forcing you to keep up with memory allocation (or use a third-party library to do so), the Java platform provides memory management out of the box. When your Java application creates an object instance at runtime, the JVM automatically allocates memory space for that object from the heap— a pool of memory set aside for your program to use. The Java garbage collector runs in the background, keeping track of which objects the application no longer needs and reclaiming memory from them. This approach to memory handling is called implicit memory management because it doesn't require you to write any memory-handling code. Garbage collection is one of the essential features of Java platform performance.

Platform

The Java platform is a suite of programs that facilitate developing and running programs written in the Java programming language. A Java platform will include an execution engine (called a virtual machine), a compiler and a set of libraries; there may also be additional servers and alternative libraries that depend on the requirements. Java is not specific to any processor or operating system as Java platforms have been implemented for a wide variety of hardware and operating systems with a view to enable Java programs to run identically on all of them. Different platforms target different classes of device and application domains:

- Java Card: A technology that allows small Java-based applications (applets) to be run securely on smart cards and similar small-memory devices.

- Java ME (Micro Edition): Specifies several different sets of libraries (known as profiles) for devices with limited storage, display, and power capacities. It is often used to develop applications for mobile devices, PDAs, TV set-top boxes, and printers.

- Java SE (Standard Edition): For general-purpose use on desktop PCs, servers and similar devices.

- Java EE (Enterprise Edition): Java SE plus various APIs which are useful for multi-tier client–server enterprise applications.

The Java platform consists of several programs, each of which provides a portion of its overall capabilities. For example, the Java compiler, which converts Java source code into Java bytecode (an intermediate language for the JVM), is provided as part of the Java Development Kit (JDK). The Java Runtime Environment (JRE), complementing the JVM with a just-in-time (JIT) compiler, converts intermediate bytecode into native machine code on the fly. The Java platform also includes an extensive set of libraries.

The essential components in the platform are the Java language compiler, the libraries, and the runtime environment in which Java intermediate bytecode executes according to the rules laid out in the virtual machine specification.

Java Virtual Machine

The heart of the Java platform is the concept of a "virtual machine" that executes Java bytecode programs. This bytecode is the same no matter what hardware or operating system the program is running under. However, newer versions, such as for Java 10 (and earlier), have made small changes, meaning the bytecode is in general only forward compatible. There is a JIT (Just In Time) compiler within the *Java Virtual Machine*, or JVM. The JIT compiler translates the Java bytecode into native processor instructions at run-time and caches the native code in memory during execution.

The use of bytecode as an intermediate language permits Java programs to run on any platform that has a virtual machine available. The use of a JIT compiler means that Java applications, after a short delay during loading and once they have "warmed up" by being all or mostly JIT-compiled, tend to run about as fast as native programs. Since JRE version 1.2, Sun's JVM implementation has included a just-in-time compiler instead of an interpreter.

Although Java programs are cross-platform or platform independent, the code of the Java Virtual Machines (JVM) that execute these programs is not. Every supported operating platform has its own JVM.

Class Libraries

In most modern operating systems (OSs), a large body of reusable code is provided to simplify the programmer's job. This code is typically provided as a set of dynamically loadable libraries that applications can call at runtime. Because the Java platform is not dependent on any specific operating system, applications cannot rely on any of the pre-existing OS libraries. Instead, the Java platform provides a comprehensive set of its own standard class libraries containing many of the same reusable functions commonly found in modern operating systems. Most of the system library is also written in Java. For instance, the Swing library paints the user interface and handles the events itself, eliminating many subtle differences between how different platforms handle components.

The Java class libraries serve three purposes within the Java platform. First, like other standard code libraries, the Java libraries provide the programmer a well-known set of functions to perform common tasks, such as maintaining lists of items or performing complex string parsing. Second, the class libraries provide an abstract interface to tasks that would normally depend heavily on the hardware and operating system. Tasks such as network access and file access are often heavily intertwined with the distinctive implementations of each platform. The java.net and java.io libraries implement an abstraction layer in native OS code, then provide a standard interface for the Java applications to perform those tasks. Finally, when some underlying platform does not support all of the features a Java application expects, the class libraries work to gracefully handle the absent components, either by emulation to provide a substitute, or at least by providing a consistent way to check for the presence of a specific feature.

Languages

The word "Java", alone, usually refers to Java programming language that was designed for use with the Java platform. Programming languages are typically outside of the scope of the phrase "platform", although the Java programming language was listed as a core part of the Java platform before Java 7. The language and runtime were therefore commonly considered a single unit. However, an effort was made with the Java 7 specification to more clearly treat the Java language and the Java virtual machine as separate entities, so that they are no longer considered a single unit.

Third parties have produced many compilers or interpreters that target the JVM. Some of these are for existing languages, while others are for extensions to the Java language. These include:

- BeanShell – A lightweight scripting language for Java

- Clojure – A dialect of the Lisp programming language

- Groovy – A fully Java interoperable, Java-syntax-compatible, static and dynamic language with features from Python, Ruby, Perl, and Smalltalk

- JRuby – A Ruby interpreter

- Jython – A Python interpreter

- Kotlin – An industrial programming language for JVM with full Java interoperability

- Rhino – A JavaScript interpreter

- Scala – A multi-paradigm programming language with non-Java compatible syntax designed as a "better Java"

- Gosu – A general-purpose Java Virtual Machine-based programming language released under the Apache License 2.0

Similar Platforms

The success of Java and its write once, run anywhere concept has led to other similar efforts, notably the .NET Framework, appearing since 2002, which incorporates many of the successful aspects of Java. .NET in its complete form (Microsoft's implementation) is currently only fully available on Windows platforms, whereas Java is fully available on many platforms. .NET was built from the ground-up to support multiple programming languages, while the Java platform was initially built to support only the Java language, although many other languages have been made for JVM since.

.NET includes a Java-like language called Visual J# (formerly named J++) that is incompatible with the Java specification, and the associated class library mostly dates to the old JDK 1.1 version of the language. For these reasons, it is more of a transitional language to switch from Java to the .NET platform than it is a first class .NET language. Visual J# was discontinued with the release of Microsoft Visual Studio 2008. The existing version shipping with Visual Studio 2005 will be supported until 2015 as per the product life-cycle strategy.

Java Development Kit

The *Java Development Kit* (*JDK*) is a Sun product aimed at Java developers. Since the introduction of Java, it has been by far the most widely used Java software development kit (SDK). It contains a Java compiler, a full copy of the Java Runtime Environment (JRE), and many other important development tools.

Usage

Desktop use

A Java program running on a Windows Vista desktop computer (supported by Java 8, but not officially by Java 10)

According to Oracle in 2010, the Java Runtime Environment was found on over 850 million PCs. Microsoft has not bundled a Java Runtime Environment (JRE) with its operating systems since Sun Microsystems sued Microsoft for adding Windows-specific classes to the bundled Java runtime environment, and for making the new classes available through Visual J++. Apple no longer includes a Java runtime with OS X as of version 10.7, but the system prompts the user to download and install it the first time an application requiring the JRE is launched. Many Linux distributions include the OpenJDK runtime as the default virtual machine, negating the need to download the proprietary Oracle JRE.

Some Java applications are in fairly widespread desktop use, including the NetBeans and Eclipse integrated development environments, and file sharing clients such as LimeWire and Vuze. Java is also used in the MATLAB mathematics programming environment, both for rendering the user interface and as part of the core system. Java provides cross platform user interface for some high end collaborative applications such as Lotus Notes.

Oracle plans to first deprecate the separately installable Java browser plugin from the Java Runtime Environment in JDK 9 then remove it completely from a future release, forcing web developers to use an alternative technology.

Mobile Devices

Java ME has become popular in mobile devices, where it competes with Symbian, BREW, and the .NET Compact Framework.

2006 era mobile phones running a Java application

The diversity of mobile phone manufacturers has led to a need for new unified standards so programs can run on phones from different suppliers – MIDP. The first standard was MIDP 1, which assumed a small screen size, no access to audio, and a 32 KB program limit. The more recent MIDP 2 allows access to audio, and up to 64 KB for the program size. With handset designs improving more rapidly than the standards, some manufacturers relax some limitations in the standards, for example, maximum program size.

Google's Android operating system uses the Java language, but not its class libraries, therefore the Android platform cannot be called Java. Android, in all supported versions, executes the code on the ART VM (formerly the Dalvik VM up to Android 4.4.4) instead of the Java VM.

Web Server and Enterprise use

Java-powered web application

The Java platform has become a mainstay of enterprise IT development since the introduction of the Enterprise Edition in 1998, in two different ways:

1. Through the coupling of Java to the web server, the Java platform has become a leading platform for integrating the Web with enterprise backend systems. This has allowed companies to move part or all of their business to the Internet environment by way of highly interactive online environments (such as highly dynamic websites) that allow the customer direct access to the business processes (e.g. online banking websites, airline booking systems and so on). This trend has continued from its initial Web-based start:

o   The Java platform has matured into an Enterprise Integration role in which legacy systems are unlocked to the outside world through bridges built on the Java platform. This trend has been supported for Java platform support for EAI standards like messaging and Web services and has fueled the inclusion of the Java platform as a development basis in such standards as SCA, XAM and others.

o   Java has become the standard development platform for many companies' IT departments, which do most or all of their corporate development in Java. This type of development is usually related to company-specific tooling (e.g. a booking tool for an airline) and the choice for the Java platform is often driven by a desire to leverage the existing Java infrastructure to build highly intelligent and interconnected tools.

2.   The Java platform has become the main development platform for many software tools and platforms that are produced by third-party software groups (commercial, open source and hybrid) and are used as configurable (rather than programmable) tools by companies. Examples in this category include Web servers, application servers, databases, enterprise service buses, business process management (BPM) tools and content management systems.

Enterprise use of Java has also long been the main driver of open source interest in the platform. This interest has inspired open source communities to produce a large amount of software, including simple function libraries, development frameworks (e.g. the Spring Framework, Apache Wicket, Dojo Toolkit, Hibernate), and open source implementations of standards and tools (e.g. Apache Tomcat, the GlassFish application server, the Mule and Apache ServiceMix enterprise service buses).

Mascot

Duke is Java's mascot.

Plain ol' Duke

When Sun announced that Java SE and Java ME would be released under a free software license (the GNU General Public License), they released the Duke graphics under the free BSD license at the same time. A new Duke personality is created every year. For example, in July 2011 "Future Tech Duke" included a bigger nose, a jetpack, and blue wings.

Licensing

The source code for Sun's implementations of Java (i.e. the de facto reference implementation) has been available for some time, but until recently, the license terms severely restricted what could be done with it without signing (and generally paying for) a contract with Sun. As such these terms did not satisfy the requirements of either the Open Source Initiative or the Free Software Foundation to be considered open source or free software, and Sun Java was therefore a proprietary platform.

While several third-party projects (e.g. GNU Classpath and Apache Harmony) created free software partial Java implementations, the large size of the Sun libraries combined with the use of clean room methods meant that their implementations of the Java libraries (the compiler and VM are comparatively small and well defined) were incomplete and not fully compatible. These implementations also tended to be far less optimized than Sun's.

Free Software

Jonathan I. Schwartz

Sun announced in JavaOne 2006 that Java would become free and open source software, and on October 25, 2006, at the Oracle OpenWorld conference, Jonathan I. Schwartz said that the company was set to announce the release of the core Java Platform as free and open source software within 30 to 60 days.

Sun released the Java HotSpot virtual machine and compiler as free software under the GNU General Public License on November 13, 2006, with a promise that the rest of the JDK (that includes the JRE) would be placed under the GPL by March 2007 ("except for a few components that Sun does not have the right to publish in distributable source form under the GPL"). According to Richard Stallman, this would mean an end to the "Java trap". Mark Shuttleworth called the initial press announcement, "A real milestone for the free software community".

Sun released the source code of the Class library under GPL on May 8, 2007, except some limited parts that were licensed by Sun from third parties who did not want their code to be released under a free software and open-source license. Some of the encumbered parts turned out to be fairly key parts of the platform such as font rendering and 2D rasterising, but these were released as open-source later by Sun.

Sun's goal was to replace the parts that remain proprietary and closed-source with alternative implementations and make the class library completely free and open source. In the meantime, a third party project called IcedTea created a completely free and highly usable JDK by replacing encumbered code with either stubs or code from GNU Classpath. However OpenJDK has since become buildable without the encumbered parts (from OpenJDK 6 b10) and has become the default runtime environment for most Linux distributions.

In June 2008, it was announced that IcedTea6 (as the packaged version of OpenJDK on Fedora 9) has passed the Technology Compatibility Kit tests and can claim to be a fully compatible Java 6 implementation.

Because OpenJDK is under the GPL, it is possible to redistribute a custom version of the JRE directly with software applications, rather than requiring the enduser (or their sysadmin) to download and install the correct version of the proprietary Oracle JRE onto each of their systems themselves.

Criticism

In most cases, Java support is unnecessary in Web browsers, and security experts recommend that it not be run in a browser unless absolutely necessary. It was suggested that, if Java is required by a few Web sites, users should have a separate browser installation specifically for those sites.

Generics

When generics were added to Java 5.0, there was already a large framework of classes (many of which were already deprecated), so generics were chosen to be implemented using erasure to allow for *migration compatibility* and re-use of these existing classes. This limited the features that could be provided by this addition as compared to some other languages. The addition of type wildcards made Java unsound.

Unsigned Integer Types

Java lacks native unsigned integer types. Unsigned data are often generated from programs written in C and the lack of these types prevents direct data interchange between C and Java. Unsigned large numbers are also used in many numeric processing fields, including cryptography, which can make Java less convenient to use for these tasks. Although it is possible to partially circumvent this problem with conversion code and using larger data types, it makes using Java cumbersome for handling the unsigned data. While a 32-bit signed integer may be used to hold a 16-bit unsigned value with relative ease, a 32-bit unsigned value would require a 64-bit signed integer. Additionally, a 64-bit unsigned value cannot be stored using any integer type in Java because no type larger than 64 bits exists in the Java language. If abstracted using functions, function calls become necessary for many operations which are native to some other languages. Alternatively, it is possible to use Java's signed integers to emulate unsigned integers of the same size, but this requires detailed knowledge of complex bitwise operations.

Floating Point Arithmetic

While Java's floating point arithmetic is largely based on IEEE 754 (*Standard for Binary Floating-Point Arithmetic*), certain features are not supported even when using the strictfp modifier, such as Exception Flags and Directed Roundings – capabilities mandated by IEEE Standard 754. Additionally, the extended precision floating-point types permitted in 754 and present in many processors are not permitted in Java.

Performance

In the early days of Java (before the HotSpot VM was implemented in Java 1.3 in 2000) there were some criticisms of performance. However, benchmarks typically report Java as being about 50% slower than C (a language which compiles to native code).

Java's performance has improved substantially since the early versions. Performance of JIT compilers relative to native compilers has in some optimized tests been shown to be quite similar.

Java bytecode can either be interpreted at run time by a virtual machine, or it can be compiled at load time or runtime into native code which runs directly on the computer's hardware. Interpretation is slower than native execution, and compilation at load time or runtime has an initial performance penalty for the compilation. Modern performant JVM implementations all use the compilation approach, so after the initial startup time the performance is equivalent to native code.

Security

The Java platform provides a security architecture which is designed to allow the user to run untrusted bytecode in a "sandboxed" manner to protect against malicious or poorly written software. This "sandboxing" feature is intended to protect the user by restricting access to certain platform features and APIs which could be exploited by malware, such as accessing the local filesystem, running arbitrary commands, or accessing communication networks.

In recent years, researchers have discovered numerous security flaws in some widely used Java implementations, including Oracle's, which allow untrusted code to bypass the sandboxing mechanism, exposing users to malicious attacks. These flaws affect only Java applications which execute arbitrary untrusted bytecode, such as web browser plug-ins that run Java applets downloaded from public websites. Applications where the user trusts, and has full control over, all code that is being executed are unaffected.

On August 31, 2012, Java 6 and 7 (then supported, but no longer) on Microsoft Windows, macOS, and Linux were found to have a serious security flaw that allowed a remote exploit to take place by simply loading a malicious web page. Java 5 was later found to be flawed as well.

On January 10, 2013, three computer specialists spoke out against Java, telling Reuters that it was not secure and that people should disable Java. Jaime Blasco, Labs Manager with AlienVault Labs, stated that "Java is a mess. It's not secure. You have to disable it." This vulnerability affects Java 7 and it is unclear if it affects Java 6, so it is suggested that consumers disable it. Security alerts from Oracle announce schedules of critical security-related patches to Java.

On January 14, 2013, security experts said that the update still failed to protect PCs from attack. This exploit hole prompted a response from the United States Department of Homeland Security encouraging users to disable or uninstall Java. Apple blacklisted Java in limited order for all computers running its macOS operating system through a virus protection program.

Responding to recent Java security and vulnerability issues, security blogger Brian Krebs has called for users to remove at least the Java browser plugin and also the entire software. "I look forward to a world without the Java plugin (and to not having to remind readers about quarterly patch updates) but it will probably be years before various versions of this plugin are mostly removed from end-user systems worldwide." "Once promising, it has outlived its usefulness in the browser, and has become a nightmare that delights cyber-criminals at the expense of computer users." "I think everyone should uninstall Java from all their PCs and Macs, and then think carefully about whether they need to add it back. If you are a typical home user, you can probably do without it. If you are a business user, you may not have a choice."

Adware

The Java runtime environment has a history of bundling sponsored software to be installed by default during installation and during the updates which roll out every month or so. This includes the "Ask.com toolbar" that will redirect browser searches to ads and "McAfee Security Scan Plus". These offers can be blocked through a setting in the Java Control Panel, although this is not obvious. This setting is located under the "Advanced" tab in the Java Control Panel, under the "Miscellaneous" heading, where the option is labelled as an option to suppress "sponsor offers".

Update System

Java has yet to release an automatic updater that does not require user intervention and administrative rights unlike Google Chrome and Flash player.

Java Card

Java Card is a Java technology used for tiny applications, known as applets, on extremely resource-limited devices. This Java technology is used on mobile phone subscriber identity module (SIM) cards, financial cards, healthcare identification cards, smart tickets and many other devices.

Like other applications created using the Java programming language, Java Card applets feature write-once-run-anywhere capabilities. This means that they will run on any Java Card technology-enabled smart card, regardless of the manufacturer of the card or the hardware being used as long as the necessary Java virtual machine (JVM) is present.

Java Card technology is widely used, with Java Card manufacturers accounting for more than 90 percent of the entire smart card industry.

Because the applets have to run on such constrained environments, the Java Card byte code is understandably tiny. In fact, only a subset of the entire Java programming language application programming interface (API) is used in writing the source code for a Java Card applet. After the source code is written and saved as a .java file, it is then compiled into a .class file, just like in an ordinary Java application. However, the development process does not end there. The .class file must then be converted into a smaller converted applet or .cap file. After conversion, the .cap file can be verified and finally installed on the card.

In most cases, the final applet will not be able to operate on its own. Rather, the elements of a complete Java Card application usually consist of a back-end application, a host application, an interface device and the applet on the card. As a simple example, the back-end application may be a program connecting to a database or the host application (an application running on a cellphone) or the interface device (the cellphone).

Portability

Java Card aims at defining a standard smart card computing environment allowing the same Java Card applet to run on different smart cards, much like a Java applet runs on different computers. As in Java, this is accomplished using the combination of a virtual machine (the Java Card Virtual Machine), and a well-defined runtime library, which largely abstracts the applet from differences between smart cards. Portability remains mitigated by issues of memory size, performance, and runtime support (e.g. for communication protocols or cryptographic algorithms).

Security

Java Card technology was originally developed for the purpose of securing sensitive information stored on smart cards. Security is determined by various aspects of this technology:

- Data encapsulation

    Data is stored within the application, and Java Card applications are executed in an isolated environment (the Java Card VM), separate from the underlying operating system and hardware.

- Applet Firewall

    Unlike other Java VMs, a Java Card VM usually manages several applications, each one controlling sensitive data. Different applications are therefore separated from each other by an applet firewall which restricts and checks access of data elements of one applet to another.

- Cryptography

    Commonly used symmetric key algorithms like DES, Triple DES, AES, and asymmetric key algorithms such as RSA, elliptic curve cryptography are supported as well as other cryptographic services like signing, key generation and key exchange.

- Applet

    The applet is a state machine which processes only incoming command requests and responds by sending data or response status words back to the interface device.

Design

At the language level, Java Card is a precise subset of Java: all language constructs of Java Card exist in Java and behave identically. This goes to the point that as part of a standard build cycle, a Java Card program is compiled into a Java class file by a Java compiler; the class file is post-processed by tools specific to the Java Card platform.

However, many Java language features are not supported by Java Card (in particular types char, double, float and long; the transient qualifier; enums; arrays of more than one dimension; finalization; object cloning; threads). Further, some common features of Java are not provided at runtime by many actual smart cards (in particular type int, which is the default type of a Java expression; and garbage collection of objects).

Bytecode

Java Card bytecode run by the Java Card Virtual Machine is a functional subset of Java 2 bytecode run by a standard Java Virtual Machine but with a different encoding to optimize for size. A Java Card applet thus typically uses less bytecode than the hypothetical Java applet obtained by compiling the same Java source code. This conserves memory, a necessity in resource constrained devices like smart cards. As a design tradeoff, there is no support for some Java language features, and size limitations. Techniques exist for overcoming the size limitations, such as dividing the application's code into packages below the 64 KiB limit.

Library and Runtime

Standard Java Card class library and runtime support differs a lot from that in Java, and the common subset is minimal. For example, the Java Security Manager class is not supported in Java Card, where security policies are implemented by the Java Card Virtual Machine; and transients (non-persistent, fast RAM variables that can be class members) are supported via a Java Card class library, while they have native language support in Java.

Specific Features

The Java Card runtime and virtual machine also support features that are specific to the Java Card platform:

- Persistence

  With Java Card, objects are by default stored in persistent memory (RAM is very scarce on smart cards, and it is only used for temporary or security-sensitive objects). The runtime environment as well as the bytecode have therefore been adapted to manage persistent objects.

- Atomicity

  As smart cards are externally powered and rely on persistent memory, persistent updates must be atomic. The individual write operations performed by individual bytecode instructions and API methods are therefore guaranteed atomic, and the Java Card Runtime includes a limited transaction mechanism.

- Applet isolation

  The Java Card firewall is a mechanism that isolates the different applets present on a card from each other. It also includes a sharing mechanism that allows an applet to explicitly make an object available to other applets.

Development

Coding techniques used in a practical Java Card program differ significantly from that used in a Java program. Still, that Java Card uses a precise subset of the Java language speeds up the learning curve, and enables using a Java environment to develop and debug a Java Card program (caveat: even if debugging occurs with Java bytecode, make sure that the class file fits the limitation of Java Card language by converting it to Java Card bytecode; and test in a real Java Card smart card early on to get an idea of the performance); further, one can run and debug both the Java Card code for the application to be embedded in a smart card, and a Java application that will be in the host using the smart card, all working jointly in the same environment.

Versions

Oracle has released several Java Card platform specifications and is providing SDK tools for application development. Usually smart card vendors implement just a subset of algorithms specified in Java Card platform target and the only way to discover what subset of specification is implemented is to test the card.

- Version 3.0.5 (03.06.2015)

    o Oracle SDK: Java Card Classic Development Kit 3.0.5u1 (03.06.2015)

    o Added support for Diffie-Hellman modular exponentiation, Domain Data Conservation for Diffie-Hellman, Elliptic Curve and DSA keys, RSA-3072, SHA3, plain ECDSA, AES CMAC, AES CTR.

- Version 3.0.4 (06.08.2011)

    o Oracle SDK: Java Card Classic Development Kit 3.0.4 (06.11.2011)

    o Added support for DES MAC8 ISO9797.

- Version 3.0.1 (15.06.2009)

    o Oracle SDK: Java Card Development Kit 3.0.3 RR (11.11.2010)

    o Added support for SHA-224, SHA-2 for all signature algorithms.

- Version 2.2.2 (03.2006)

    o Oracle SDK: Java Card Development Kit 2.2.2 (03.2006)

    o Added support for SHA-256, SHA-384, SHA-512, ISO9796-2, HMAC, Korean SEED MAC NOPAD, Korean SEED NOPAD.

- Version 2.2.1 (10.2003)

    o Oracle SDK: Java Card Development Kit 2.2.1 (10.2003)

- Version 2.2 (11.2002)

○ Added support for AES cryptography key encapsulation, CRC algorithms, Elliptic Curve Cryptography key encapsulation,Diffie-Hellman key exchange using ECC, ECC keys for binary polynomial curves and for prime integer curves, AES, ECC and RSA with variable key lengths.

- Version 2.1.1 (18.05.2000)

  ○ Oracle SDK: Java Card Development Kit 2.1.2 (05.04.2001)

  ○ Added support for RSA without padding.

- Version 2.1 (07.06.1999)

Java Card 3.0

The version 3.0 of the Java Card specification (draft released in March 2008) is separated in two editions: the *Classic Edition* and the *Connected Edition*.

- The *Classic Edition* (currently at version 3.0.5 released in June 2015) is an evolution of the Java Card Platform version 2 (which last version 2.2.2 was released in March 2006), which supports traditional card applets on resource-constrained devices such as Smart Cards. Older applets are generally compatible with newer Classic Edition devices, and applets for these newer devices can be compatible with older devices if not referring to new library functions. Smart Cards implementing Java Card Classic Edition have been security-certified by multiple vendors, and are commercially available.

- The *Connected Edition* (currently at version 3.0.2 released in December 2009) aims to provide a new virtual machine and an enhanced execution environment with network-oriented features. Applications can be developed as classic card applets requested by APDU commands or as servlets using HTTP to support web-based schemes of communication (HTML, REST, SOAP ...) with the card. The runtime uses a subset of the Java (1.)6 bytecode, without Floating Point; it supports volatile objects (garbage collection), multi-threading, inter-application communications facilities, persistence, transactions, card management facilities ... As of 2017 there has been little adoption in commercially available Smart Cards, so much that reference to Java Card often implicitly excludes the *Connected Edition*.

Applications

Java Card technology is used in a wide range of smart card applications, including:

- Smart ID badges for logical and physical access to enterprise resources

- Subscriber Identity Modules used in mobile phones on wireless networks

- Machine Identity Modules used in M2M applications

- Banking cards for traditional and online bank transactions

- Government and health-care identity cards

Advantages

Its unique features provide several advantages. Applets are interoperable and will run on any Java Card-based smart card device, thereby reduces hardware costs. In addition, multiple applications can reside on a single device. New applications can be installed securely after a card has been issued using Over-The-Air (OTA) platforms, enabling card issuers to respond to their customer's changing needs dynamically.

Java Cards enable easy and fast updates through an open OS architecture that separates the platform from the application. This partitioning also reduces migration constraints, even after initial card issuance. Compliant applications can be loaded and cards that are compatible with existing ones can be produced quickly.

The strong security of the Java programming language provides the foundation for Java Card's secure execution environment. As an open standard backed by all the leading smart card manufacturers, it offers one of the most secure technology platforms available. In addition, this technology enables various business models between issuer, application providers and operators, thanks to multiple security domains and dynamic application partitioning.

Java Platform, Micro Edition

Java Platform, Micro Edition (Java ME) is a Java platform, developed by Sun Microsystems (now part of Oracle), for mobile devices and other embedded systems. Java ME is one of the most ubiquitous mobile platform in the world. Java ME runs on a wide range of feature phones, smartphones, pocket PCs, PDAs, set-top boxes and even printers. Java ME theoretically employs the Java mantra of write-once-run-anywhere, which means that code written for one device can run on all similar devices.

Java ME is made up of two sets of libraries, which are known as the connected limited device configuration (CLDC) and the connected device configuration (CDC). The CLDC is designed for significantly constrained devices characterized by low processing power, storage space, RAM and graphics capabilities. Devices that are best suited for the CLDC can have a CPU clock speed of as low as 16 MHz, a ROM size as small as 180 KB, RAM as small as 192 KB and zero graphics. CDC devices can be more powerful. Examples of such devices include smartphones, pocket PCs and PDAs. Java ME applications are most often associated with tiny applications called MIDlets, which are just one group of applications written using Java ME. MIDlets, however, are actually applications written using the mobile information device profile, which sits on top of the CLDC.

An aspiring Java ME developer would normally need the Java ME software development kit (SDK). It contains all the necessary tools needed for Java mobile application development, including the API, debugger, compiler and emulator. To simplify the development process, developers may use the SDK in conjunction with integrated development environments (IDEs) like Netbeans and Eclipse. These IDEs allow developers to take advantage of GUIs, which allow drag-and-drop and point-and-click procedures, to design the layout of the Java ME application's own GUI. Coupled with the SDK, IDEs allow users to see how an application would appear on a device, through emulators.

Java Platform, Micro Edition (Java ME) provides a robust, flexible environment for applications running on embedded and mobile devices in the Internet of Things: micro-controllers, sensors, gateways, mobile phones, personal digital assistants (PDAs), TV set-top boxes, printers and more. Java ME includes flexible user interfaces, robust security, built-in network protocols, and support for networked and offline applications that can be downloaded dynamically. Applications based on Java ME are portable across many devices, yet leverage each device's native capabilities.

Oracle Java ME Embedded

Oracle Java ME Embedded is a Java runtime that leverages the core Java ME technologies deployed in billions of devices around the world in the Internet of Things. The Java ME specifications are designed to be rich in functionality, portable to a wide range of devices, flexible, and secure while being very resource-efficient and keeping the demands on the underlying platform low.

Java ME SDK

The Java ME Software Development Kit (SDK) provides device emulation, a standalone development environment and a set of utilities for rapid development of Java ME applications. It integrates the Connected Limited Device Configuration (CLDC) and the Connected Device Configuration (CDC) technology into one simple development environment.

Oracle Java ME Embedded Client

Oracle Java ME Embedded Client enables you to develop highly functional, reliable, and portable applications for today's most powerful embedded systems. The flexibility of the Java Platform coupled with and established developer base enables you to develop secure, innovative products while achieving enhanced cost savings and time to market advantage. A vital platform that offers industry-leading reliability, performance, throughput, security, and cross-platform support.

Java for Mobile

The Connected Limited Device Configuration and the Java ME APIs are used by a vast number of Java mobile phone developers, carriers, and OEMs to create feature phone products around the globe. Oracle is the leader in providing mobile phone technology found on over three billion devices and counting.

Java TV

Java TV is a Java ME-based technology that provides a performant, secure, and easy to implement solution for developing Java applications that run on TV and set top box devices. Using the Java TV runtime, a developers can easily create applications, such as Electronic Program Guides (EPG's), Video-on-Demand (VOD) clients, games and educational applications, applications for accessing internet data (e.g. weather, news tickers, social networking), and, on most Blu-ray Disc titles, the user interface and bonus content.

Oracle Java Platform Integrator

Extend the reach of Java in the Internet of Things (IoT) with OJPI. Oracle has introduced the Oracle Java Platform Integrator program to provide partners with the ability to customize Oracle Java Embedded products, including Oracle Java SE Embedded, Oracle Java ME Embedded, and Oracle Java ME Embedded Client, to reach different device types and market segments. Coupled with the massive Java ecosystem of over 9 million Java developers worldwide, this new program will help enable greater development and deployment flexibility for the IoT.

Java ME technology was originally created in order to deal with the constraints associated with building applications for small devices. For this purpose Oracle defined the basics for Java ME technology to fit such a limited environment and make it possible to create Java applications running on small devices with limited memory, display and power capacity.

Connected Limited Device Configuration

The Connected Limited Device Configuration (CLDC) contains a strict subset of the Java-class libraries, and is the minimum amount needed for a Java virtual machine to operate. CLDC is basically used for classifying myriad devices into a fixed configuration.

A configuration provides the most basic set of libraries and virtual-machine features that must be present in each implementation of a J2ME environment. When coupled with one or more profiles, the Connected Limited Device Configuration gives developers a solid Java platform for creating applications for consumer and embedded devices. The configuration is designed for devices with 160KB to 512KB total memory, which has a minimum of 160KB of ROM and 32KB of RAM available for the Java platform.

Mobile Information Device Profile

Designed for mobile phones, the Mobile Information Device Profile includes a GUI, and a data storage API, and MIDP 2.0 includes a basic 2D gaming API. Applications written for this profile are called MIDlets. Almost all new cell phones come with a MIDP implementation, and it is now the de facto standard for downloadable cell phone games. However, many cellphones can run only those MIDlets that have been approved by the carrier, especially in North America.

JSR 271: Mobile Information Device Profile 3 (Final release on 09 Dec, 2009) specified the 3rd generation Mobile Information Device Profile (MIDP3), expanding upon the functionality in all areas as well as improving interoperability across devices. A key design goal of MIDP3 is backward compatibility with MIDP2 content.

Information Module Profile

The Information Module Profile (IMP) is a profile for embedded, "headless" devices such as vending machines, industrial embedded applications, security systems, and similar devices with either simple or no display and with some limited network connectivity.

Originally introduced by Siemens Mobile and Nokia as JSR-195, IMP 1.0 is a strict subset of MIDP 1.0 except that it doesn't include user interface APIs — in other words, it doesn't include support for the Java package javax.microedition.lcdui. JSR-228, also known as IMP-NG, is IMP's next generation that is based on MIDP 2.0, leveraging MIDP 2.0's new security and networking types and APIs, and other APIs such as PushRegistry and platformRequest(), but again it doesn't include UI APIs, nor the game API.

Connected Device Configuration

The Connected Device Configuration is a subset of Java SE, containing almost all the libraries that are not GUI related. It is richer than CLDC.

Foundation Profile

The Foundation Profile is a Java ME Connected Device Configuration (CDC) profile. This profile is intended to be used by devices requiring a complete implementation of the Java virtual machine up to and including the entire Java Platform, Standard Edition API. Typical implementations will use some subset of that API set depending on the additional profiles supported. This specification was developed under the Java Community Process.

Personal Basis Profile

The Personal Basis Profile extends the Foundation Profile to include lightweight GUI support in the form of an AWT subset. This is the platform that BD-J is built upon.

Implementations

Sun provides a reference implementation of these configurations and profiles for MIDP and CDC. Starting with the JavaME 3.0 SDK, a NetBeans-based IDE will support them in a single IDE.

In contrast to the numerous binary implementations of the Java Platform built by Sun for servers and workstations, Sun does not provide any binaries for the platforms of Java ME targets with the exception of an MIDP 1.0 JRE (JVM) for Palm OS. Sun provides no J2ME JRE for the Microsoft Windows Mobile (Pocket PC) based devices, despite an open-letter campaign to Sun to release a rumored internal implementation of PersonalJava known by the code name "Captain America". Third party implementations like JBlend and JBed are widely used by Windows Mobile vendors like HTC and Samsung.

Operating systems targeting Java ME have been implemented by DoCoMo in the form of DoJa, and by SavaJe as SavaJe OS. The latter company was purchased by Sun in April 2007 and now forms the basis of Sun's JavaFX Mobile. The company IS2T provides a Java ME virtual machine (MicroJvm) for any RTOS and even with no RTOS (then qualified as baremetal). When baremetal, the virtual machine is the OS/RTOS: the device boots in Java.

MicroEmu provides an open source (LGPL) implementation of an MIDP emulator. This is a Java Applet-based emulator and can be embedded in web pages.

The open-source Mika VM aims to implement JavaME CDC/FP, but is not certified as such (certified implementations are required to charge royalties, which is impractical for an open-source project). Consequently, devices which use this implementation are not allowed to claim JavaME CDC compatibility.

The linux-based Android operating system uses a proprietary version of Java that is similar, but not identical to Java Me.

JSRs (Java Specification Requests)

Foundation

JSR #	Name	Description
68	J2ME Platform Specification	
30	CLDC 1.x	
37	MIDP 1.0	
118	MIDP 2.x	
139	CLDC 1.1	
271	MIDP 3.0	Java ME 3.4 and earlier only, Last Specification for Mobile Phones, Java Language features as Java SE 1.3
360	CLDC 8	New in Java ME 8
361	MEEP 8	New in Java ME 8, Language feature as Java SE 8, for Internet of Everything devices

Main Extensions

JSR #	Name	Description	MSA
75	File Connection and PIM	File system, contacts, calendar, to-do	✓
82	Bluetooth		✓
120	Wireless Messaging API (WMA)		
135	Mobile Media API (MMAPI)	Audio, video, multimedia	✓
172	Web Services		✓
177	Security and Trust Services		✓
179	Location API		✓
180	SIP API		✓
184	Mobile 3D Graphics	High level 3D graphics	✓
185	Java Technology for the Wireless Industry (JTWI)	General	
205	Wireless Messaging 2.0 (WMA)		
211	Content Handler API		✓
226	Scalable 2D Vector Graphics API for J2ME		✓
228	Information Module Profile - Next Generation		
229	Payment API		✓
234	Advanced Multimedia Supplements (AMMS)	MMAPI extensions	✓
238	Mobile Internationalization API		✓
239	Java Bindings for the OpenGL ES API		
248	Mobile Service Architecture		✓
253	Mobile Telephony API		
256	Mobile Sensor API		
257	Contactless Communication API		

258	Mobile User Interface Customization API		
272	Mobile Broadcast Service API for Handheld Terminals		
280	XML API for Java ME		
281	IMS Services API		
287	Scalable 2D Vector Graphics API 2.0 for Java ME		
293	Location API 2.0		
298	Telematics API for Java ME		
300	DRM API for Java ME		
325	IMS Communication Enablers		

Future

JSR #	Name	Description
297	Mobile 3D Graphics API (M3G) 2.0	

ESR

The ESR consortium is devoted to Standards for embedded Java. Especially cost effective Standards. Typical applications domains are industrial control, machine-to-machine, medical, e-metering, home automation, consumer, human-to-machine-interface.

ESR #	Name	Description
001	B-ON (Beyond CLDC)	B-ON serves as a very robust foundation for implementing embedded Java software. It specifies a reliable initialization phase of the Java device, and 3 kind of objects: immutable, immortal and regular (mortal) objects.
002	MicroUI	MicroUI defines an enhanced architecture to enable an open, third-party, application development environment for embedded HMI devices. Such devices typically have some form of display, some input sensors and potentially some sound rendering capabilities. This specification spans a potentially wide set of devices.
011	MWT	MWT defines three distinct roles: Widget Designers, Look and Feel Designers, and Application Designers. MWT allows a binary HMI application to run the same on all devices that provide a compliant MWT framework (embedded devices, cellphones, set-top box TV's, PC's, etc...) allowing for true consistency and ubiquity of applications across product lines (ME, SE, EE).
015	ECLASSPATH	ECLASSPATH unifies CLDC, CDC, Foundation, SE, and EE execution environments with a set of around 300 classes API. Compiling against CLDC1.1/ECLASSPATH makes binary code portable across all Java execution environments.

Java Platform, Standard Edition

Java Platform, Standard Edition (Java SE) lets you develop and deploy Java applications on desktops and servers, as well as in today's demanding embedded environments. Java offers the rich user interface, performance, versatility, portability, and security that today's applications require. For learning Java or for small business applications Java SE is the platform of choice.

When most people think of the Java programming language, they think of the Java SE API. Java SE's API provides the core functionality of the Java programming language. It defines everything from the basic types and objects of the Java programming language to high-level classes that are used for networking, security, database access, graphical user interface (GUI) development, and XML parsing.

In addition to the core API, the Java SE platform consists of a virtual machine, development tools, deployment technologies, and other class libraries and toolkits commonly used in Java technology applications.

Nomenclature, Standards and Specifications

The platform was known as *Java 2 Platform, Standard Edition* or *J2SE* from version 1.2, until the name was changed to *Java Platform, Standard Edition* or *Java SE* in version 1.5. The "SE" is used to distinguish the base platform from the Enterprise Edition (Java EE) and Micro Edition (Java ME) platforms. The "2" was originally intended to emphasize the major changes introduced in version 1.2, but was removed in version 1.6. The naming convention has been changed several times over the Java version history. Starting with J2SE 1.4 (Merlin), Java SE has been developed under the Java Community Process, which produces descriptions of proposed and final specifications for the Java platform called Java Specification Requests (JSR). JSR 59 was the umbrella specification for J2SE 1.4 and JSR 176 specified J2SE 5.0 (Tiger). Java SE 6 (Mustang) was released under JSR 270.

Java Platform, Enterprise Edition (Java EE) is a related specification that includes all the classes in Java SE, plus a number that are more useful to programs that run on servers as opposed to workstations.

Java Platform, Micro Edition (Java ME) is a related specification intended to provide a certified collection of Java APIs for the development of software for small, resource-constrained devices such as cell phones, PDAs and set-top boxes.

The Java Runtime Environment (JRE) and Java Development Kit (JDK) are the actual files downloaded and installed on a computer to run or develop Java programs, respectively.

General Purpose Packages

java.lang

The Java package java.lang contains fundamental classes and interfaces closely tied to the language and runtime system. This includes the root classes that form the class hierarchy, types tied to the language definition, basic exceptions, math functions, threading, security functions, as well as some information on the underlying native system. This package contains 22 of 32 Error classes provided in JDK 6.

The main classes and interfaces in java.lang are:

- Object – the class that is the root of every class hierarchy.
- Enum – the base class for enumeration classes (as of J2SE 5.0).

- Class – the class that is the root of the Java reflection system.

- Throwable – the class that is the base class of the exception class hierarchy.

- Error, Exception, and RuntimeException – the base classes for each exception type.

- Thread – the class that allows operations on threads.

- String – the class for strings and string literals.

- StringBuffer and StringBuilder – classes for performing string manipulation (StringBuilder as of J2SE 5.0).

- Comparable – the interface that allows generic comparison and ordering of objects (as of J2SE 1.2).

- Iterable – the interface that allows generic iteration using the enhanced for loop (as of J2SE 5.0).

- ClassLoader, Process, Runtime, SecurityManager, and System – classes that provide "system operations" that manage the dynamic loading of classes, creation of external processes, host environment inquiries such as the time of day, and enforcement of security policies.

- Math and StrictMath – classes that provide basic math functions such as sine, cosine, and square root (StrictMath as of J2SE 1.3).

- The primitive wrapper classes that encapsulate primitive types as objects.

- The basic exception classes thrown for language-level and other common exceptions.

Classes in java.lang are automatically imported into every source file.

java.lang.ref

The java.lang.ref package provides more flexible types of references than are otherwise available, permitting limited interaction between the application and the Java Virtual Machine (JVM) garbage collector. It is an important package, central enough to the language for the language designers to give it a name that starts with "java.lang", but it is somewhat special-purpose and not used by a lot of developers. This package was added in J2SE 1.2.

Java has an expressive system of references and allows for special behavior for garbage collection. A normal reference in Java is known as a "strong reference." The java.lang.ref package defines three other types of references—soft, weak, and phantom references. Each type of reference is designed for a specific use.

- A SoftReference can be used to implement a cache. An object that is not reachable by a strong reference (that is, not strongly reachable), but is referenced by a soft reference is called "softly reachable." A softly reachable object may be garbage collected at the discretion of the garbage collector. This generally means that softly reachable objects are only garbage collected when free memory is low—but again, this is at the garbage collector's discretion. Semantically, a soft reference means, "Keep this object when nothing else references it, unless the memory is needed."

- A WeakReference is used to implement weak maps. An object that is not strongly or softly reachable, but is referenced by a weak reference is called "weakly reachable". A weakly reachable object is garbage collected in the next collection cycle. This behavior is used in the class java.util.WeakHashMap. A weak map allows the programmer to put key/value pairs in the map and not worry about the objects taking up memory when the key is no longer reachable anywhere else. Another possible application of weak references is the string intern pool. Semantically, a weak reference means "get rid of this object when nothing else references it at the next garbage collection."

- A PhantomReference is used to reference objects that have been marked for garbage collection and have been finalized, but have not yet been reclaimed. An object that is not strongly, softly or weakly reachable, but is referenced by a phantom reference is called "phantom reachable." This allows for more flexible cleanup than is possible with the finalization mechanism alone. Semantically, a phantom reference means "this object is no longer needed and has been finalized in preparation for being collected."

Each of these reference types extends the Reference class, which provides the get() method to return a strong reference to the referent object (or null if the reference has been cleared or if the reference type is phantom), and the clear() method to clear the reference.

The java.lang.ref also defines the class ReferenceQueue, which can be used in each of the applications discussed above to keep track of objects that have changed reference type. When a Reference is created it is optionally registered with a reference queue. The application polls the reference queue to get references that have changed reachability state.

java.lang.reflect

Reflection is a constituent of the Java API that lets Java code examine and "reflect" on Java components at runtime and use the reflected members. Classes in the java.lang.reflect package, along with java.lang.Class and java.lang.Package accommodate applications such as debuggers, interpreters, object inspectors, class browsers, and services such as object serialization and JavaBeans that need access to either the public members of a target object (based on its runtime class) or the members declared by a given class. This package was added in JDK 1.1.

Reflection is used to instantiate classes and invoke methods using their names, a concept that allows for dynamic programming. Classes, interfaces, methods, fields, and constructors can all be discovered and used at runtime. Reflection is supported by metadata that the JVM has about the program.

Techniques

There are basic techniques involved in reflection:

- Discovery – this involves taking an object or class and discovering the members, superclasses, implemented interfaces, and then possibly using the discovered elements.

- Use by name – involves starting with the symbolic name of an element and using the named element.

Discovery

Discovery typically starts with an object and calling the Object. getClass() method to get the object's Class. The Class object has several methods for discovering the contents of the class, for example:

- getMethods() – returns an array of Method objects representing all the public methods of the class or interface

- getConstructors() – returns an array of Constructor objects representing all the public constructors of the class

- getFields() – returns an array of Field objects representing all the public fields of the class or interface

- getClasses() – returns an array of Class objects representing all the public classes and interfaces that are members (e.g. inner classes) of the class or interface

- getSuperclass() – returns the Class object representing the superclass of the class or interface (null is returned for interfaces)

- getInterfaces() – returns an array of Class objects representing all the interfaces that are implemented by the class or interface

Use by Name

The Class object can be obtained either through discovery, by using the *class literal* (e.g. MyClass. class) or by using the name of the class (e.g. Class.forName("mypackage.MyClass")). With a Class object, member Method, Constructor, or Field objects can be obtained using the symbolic name of the member. For example:

- getMethod("methodName", Class...) – returns the Method object representing the public method with the name "methodName" of the class or interface that accepts the parameters specified by the Class... parameters.

- getConstructor(Class...) – returns the Constructor object representing the public constructor of the class that accepts the parameters specified by the Class... parameters.

- getField("fieldName") – returns the Field object representing the public field with the name "fieldName" of the class or interface.

Method, Constructor, and Field objects can be used to dynamically access the represented member of the class. For example:

- Field.get(Object) – returns an Object containing the value of the field from the instance of the object passed to get(). (If the Field object represents a static field then the Object parameter is ignored and may be null.)

- Method.invoke(Object, Object...) – returns an Object containing the result of invoking the method for the instance of the first Object parameter passed to invoke(). The remaining Object... parameters are passed to the method. (If the Method object represents a static method then the first Object parameter is ignored and may be null.)

- Constructor.newInstance(Object...) – returns the new Object instance from invoking the constructor. The Object... parameters are passed to the constructor. (Note that the parameterless constructor for a class can also be invoked by calling newInstance().)

Arrays and Proxies

The java.lang.reflect package also provides an Array class that contains static methods for creating and manipulating array objects, and since J2SE 1.3, a Proxy class that supports dynamic creation of proxy classes that implement specified interfaces.

The implementation of a Proxy class is provided by a supplied object that implements the InvocationHandler interface. The InvocationHandler's invoke(Object, Method, Object[]) method is called for each method invoked on the proxy object—the first parameter is the proxy object, the second parameter is the Method object representing the method from the interface implemented by the proxy, and the third parameter is the array of parameters passed to the interface method. The invoke() method returns an Object result that contains the result returned to the code that called the proxy interface method.

java.io

The java.io package contains classes that support input and output. The classes in the package are primarily stream-oriented; however, a class for random access files is also provided. The central classes in the package are InputStream and OutputStream, which are abstract base classes for reading from and writing to byte streams, respectively. The related classes Reader and Writer are abstract base classes for reading from and writing to character streams, respectively. The package also has a few miscellaneous classes to support interactions with the host file system.

Streams

The stream classes follow the decorator pattern by extending the base subclass to add features to the stream classes. Subclasses of the base stream classes are typically named for one of the following attributes:

- the source/destination of the stream data

- the type of data written to/read from the stream

- additional processing or filtering performed on the stream data

The stream subclasses are named using the naming pattern XxxStreamType where Xxx is the name describing the feature and StreamType is one of InputStream, OutputStream, Reader, or Writer.

The following table shows the sources/destinations supported directly by the java.io package:

Source/Destination	Name	Stream types	In/Out	Classes
byte array (`byte[]`)	`ByteArray`	`byte`	in, out	ByteArrayInputStream, ByteArrayOutputStream
char array (`char[]`)	`CharArray`	`char`	in, out	CharArrayReader, CharArrayWriter
file	`File`	`byte, char`	in, out	FileInputStream, FileOutputStream, FileReader, FileWriter
string (StringBuffer)	`String`	`char`	in, out	StringReader, StringWriter
thread (`Thread`)	`Piped`	`byte, char`	in, out	PipedInputStream, PipedOutputStream, PipedReader, PipedWriter

Other standard library packages provide stream implementations for other destinations, such as the InputStream returned by the java.net.Socket.getInputStream() method or the Java EE javax.servlet.ServletOutputStream class.

Data type handling and processing or filtering of stream data is accomplished through stream filters. The filter classes all accept another compatible stream object as a parameter to the constructor and *decorate* the enclosed stream with additional features. Filters are created by extending one of the base filter classes FilterInputStream, FilterOutputStream, FilterReader, or FilterWriter.

The Reader and Writer classes are really just byte streams with additional processing performed on the data stream to convert the bytes to characters. They use the default character encoding for the platform, which as of J2SE 5.0 is represented by the Charset returned by the java.nio.charset.Charset.defaultCharset() static method. The InputStreamReader class converts an InputStream to a Reader and the OutputStreamWriter class converts an OutputStream to a Writer. Both these classes have constructors that support specifying the character encoding to use. If no encoding is specified, the program uses the default encoding for the platform.

The following table shows the other processes and filters that the java.io package directly supports. All these classes extend the corresponding Filter class.

Operation	Name	Stream types	In/Out	Classes
buffering	`Buffered`	`byte, char`	in, out	BufferedInputStream, BufferedOutputStream, BufferedReader, BufferedWriter
"push back" last value read	`Pushback`	`byte, char`	in	PushbackInputStream, PushbackReader
read/write primitive types	`Data`	`byte`	in, out	DataInputStream, DataOutputStream
object serialization (read/write objects)	`Object`	`byte`	in, out	ObjectInputStream, ObjectOutputStream

Random Access

The RandomAccessFile class supports *random access* reading and writing of files. The class uses a *file pointer* that represents a byte-offset within the file for the next read or write operation. The file pointer is moved implicitly by reading or writing and explicitly by calling the seek(long) or skipBytes(int) methods. The current position of the file pointer is returned by the getFilePointer() method.

File System

The File class represents a file or directory path in a file system. File objects support the creation, deletion and renaming of files and directories and the manipulation of file attributes such as *read-only* and *last modified timestamp*. File objects that represent directories can be used to get a list of all the contained files and directories.

The FileDescriptor class is a file descriptor that represents a source or sink (destination) of bytes. Typically this is a file, but can also be a console or network socket. FileDescriptor objects are used to create File streams. They are obtained from File streams and java.net sockets and datagram sockets.

java.nio

In J2SE 1.4, the package java.nio (NIO or Non-blocking I/O) was added to support memory-mapped I/O, facilitating I/O operations closer to the underlying hardware with sometimes dramatically better performance. The java.nio package provides support for a number of buffer types. The subpackage java.nio.charset provides support for different character encodings for character data. The subpackage java.nio.channels provides support for *channels,* which represent connections to entities that are capable of performing I/O operations, such as files and sockets. The java. nio.channels package also provides support for fine-grained locking of files.

java.math

The java.math package supports multiprecision arithmetic (including modular arithmetic operations) and provides multiprecision prime number generators used for cryptographic key generation. The main classes of the package are:

- BigDecimal – provides arbitrary-precision signed decimal numbers. BigDecimal gives the user control over rounding behavior through RoundingMode.

- BigInteger – provides arbitrary-precision integers. Operations on BigInteger do not overflow or lose precision. In addition to standard arithmetic operations, it provides modular arithmetic, GCD calculation, primality testing, prime number generation, bit manipulation, and other miscellaneous operations.

- MathContext – encapsulate the context settings that describe certain rules for numerical operators.

- RoundingMode – an enumeration that provides eight rounding behaviors.

java.net

The java.net package provides special IO routines for networks, allowing HTTP requests, as well as other common transactions.

java.text

The java.text package implements parsing routines for strings and supports various human-readable languages and locale-specific parsing.

Java.util

Data structures that aggregate objects are the focus of the java.util package. Included in the package is the Collections API, an organized data structure hierarchy influenced heavily by the design patterns considerations.

Special Purpose Packages

java.applet

Created to support Java applet creation, the java.applet package lets applications be downloaded over a network and run within a guarded sandbox. Security restrictions are easily imposed on the sandbox. A developer, for example, may apply a digital signature to an applet, thereby labeling it as safe. Doing so allows the user to grant the applet permission to perform restricted operations (such as accessing the local hard drive), and removes some or all the sandbox restrictions. Digital certificates are issued by certificate authorities.

java.beans

Included in the java.beans package are various classes for developing and manipulating beans, reusable components defined by the JavaBeans architecture. The architecture provides mechanisms for manipulating properties of components and firing events when those properties change.

The APIs in java.beans are intended for use by a bean editing tool, in which beans can be combined, customized, and manipulated. One type of bean editor is a GUI designer in an integrated development environment.

java.awt

The java.awt, or Abstract Window Toolkit, provides access to a basic set of GUI widgets based on the underlying native platform's widget set, the core of the GUI event subsystem, and the interface between the native windowing system and the Java application. It also provides several basic layout managers, a datatransfer package for use with the Clipboard and Drag and Drop, the interface to input devices such as mice and keyboards, as well as access to the system tray on supporting systems. This package, along with javax.swing contains the largest number of enums (7 in all) in JDK 6.

java.rmi

The java.rmi package provides Java remote method invocation to support remote procedure calls between two java applications running in different JVMs.

java.security

Support for security, including the message digest algorithm, is included in the java.security package.

java.sql

An implementation of the JDBC API (used to access SQL databases) is grouped into the java.sql package.

javax.rmi

The javax.rmi package provides the support for the remote communication between applications, using the RMI over IIOP protocol. This protocol combines RMI and CORBA features.

Java SE Core Technologies - CORBA / RMI-IIOP

javax.swing

Swing is a collection of routines that build on java.awt to provide a platform independent widget toolkit. javax.swing uses the 2D drawing routines to render the user interface components instead of relying on the underlying native operating system GUI support.

This package contains the largest number of classes (133 in all) in JDK 6. This package, along with java.awt also contains the largest number of enums (7 in all) in JDK 6. It supports pluggable looks and feels (PLAFs) so that widgets in the GUI can imitate those from the underlying native system. Design patterns permeate the system, especially a modification of the model-view-controller pattern, which loosens the coupling between function and appearance. One inconsistency is that (as of J2SE 1.3) fonts are drawn by the underlying native system, and not by Java, limiting text portability. Workarounds, such as using bitmap fonts, do exist. In general, "layouts" are used and keep elements within an aesthetically consistent GUI across platforms.

javax.swing.text.html.parser

The javax.swing.text.html.parser package provides the error tolerant HTML parser that is used for writing various web browsers and web bots.

javax.xml.bind.annotation

The javax.xml.bind.annotation package contains the largest number of Annotation Types (30 in all) in JDK 6. It defines annotations for customizing Java program elements to XML Schema mapping.

OMG Packages

org.omg.CORBA

The org.omg.CORBA package provides the support for the remote communication between applications using the General Inter-ORB Protocol and supports other features of the common object request broker architecture. Same as RMI and RMI-IIOP, this package is for calling remote methods of objects on other virtual machines (usually via network).

This package contains the largest number of Exception classes (45 in all) in JDK 6. From all communication possibilities CORBA is portable between various languages; however, with this comes more complexity.

org.omg.PortableInterceptor

The org.omg.PortableInterceptor package contains the largest number of interfaces (39 in all) in JDK 6. It provides a mechanism to register ORB hooks through which ORB services intercept the normal flow of execution of the ORB.

Java SE plugin

Several critical security vulnerabilities have been reported, the most recent in January 2013. Security alerts from Oracle announce critical security-related patches to Java SE.

Java Platform, Enterprise Edition

The Java Platform, Enterprise Edition (Java EE) is a collection of Java APIs owned by Oracle that software developers can use to write server-side applications. It was formerly known as Java 2 Platform, Enterprise Edition, or J2EE.

Sun Microsystems (together with industry partners such as IBM) originally designed Java EE to simplify application development in a thin-client-tiered environment. Java EE simplifies app development and decreases the need for programming by creating standardized, reusable modular components and by enabling the tier to handle many aspects of programming automatically.

Java EE applications are hosted on application servers, such as IBM's WebSphere, Oracle's Glass-Fish or Red Hat's WildFly server, all of which run either in the cloud or within a corporate data center. While Java EE apps are hosted on the server side, examples of Java EE clients include an internet of things (IoT) device, smartphone, RESTful web service, standard web-based application, WebSocket or even microservices running in a Docker container.

Java EE Architecture Goals

The Java EE architecture provides services that simplify the most common challenges facing developers when building modern applications, in many cases through APIs, thus making it easier to use popular design patterns and industry-accepted best practices.

For example, one common challenge enterprise developers face is how to handle requests coming in from web-based clients. To simplify this challenge, Java EE provides the Servlet and JavaServer Pages (JSP) APIs, which provide methods for activities like finding out what a user typed into a text field in an online form or storing a cookie on a user's browser.

Another common task is how to store and retrieve information in a database. To address this goal, Java EE provides the Java Persistence API (JPA,) which makes it easy to map data used within a program to information stored in the tables and rows of a database. Also, creating web services or highly scalable logic components is simplified through the use of the Enterprise JavaBeans (EJB) specification. All of these APIs are well tested, relatively easy for Java developers to learn and can greatly simplify some of the hardest parts of enterprise development.

Java EE Core Technologies

Along with the four aforementioned APIs, there are more than 30 Java APIs included as Java EE core technologies, with that number to approach 50 with the eventual release of Java EE 8. These Java EE core technologies broadly fall into the following file categories:

- HTTP client technologies. For dealing with HTTP-based clients, Java EE includes the Java API for WebSocket programming, an API for JSON Processing, the JSF and Servlet APIs and the JSP Standard Tag Library (JSTL).

- Database and resource access technologies. For interacting with external and back-end systems, Java EE includes JavaMail, a standard connector architecture, a Java Message Service (JMS) API and a Java Transaction API (JTA) for enforcing two-phase commits.

- REST and web service technologies: To help with the development and deployment of REST-, SOAP-, XML- and JSON-based web services, the Java APIs for RESTful Web Services (JAX-RS) and XML-based web services (JAX-WS) are included, along with APIs for XML messaging and XML registries (JAXR).

- Java EE security and container management: For implementing custom Java EE security and managing Java EE containers, software developers have access to the Java Authorization Contract for Containers and the Java Authentication Service Provider Interface for Containers.

Java EE vs. Java SE

The APIs listed above are just a sampling of the various Java EE components available to developers. All of the APIs defined in the Java Standard Edition, or Java SE, are also offered to Java EE applications.

Java EE does not compete with Java SE, but is instead a superset of APIs that builds upon the foundation provided by Java SE and the standard Java Development Kit (JDK).

Java EE applications build upon the foundation provided by Java SE, and all Java EE applications run on a Java virtual machine that supports all of the APIs defined by Java SE.

Developing and Deploying Java EE Applications

The server-side application development process in Java involves:

1. Writing code that utilizes Java EE core technologies
2. Compiling that code into bytecode
3. Packaging that bytecode and any associated resources into an Enterprise Archive (EAR) file
4. Deploying the EAR to an application server

This process could be accomplished simply using nothing but a text editor and the Java compiler that comes standard with an installation of the JDK. However, there is a rich ecosystem of integrated development environment (IDE) tools that assist in the rapid application development of Java EE code.

In terms of open source IDEs, the Eclipse IDE and Oracle's NetBeans IDE are two of the most popular for Java EE development. Both provide source code formatting, syntax checking and project organization, and they also have a rich plug-in community, allowing users to create components that will add extra functionality to the IDE.

Plug-ins are commonly required to build, deploy and perform continuous integration to Java EE applications. In this space, plug-ins for build projects like Maven, deployment tools like Gradle and continuous integration technologies, such as Jenkins and Hudson, are popular.

Java EE vs. Spring Framework

A standard for enterprise Java was first established with the release of the J2EE specification in December of 1999. This first foray into establishing a baseline of support for server-side compliance defined less than a dozen APIs, with the focus being on front-end development with Servlets and JSPs and back-end development being done with EJBs.

There were incremental improvements with the release of J2EE 1.3 in September 2001, with the addition of the JSTL being one of the release's most significant accomplishments. The inclusion of the HTML framework JSF was a further highlight in the release of J2EE 1.4 in November 2003.

Many people in the development community derided the J2EE approach to enterprise software development as being too academic, too cumbersome and heavy. As an alternative to J2EE development, with a significant focus on eliminating the use of J2EE's EJBs, programmer Rod Johnson created the Spring Framework. Working independently of Sun Microsystems, which was the steward of the J2EE framework at the time, Spring proved that enterprise-grade applications could be written in Java without needing the entire J2EE stack.

The Spring Framework took a more lightweight approach to the Java-based development of enterprise software, and developers began to embrace this simpler approach to application design.

Java EE 5 and Lightweight EJB Development

Recognizing the rising level of dissatisfaction with traditional EJBs, a new lightweight approach was introduced, with the new EJB 3.0 specification becoming part of the May 2006 rebranding of J2EE to Java EE.

Being released at a time when the current JDK was on its fifth version, the newly branded enterprise Java specification was named Java EE 5. Other major additions with Java EE 5 included the JPA and JAX-WS.

Java EE 6 and RESTful Web Services

While Java EE 5 provided API support for SOAP- and XML-based web services, the December 2009 release of Java EE 6 introduced support for REST by including the Java API for RESTful Web Services (JAX-RS).

The other big change in Java EE 6 was the introduction of a web profile. This feature allowed vendors to create Java-EE-6-compliant servers that provided only a subset of the overall Java

EE functionality. These profiles, which are essentially scaled down software stacks, reduced the distribution size of a Java EE application, making it easier to deploy apps to devices with limited computing capacity.

This new approach opened opportunities to use Java EE for IoT devices and embedded software. For example, the Java EE 6 Web Profile required Servlet and JSP support, but did not require support for APIs like JavaMail or the Java Authentication Service Provider Interface for Containers (JASPIC).

Java EE 7 and WebSockets

Released in June 2013, Java EE 7 took advantage of the emergence of HTML5 and the need for Java EE web browser support.

The Java API for WebSocket development was introduced, as was the Java API for JSON Processing, making it easier to send information formatted in JavaScript Object Notation (JSON) back and forth from the client to the server.

Java EE 8, Containers and Cloud Computing

When scheduled for release in late 2017, the Java Community Process (JCP) had stated the main focus on the latest Java EE release will be about "support for HTML5 and the emerging HTTP 2.0 standard; enhanced simplification and managed bean integration; and improved infrastructure for applications running in the cloud

Specifications

Java EE includes several specifications that serve different purposes, like generating web pages, reading and writing from a database in a transactional way, managing distributed queues.

The Java EE APIs include several technologies that extend the functionality of the base Java SE APIs, such as Enterprise JavaBeans, connectors, servlets, JavaServer Pages and several web service technologies.

Web Specifications

- Servlet: defines how to manage HTTP requests, in a synchronous or asynchronous way. It is low level and other Java EE specifications rely on it;

- WebSocket: The Java API for WebSocket specification defines a set of APIs to service WebSocket connections;

- Java Server Faces: a technology for constructing user interfaces out of components;

- Unified Expression Language (*EL*) is a simple language originally designed to satisfy the specific needs of web application developers. It is used specifically in Java Server Faces to bind components to (backing) beans and in Contexts and Dependency Injection to name beans, but can be used throughout the entire platform.

Web Service Specifications

- Java API for RESTful Web Services provides support in creating web services according to the Representational State Transfer (REST) architectural pattern;

- Java API for JSON Processing is a set of specifications to manage information encoded in JSON format;

- Java API for JSON Binding provides specifications to convert JSON information into or from Java classes;

- Java Architecture for XML Binding allows mapping XML into Java objects;

- Java API for XML Web Services can be used to create SOAP web services.

Enterprise Specifications

- Contexts and Dependency Injection is a specification to provide a depencency injection container, as in Spring;

- Enterprise JavaBean (*EJB*) specification defines a set of lightweight APIs that an object container (the EJB container) will support in order to provide transactions (using JTA), remote procedure calls (using RMI or RMI-IIOP), concurrency control, dependency injection and access control for business objects. This package contains the Enterprise JavaBeans classes and interfaces that define the contracts between the enterprise bean and its clients and between the enterprise bean and the ejb container.

- Java Persistence API are specifications about object-relational mapping between relation database tables and Java classes.

- Java Transaction API contains the interfaces and annotations to interact with the transaction support offered by Java EE. Even though this API abstracts from the really low-level details, the interfaces are also considered somewhat low-level and the average application developer in Java EE is either assumed to be relying on transparent handling of transactions by the higher level EJB abstractions, or using the annotations provided by this API in combination with CDI managed beans.

- Java Message Service provides a common way for Java programs to create, send, receive and read an enterprise messaging system's messages.

Other Specifications

- Validation: This package contains the annotations and interfaces for the declarative validation support offered by the Bean Validation API. Bean Validation provides a unified way to provide constraints on beans (e.g. JPA model classes) that can be enforced cross-layer. In Java EE, JPA honors bean validation constraints in the persistence layer, while JSF does so in the view layer.

- Batch Applications provides the means to run long running background tasks that possibly involve a large volume of data and which may need to be periodically executed.

- Java EE Connector Architecture is a Java-based technology solution for connecting application servers and enterprise information systems (*EIS*) as part of enterprise application integration (*EAI*) solutions. This is a low-level API aimed at vendors that the average application developer typically does not come in contact with.

What is JavaFX?

JavaFX is a Java library used to build Rich Internet Applications. The applications written using this library can run consistently across multiple platforms. The applications developed using JavaFX can run on various devices such as Desktop Computers, Mobile Phones, TVs, Tablets, etc.

To develop GUI Applications using Java programming language, the programmers rely on libraries such as Advanced Windowing Toolkit and Swing. After the advent of JavaFX, these Java programmers can now develop GUI applications effectively with rich content.

Need for JavaFX

To develop Client Side Applications with rich features, the programmers used to depend on various libraries to add features such as Media, UI controls, Web, 2D and 3D, etc. JavaFX includes all these features in a single library. In addition to these, the developers can also access the existing features of a Java library such as Swing.

JavaFX provides a rich set of graphics and media API's and it leverages the modern Graphical Processing Unit through hardware accelerated graphics. JavaFX also provides interfaces using which developers can combine graphics animation and UI control.

One can use JavaFX with JVM based technologies such as Java, Groovy and JRuby. If developers opt for JavaFX, there is no need to learn additional technologies, as prior knowledge of any of the above-mentioned technologies will be good enough to develop RIA's using JavaFX.

Features of JavaFX

Following are some of the important features of JavaFX –

- Written in Java – The JavaFX library is written in Java and is available for the languages that can be executed on a JVM, which include – Java, Groovy and JRuby. These JavaFX applications are also platform independent.

- FXML – JavaFX features a language known as FXML, which is a HTML like declarative markup language. The sole purpose of this language is to define a user Interface.

- Scene Builder – JavaFX provides an application named Scene Builder. On integrating this application in IDE's such as Eclipse and NetBeans, the users can access a drag and drop design interface, which is used to develop FXML applications (just like Swing Drag & Drop and DreamWeaver Applications).

- Swing Interoperability – In a JavaFX application, you can embed Swing content using the Swing Node class. Similarly, you can update the existing Swing applications with JavaFX features like embedded web content and rich graphics media.

- Built-in UI controls – JavaFX library caters UI controls using which we can develop a full-featured application.

- CSS like Styling – JavaFX provides a CSS like styling. By using this, you can improve the design of your application with a simple knowledge of CSS.

- Canvas and Printing API – JavaFX provides Canvas, an immediate mode style of rendering API. Within the package javafx.scene.canvas it holds a set of classes for canvas, using which we can draw directly within an area of the JavaFX scene. JavaFX also provides classes for Printing purposes in the package javafx.print.

- Rich set of API's – JavaFX library provides a rich set of API's to develop GUI applications, 2D and 3D graphics, etc. This set of API's also includes capabilities of Java platform. Therefore, using this API, you can access the features of Java languages such as Generics, Annotations, Multithreading, and Lambda Expressions. The traditional Java Collections library was enhanced and concepts like observable lists and maps were included in it. Using these, the users can observe the changes in the data models.

- Integrated Graphics library – JavaFX provides classes for 2d and 3d graphics.

- Graphics pipeline – JavaFX supports graphics based on the Hardware-accelerated graphics pipeline known as Prism. When used with a supported Graphic Card or GPU it offers smooth graphics. In case the system does not support graphic card then prism defaults to the software rendering stack.

Technical Highlights

JavaFX 1.1 was based on the concept of a "common profile" that is intended to span across all devices supported by JavaFX. This approach makes it possible for developers to use a common programming model while building an application targeted for both desktop and mobile devices and to share much of the code, graphics assets and content between desktop and mobile versions. To address the need for tuning applications on a specific class of devices, the JavaFX 1.1 platform includes API that are desktop or mobile-specific. For example, JavaFX Desktop profile includes Swing and advanced visual effects.

From the point of view of the end user "Drag-to-Install" allows them to drag a JavaFX widget (or application residing in a website and is visible within the browser window) and drop it onto their desktop. The application will not lose its state or context even after the browser is closed. An application can also be re-launched by clicking on a shortcut that gets created automatically on the user's desktop. This behavior is enabled out-of-the-box by the Java applet mechanism since Java 6 update 10 and is leveraged by JavaFX from the underlying Java layer. Sun touts "Drag-to-Install" as opening up of a new distribution model and allowing developers to "break away from the browser".

JavaFX 1.x included a set of plug-ins for Adobe Photoshop and Illustrator that enable advanced graphics to be integrated directly into JavaFX applications. The plug-ins generate JavaFX Script code that preserves layers and structure of the graphics. Developers can then easily add animation or effects to the static graphics imported. There was also an SVG graphics converter tool (also known as Media Factory) that allows for importing graphics and previewing assets after the conversion to JavaFX format.

Design Highlights

Sun Microsystems licensed a custom typeface called Amble for use on JavaFX-powered devices. The font family was designed by mobile user interface design specialists Punchcut and is available as part of the JavaFX SDK 1.3 Release.

JavaFX Platform Components

JavaFX 2.x platform includes the following components:

1. The JavaFX SDK: runtime tools. Graphics, media web services, and rich text libraries. Java FX 1.x also included JavaFX compiler, which is now obsolete as JavaFX user code is written in Java.

2. NetBeans IDE for JavaFX: NetBeans with drag-and-drop palette to add objects with transformations, effects and animations plus a set of samples and best practices. For JavaFX 2 support you need at least NetBeans 7.1.1. For Eclipse users there is a community-supported plugin hosted on e(fx)clipse.

3. JavaFX scene builder: This was introduced for Java FX 2.1 and later. A user interface (UI) is created by dragging and dropping controls from a palette. This information is saved as an FXML file, a special XML format.

4. Tools and plugins for creative tools (a.k.a. Production Suite): Plugins for Adobe Photoshop and Adobe Illustrator that can export graphics assets to JavaFX Script code, tools to convert SVG graphics into JavaFX Script code and preview assets converted to JavaFX from other tools (currently not supported in JavaFX 2.x versions)

JavaFX Mobile

JavaFX Mobile was the implementation of the JavaFX platform for rich Internet applications aimed at mobile devices. JavaFX Mobile 1.x applications can be developed in the same language, JavaFX Script, as JavaFX 1.x applications for browser or desktop, and using the same tools: JavaFX SDK and the JavaFX Production Suite. This concept makes it possible to share code-base and graphics assets for desktop and mobile applications. Through integration with Java ME, the JavaFX applications have access to capabilities of the underlying handset, such as the filesystem, camera, GPS, bluetooth or accelerometer.

An independent application platform built on Java, JavaFX Mobile is capable of running on multiple mobile operating systems, including Android, Windows Mobile, and proprietary real-time operating systems.

JavaFX Mobile was publicly available as part of the JavaFX 1.1 release announced by Sun Microsystems on February 12, 2009.

Sun planned to enable out-of-the-box support of JavaFX on the devices by working with handset manufacturers and mobile operators to preload the JavaFX Mobile runtime on the handsets. JavaFX Mobile running on an Android was demonstrated at JavaOne 2008 and selected partnerships (incl. LG Electronics, Sony Ericsson) were announced at the JavaFX Mobile launch in February, 2009.

Versions

JavaFX Script, the scripting component of JavaFX, began life as a project by Chris Oliver called F3.

Sun Microsystems first announced JavaFX at the JavaOne Worldwide Java Developer conference on May 2007.

In May 2008 Sun Microsystems announced plans to deliver JavaFX for the browser and desktop by the third quarter of 2008, and JavaFX for mobile devices in the second quarter of 2009. Sun also announced a multi-year agreement with On2 Technologies to bring comprehensive video capabilities to the JavaFX product family using the company's TrueMotion Video codec. Since end of July 2008, developers could download a preview of the JavaFX SDK for Windows and Macintosh, as well as the JavaFX plugin for NetBeans 6.1.

Major releases since JavaFX 1.1 have a release name based on a street or neighborhood in San Francisco. Update releases typically do not have a release name.

JavaFX 1.0

On December 4, 2008 Sun released JavaFX 1.0.2

JavaFX 1.1

JavaFX for mobile development was finally made available as part of the JavaFX 1.1 release (named Franca) announced officially on February 12, 2009.

JavaFX 2.2

On August 14, 2012, Oracle released version 2.2 of JavaFX, which includes the following main features:

- Linux support (including plugin and webstart)
- Canvas
- New controls: Color Picker, Pagination
- HTTP Live Streaming support
- Touch events and gestures
- Image manipulation API
- Native Packaging

JavaFX 2.2 adds new packaging option called Native Packaging, allowing packaging of an application as a "native bundle". This gives users a way to install and run an application without any external dependencies on a system JRE or FX SDK.

As of Oracle Java SE 7 update 6 and Java FX 2.2, JavaFX is bundled to be installed with Oracle Java SE platform.

JavaFX 8

JavaFX is now part of the JRE/JDK for Java 8 (released on March 18, 2014) and has the same numbering, i.e., JavaFX 8.

JavaFX 8 adds several new features, including:

- Support for 3D graphics
- Sensor Support
- Printing and rich text support
- Generic dialog templates via inclusion of ControlsFX to replace JOptionPane as of JavaFX 8u40.

JavaFX 9

JavaFX 9 features were centered on extracting some useful private APIs from the JavaFX code to make these APIs public:

- JEP 253: Prepare JavaFX UI Controls and CSS APIs for Modularization

Future Work

Oracle also announced in November 2012 the open sourcing of Decora, a DSL Shader language for JavaFX allowing to generate Shaders for OpenGL and Direct3D.

Oracle announced their intention to stop shipping JavaFX with JDK 11 and later. Oracle wrote in a white paper that JavaFX new fixes will continue to be supported on Java SE 8 through March 2022 and announced that they are "working with interested third parties to make it easier to build and maintain JavaFX as a separately distributable open-source module." JavaFX will continue to be supported in the future by the company Gluon as a downloadable module in addition to the JDK.

JavaFX Application Example

Example Code

The following is a rather simple JavaFX-based program. It displays a window (a Stage) containing a button.

Hello world program in JavaFX

```
package javafxtuts;


import javafx.application.Application;
```

```java
import javafx.event.ActionEvent;
import javafx.event.EventHandler;
import javafx.scene.Scene;
import javafx.scene.control.Button;
import javafx.scene.layout.StackPane;
import javafx.stage.Stage;


public class JavaFxTuts extends Application {
    public JavaFxTuts()
    {
        //Optional constructor
    }
    @Override
    public void init()
    {
        //By default this does nothing, but it
        //can carry out code to set up your app.
        //It runs once before the start method,
        //and after the constructor.
    }


    @Override
    public void start(Stage primaryStage) {
        // Creating the Java button
        final Button button = new Button();
        // Setting text to button
        button.setText("Hello World");
        // Registering a handler for button
        button.setOnAction((ActionEvent event) -> {
            // Printing Hello World! to the console
            System.out.println("Hello World!");
        });
        // Initializing the StackPane class
        final StackPane root = new StackPane();
```

```java
        // Adding all the nodes to the StackPane
        root.getChildren().add(button);
        // Creating a scene object
        final Scene scene = new Scene(root, 300, 250);
        // Adding the title to the window (primaryStage)
        primaryStage.setTitle("Hello World!");
        primaryStage.setScene(scene);
        // Show the window(primaryStage)
        primaryStage.show();
    }
    @Override
    public void stop()
    {
        //By default this does nothing
        //It runs if the user clicks the go-away button
        //closing the window or if Platform.exit() is called.
        //Use Platform.exit() instead of System.exit(0).
        //This is where you should offer to save any unsaved
        //stuff that the user may have generated.
    }


    /**
     * Main function that opens the "Hello World!" window
     *
     * @param args the command line arguments
     */
    public static void main(final String[] arguments) {
        launch(arguments);
    }
}
```

Platforms

As of March 2014 JavaFX is deployed on Microsoft Windows, OS X, and Linux. Oracle has an internal port of JavaFX on iOS and Android. Support for ARM is available starting with JavaFX 8 On February 11, 2013, Richard Bair, chief architect of the Client Java Platform at Oracle, announced that Oracle would open-source the iOS and Android implementations of its JavaFX platform in the next two months. Starting with version 8u33 of JDK for ARM, support for JavaFX Embedded has been removed. Support will continue for x86-based architectures.

A commercial port of JavaFX for Android and iOS has been created under the name "Gluon".

License

There are various licenses for the modules that compose the JavaFX runtime:

- Parts of the core JavaFX runtime are still proprietary software and its code has not yet been released to the public, however developers and executives behind the technology are moving toward a full opening of the code,

- The JavaFX compiler and an older version of the 2D Scene graph are released under a GPL v2 license,

- The NetBeans plugin for JavaFX is dual licensed under GPL v2 and CDDL.

During development, Sun explained they will roll out their strategy for the JavaFX licensing model for JavaFX first release. After the release in 2008, Jeet Kaul, Sun's Vice president for Client Software, explained that they will soon publish a specification for JavaFX and its associated file formats, and will continue to open-source the JavaFX runtime, and decouple this core from the proprietary parts licensed by external parties.

At JavaOne 2011, Oracle Corporation announced that JavaFX 2.0 would become open-source. Since December 2011, Oracle began to open-source the JavaFX code under the GPL+linking exception.

In December 2012, new portions of the JavaFX source code have been open-sourced by Oracle:

- the animations and timelines classes

- the event delivery mechanism and other various core classes

- the render tree interface, and the implementation of this interface

- the geometry and shapes implementation

- the java part of the rendering engine used in the rendering pipeline

- the logging support

Java Development Kit

The Java Development Kit (JDK) is a software development environment used for developing Java applications and applets. It includes the Java Runtime Environment (JRE), an interpreter/loader (java), a compiler (javac), an archiver (jar), a documentation generator (javadoc) and other tools needed in Java development.

People new to Java may be confused about whether to use the JRE or the JDK. To run Java applications and applets, simply download the JRE. However, to develop Java applications and applets as well as run them, the JDK is needed.

Java developers are initially presented with two JDK tools, java and javac. Both are run from the command prompt. Java source files are simple text files saved with an extension of .java. After writing and saving Java source code, the javac compiler is invoked to create .class files. Once the .class files are created, the 'java' command can be used to run the java program.

For developers who wish to work in an integrated development environment (IDE), a JDK bundled with Netbeans can be downloaded from the Oracle website. Such IDEs speed up the development process by introducing point-and-click and drag-and-drop features for creating an application.

There are different JDKs for various platforms. The supported platforms include Windows, Linux and Solaris. Mac users need a different software development kit, which includes adaptations of some tools found in the JDK.

Ambiguity between a JDK and an SDK

The JDK forms an extended subset of a software development kit (SDK). It includes "tools for developing, debugging, and monitoring Java applications". Oracle strongly suggests to now use the term *JDK* to refer to the Java SE Development Kit. The Java EE SDK is available with or without the JDK, by which they specifically mean the Java SE 7 JDK.

Other JDKs

In addition to the most widely used JDK, there are other JDKs commonly available for a variety of platforms, some of which started from the Sun JDK source and some that did not. All adhere to the basic Java specifications, but often differ in explicitly unspecified areas, such as garbage collection, compilation strategies, and optimization techniques. They include:

In development or in maintenance mode:

- Azul Systems Zing, low latency JDK for Linux;
- Azul Systems / OpenJDK-based Zulu for Linux, Windows, Mac OS X, embedded and the cloud;
- OpenJDK / IcedTea;
- GNU's Classpath and GCJ (The GNU Compiler for Java);
- Aicas JamaicaVM;
- IBM J9 JDK, for AIX, Linux, Windows, MVS, OS/400, Pocket PC, z/OS;

Not being maintained or discontinued:

- Apache Harmony
- Apple's Mac OS Runtime for Java JVM/JDK for Classic Mac OS

- Blackdown Java – Port of Sun's JDK for Linux

- Oracle Corporation's JRockit JDK, for Windows, Linux, and Solaris;

Major JDK Components

Java Development Kit (JDK) is a bundle of software components that is used to develop Java based applications. JDK is an implementation of either of Java SE, Java EE or Java ME. Usually, learners start from JDK implementation of Java SE to learn core Java features, which is also known as Java SDK. JDK includes the JRE, set of API classes, Java compiler, Webstart and additional files needed to write Java applets and applications. Java Development Kit is a bundle of the following software components that are needed to develop Java based applications.

- Java Compiler: Java compiler is javac tool located in */bin* folder of the JDK installation directory. The javac tool (accessed using javac command) reads class and interface definitions, written in the Java programming language, and compiles them into bytecode class files. It can also process annotations in Java source files and classes.

  There are two ways to pass source code file names to javac:

  o For a small number of source files, simply list the file names on the command line separated by blank space. For example:

  ```
  D:\JavaPrograms>javac SelectionSortDemo.java SequentialSearch-
  Demo.java
  ```

  o For a large number of source files, list the file names in a file, separated by blanks or line breaks. Then use the list file name on the javac command line, preceded by an @ character. For an example, store three source file names *SelectionSortDemo.java*, *SequentialSearchDemo.java*, *SystemOutPrintlnDemo.java* in a file named *source-file-list* and then supply following command in order to compile the source code files stored in *source-file-list*.

  ```
  D:\JavaPrograms>javac @source-file-list
  ```

Inner class definitions produce additional class files. These class files have names combining the inner and outer class names, such as MyClass$MyInnerClass.class.

- Java Interpreter: Java interpreter is used to interpret the .class Java files that have been compiled by Java compiler (javac). Java interpreter is accessed using java command. The java command starts a Java application. It does this by starting a Java runtime environment, loading a specified class, and calling that class's main method.

  The method must be declared public and static, it must not return any value, and it must accept a String array as a parameter. The method declaration has the following form:

  ```
  public static void main(String[] args)
  ```

  By default, the first argument without an option is the name of the class to be called. A fully qualified class name should be used. If the -jar option is specified, then the first non-option argument is the name of a JAR file containing class and resource files for the application, with the startup class indicated by the Main-Class manifest header.

The Java runtime searches for the startup class, and other classes used, in three sets of locations: the bootstrap class path, the installed extensions, and the user class path.

Non-option arguments after the class name or JAR file name are passed to the main function.

- Java Disassembler: The javap command is the disassembly tool of JDK that disassembles one or more class files. Its output depends on the options used. If no options are used, javap prints out the package, protected, and public fields and methods of the classes passed to it. The javap prints its output to stdout.

- Java Header File Generator: Java Header File Generator (javah command-line tool) generates C header and source files that are needed to implement native methods. The generated header and source files are used by C programs to reference an object's instance variables from native source code. The .h file contains a struct definition whose layout parallels the layout of the corresponding class. The fields in the struct correspond to instance variables in the class.

The name of the header file and the structure declared within it are derived from the name of the class. If the class passed to javah is inside a package, the package name is prepended to both the header file name and the structure name. Underscores (_) are used as name delimiters.

By default javah creates a header file for each class listed on the command line and puts the files in the current directory. Use the -stubs option to create source files. Use the -o option to concatenate the results for all listed classes into a single file.

The new native method interface, Java Native Interface (JNI), does not require header information or stub files. The javah tool can still be used to generate native method function prototypes needed for JNI-style native methods. The javah tool produces JNI-style output by default, and places the result in the .h file.

- Java Documentation: Java Documentation helps to maintain code. The javadoc tool comes as part of Java Development Kit that parses the declarations and documentation comments in a set of Java source files and produces a corresponding set of HTML pages describing (by default) the public and protected classes, nested classes (but not anonymous inner classes), interfaces, constructors, methods, and fields. You can use it to generate the API (Application Programming Interface) documentation or the implementation documentation for a set of source files.

You can run the javadoc tool on entire packages, individual source files, or both. When documenting entire packages, you can either use -subpackages for traversing recursively down from a top-level directory, or pass in an explicit list of package names. When documenting individual source files, you pass in a list of source (.java) file names.

- Java Debugger: The Java Debugger, jdb, is a simple command-line debugger for Java classes. It is a demonstration of the Java Platform Debugger Architecture that provides inspection and debugging of a local or remote Java Virtual Machine.

- Java Applet Viewer: This is used to view the Java applets. The appletviewer command connects to the documents or resources designated by *urls* and displays each applet referenced by the documents in its own window. Note: if the documents referred to by *urls* do not reference any applets with the OBJECT, EMBED, or APPLET tag, then appletviewer does nothing.

References

- Ortiz, C. Enrique; Giguère, Éric (2001). Mobile Information Device Profile for Java 2 Micro Edition: Developer's Guide (PDF). John Wiley & Sons. ISBN 978-0471034650. Retrieved 2012-05-30

- O'Hair, Kelly (December 2010). "OpenJDK7 and OpenJDK6 Binary Plugs Logic Removed". Oracle Corporation. Retrieved 2011-11-25

- Southwick, Karen (1999). High Noon: the inside story of Scott McNealy and the rise of Sun Microsystems. New York [u.a.]: Wiley. pp. 120–122. ISBN 0471297135

- Brook, Chris. "The first stop for security news". Threatpost. Archived from the original on 2013-03-08. Retrieved 2016-02-09

- Southwick, Karen (1999). High Noon: the inside story of Scott McNealy and the rise of Sun Microsystems. New York [u.a.]: Wiley. p. 124. ISBN 0471297135

Java Compiler

The compiler used for the Java programming language is known as the Java compiler. It produces Java class files that contain platform-neutral Java bytecode. There are different types of Java compilers such as Jikes, Javac, Graal, GNU compiler for Java, etc. which have been discussed in comprehensive detail in this chapter.

All *high-level* (also called third-*generation*) programming languages allow you to write programs in a language similar (although much simpler) than natural language. The high-level program is called the *source code*.

A *low-level* programming language is something closer to what makes sense to a computer. Details for low-level languages are unimportant in the intro CS courses.

Compilers

Most computer languages use the "compile-link-execute" format. You start with source code and the *compiler* converts this program into a low-level program.

In most compiled languages, the file containing the resulting low-level code is called an *object* file. A collection of object files are *linked* together to create an *executable* file (i.e., the operating system can load the executable into RAM to run the program). Another term for an executable is "(relocatable) machine code".

An object file isn't easily read by a human but it may not be runnable on a computer. For example, if your program takes a square root of a number, your program will rely on the mathematical program (provided by the math library of the language) that actually determines how to compute a square root. The object file for the program will refer to the square root but will not have the code explaining how the square root computation works. Similarly, when you start solving bigger problems, you will likely divide your project into multiple programs that communicate.

The process of *linking* connects the object files that you have created along with other pre-existing object files to form an executable file. The *linker* does this job. You shouldn't expect to find *link errors* until you're writing larger programs that have multiple parts; link errors occur when the object files for your program don't completely communicate appropriately.

Interpreters

There are a smaller number of languages (Lisp and Scheme are most famous; CMU uses ML in 15-212) that avoid the "compile-link-execute" sequence and instead try to do the conversion "on-the-fly" (also called "as needed").

In other words, an *interpreted* language takes each high-level statement, determines its low-level version and executes (while linking if need be) the result. This is done for each statement in succession (before the next high-level statement is even looked at).

As an analogy to foreign languages, a compiler acts as a translator (say, someone who translates a book) and an interpreter acts like, well, an interpreter.

While debugging programs, you wouldn't notice much of a difference between compilers and interpreters because the executable file needs to be regenerated whenever the source code changes. However, once debugging is completed, an executable created by a compiler will run much faster than a similar piece of source code that always has to run through its interpreter. Using the analogy, reading a translation of a poem will always be "faster" than having to interpret the poem on the fly every time you read it.

However, there are advantages to interpreted languages. In artificial intelligence, interpreted languages are prefered since programs may have to adapt to new stimuli. Also, it is generally easier to build a prototype program using an interpreter. Many interpreted languages also provide a "compile mode" to create executables which will run about as fast as an executable created by a compiler.

To understand the primary advantage of Java, you'll have to learn about platforms. In most programming languages, a compiler (or interpreter) generates code that can execute on a specific target machine. For example, if you compile a C++ program on a Windows machine, the executable file can be copied to any other machine but it will only run on other Windows machines but never another machine (e.g., a Mac or a Linux machine). A platform is determined by the target machine (along with its operating system). For earlier languages, language designers needed to create a specialized version of the compiler (or interpreter) for every platform. If you wrote a program that you wanted to make available on multiple platforms, you, as the programmer, would have to do quite a bit of additional work. You would have to create multiple versions of your source code for each platform.

Java succeeded in eliminating the platform issue for high-level programmers (such as you) because it has reorganized the compile-link-execute sequence at an underlying level of the compiler. Details are complicated but, essentially, the designers of the Java language isolated those programming issues which are dependent on the platform and developed low-level means to abstractly refer to these issues.

Java Compiler Definition

A Java compiler is a program that takes the text file work of a developer and compiles it into a platform-independent Java file. Java compilers include the Java Programming Language Compiler (javac), the GNU Compiler for Java (GCJ), the Eclipse Compiler for Java (ECJ) and Jikes.

Programmers typically write language statements in a given programming language one line at a time using a code editor or an integrated development environment (IDE). The resulting file contains what are called the source statements. The programmer then runs a compiler for the appropriate language, specifying the name of the file that contains the source statements.

At run time, the compiler first parses (analyzes) all of the language statements syntactically and then, in one or more successive stages or "passes," builds the output code, making sure that statements that refer to other statements are referred to correctly in the final code.

Generally, Java compilers are run and pointed to a programmer's code in a text file to produce a class file for use by the Java virtual machine (JVM) on different platforms. Jikes, for example, is an open source compiler that works in this way.

A JIT (just in time) Java compiler comes along with the Java VM. Its use is optional, and it is run on the platform-independent code. The JIT compiler then translates the code into the machine code for different hardware so that it is optimized for different architectures. Once the code has been (re-)compiled by the JIT compiler, it will usually run more quickly than the Java code that can only be executed one instruction at a time.

The Java compiler doesn't create an object file, but instead it creates a *bytecode* file which is, essentially, an object file for a *virtual machine*. In fact, the Java compiler is often called the JVM compiler (for Java Virtual Machine).

Consequently, you can write a Java program (on any platform) and use the JVM compiler (called javac) to generate a bytecode file (bytecode files use the extension .class). This bytecode file can be used on any platform (that has installed Java). However, bytecode is not an executable file. To execute a bytecode file, you actually need to invoke a Java interpreter (called java). Every platform has its own Java interpreter which will automatically address the platform-specific issues that can no longer be put off. When platform-specific operations are required by the bytecode, the Java interpreter links in appropriate code specific to the platform.

To summarize how Java works (to achieve platform independence), think about the compile-link-execute cycle. In earlier programming languages, the cycle is more closely defined as "compile-link then execute". In Java, the cycle is closer to *"compile then link-execute"*.

As with interpreted languages, it is possible to get Java programs to run faster by compiling the bytecode into an executable; the disadvantage is that such executables will only work on the platform in which it is created.

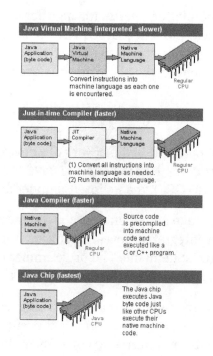

Major Java Compilers

As of 2012, the following are major Java compilers:

- The java Programming Language Compiler (javac), included in the Java Development Kit from Oracle Corporation, open-sourced since 13 November 2006.

- GNU Compiler for Java (GCJ), a part of the GNU Compiler Collection, which compiles C, C++, Fortran, Pascal and other programming languages besides Java. It can also generate native code using the back-end of Gcc.

- Eclipse Compiler for Java (ECJ), an open source incremental compiler used by the Eclipse project.

Javac

Javac is the standard Java compiler and part of the Java Development Kit. It creates bytecode for the Java Virtual Machine from valid Java code. While it is primarily run from the command line, it can be run programmatically using the Java compiler API.

javac

Arguments can be in any order:

options

> Command-line options.

sourcefiles

> One or more source files to be compiled (such as MyClass.java).

classes

> One or more classes to be processed for annotations (such as MyPackage.MyClass).

@argfiles

> One or more files that list options and source files. The -J options are not allowed in these files.

Description

The javac command reads class and interface definitions, written in the Java programming language, and compiles them into bytecode class files. The javac command can also process annotations in Java source files and classes.

There are two ways to pass source code file names to javac.

- For a small number of source files, list the file names on the command line.

- For a large number of source files, list the file names in a file that is separated by blanks or line breaks. Use the list file name preceded by an at sign (@) with the javac command.

Source code file names must have .java suffixes, class file names must have .class suffixes, and both source and class files must have root names that identify the class. For example, a class called MyClass would be written in a source file called MyClass.java and compiled into a bytecode class file called MyClass.class.

Inner class definitions produce additional class files. These class files have names that combine the inner and outer class names, such as MyClass$MyInnerClass.class.

Arrange source files in a directory tree that reflects their package tree. For example, if all of your source files are in \workspace, then put the source code for com.mysoft.mypack.MyClass in /workspace in \workspace\com\mysoft\mypack\MyClass.java.

By default, the compiler puts each class file in the same directory as its source file. You can specify a separate destination directory with the -d option.

Options

The compiler has a set of standard options that are supported on the current development environment. An additional set of nonstandard options are specific to the current virtual machine and compiler implementations and are subject to change in the future. Nonstandard options begin with the -X option.

Standard Options

- A*key*[=*value*]

  Specifies options to pass to annotation processors. These options are not interpreted by javac directly, but are made available for use by individual processors. The key value should be one or more identifiers separated by a dot (.).

- cp *path* or -classpath *path*

  Specifies where to find user class files, and (optionally) annotation processors and source files. This class path overrides the user class path in the CLASSPATH environment variable. If neither CLASSPATH, -cp nor -classpath is specified, then the user *class path* is the current directory.

  If the -sourcepath option is not specified, then the user class path is also searched for source files.

  If the -processorpath option is not specified, then the class path is also searched for annotation processors.

- Djava.ext.dirs=*directories*

  Overrides the location of installed extensions.

- Djava.endorsed.diro- *directories*

    Overrides the location of the endorsed standards path.

- d *directory*

    Sets the destination directory for class files. The directory must already exist because javac does not create it. If a class is part of a package, then javac puts the class file in a subdirectory that reflects the package name and creates directories as needed.

    If you specify -d C:\myclasses and the class is called com.mypackage.MyClass, then the class file is C:\myclasses\com\mypackage\MyClass.class.

    If the *-d* option is not specified, then javac puts each class file in the same directory as the source file from which it was generated.

    Note: The directory specified by the *-d* option is not automatically added to your user class path.

- deprecation

    Shows a description of each use or override of a deprecated member or class. Without the -deprecation option, javac shows a summary of the source files that use or override deprecated members or classes. The -deprecation option is shorthand for -Xlint:deprecation.

- encoding *encoding*

    Sets the source file encoding name, such as EUC-JP and UTF-8. If the -encoding option is not specified, then the platform default converter is used.

- endorseddirs *directories*

    Overrides the location of the endorsed standards path.

- extdirs *directories*

    Overrides the location of the ext directory. The directories variable is a colon-separated list of directories. Each JAR file in the specified directories is searched for class files. All JAR files found become part of the class path.

    If you are cross-compiling (compiling classes against bootstrap and extension classes of a different Java platform implementation), then this option specifies the directories that contain the extension classes.

- g

    Generates all debugging information, including local variables. By default, only line number and source file information is generated.

- g:none

    Does not generate any debugging information.

•g:[*keyword list*]

Generates only some kinds of debugging information, specified by a comma separated list of keywords. Valid keywords are:

source

Source file debugging information.

lines

Line number debugging information.

vars

Local variable debugging information.

•help

Prints a synopsis of standard options.

•implicit:[*class, none*]

Controls the generation of class files for implicitly loaded source files. To automatically generate class files, use -implicit:class. To suppress class file generation, use -implicit:-none. If this option is not specified, then the default is to automatically generate class files. In this case, the compiler issues a warning if any such class files are generated when also doing annotation processing. The warning is not issued when the -implicit option is set explicitly.

•J*option*

Passes option to the Java Virtual Machine (JVM), where option is one of the options described on the reference page for the Java launcher. For example, -J-Xms48m sets the startup memory to 48 MB. Note: The *CLASSPATH*, -classpath, -bootclasspath, and -ext-dirs options do not specify the classes used to run javac. Trying to customize the compiler implementation with these options and variables is risky and often does not accomplish what you want. If you must customize the complier implementation, then use the -J option to pass options through to the underlying Java launcher.

•nowarn

Disables warning messages. This option operates the same as the -Xlint:none option.

•parameters

Stores formal parameter names of constructors and methods in the generated class file so that the method java.lang.reflect.Executable.getParameters from the Reflection API can retrieve them.

•proc: [*none, only*]

Controls whether annotation processing and compilation are done. -proc:none means that compilation takes place without annotation processing. -proc:only means that only annotation processing is done, without any subsequent compilation.

- processor *class1* [,*class2,class3...*]

  Names of the annotation processors to run. This bypasses the default discovery process.

- processorpath *path*

  Specifies where to find annotation processors. If this option is not used, then the class path is searched for processors.

- s *dir*

  Specifies the directory where to place the generated source files. The directory must already exist because javac does not create it. If a class is part of a package, then the compiler puts the source file in a subdirectory that reflects the package name and creates directories as needed.

  If you specify -s C:\mysrc and the class is called com.mypackage.MyClass, then the source file is put in in C:\mysrc\com\mypackage\MyClass.java.

- source *release*

  Specifies the version of source code accepted. The following values for release are allowed:

  1.3

  The compiler does not support assertions, generics, or other language features introduced after Java SE 1.3.

  1.4

  The compiler accepts code containing assertions, which were introduced in Java SE 1.4.

  1.5

  The compiler accepts code containing generics and other language features introduced in Java SE 5.

  5

  Synonym for 1.5.

  1.6

  No language changes were introduced in Java SE 6. However, encoding errors in source files are now reported as errors instead of warnings as in earlier releases of Java Platform, Standard Edition.

  6

  Synonym for 1.6.

1.7

The compiler accepts code with features introduced in Java SE 7.

7

Synonym for 1.7.

1.8

This is the default value. The compiler accepts code with features introduced in Java SE 8.

8

Synonym for 1.8.

- sourcepath *sourcepath*

    Specifies the source code path to search for class or interface definitions. As with the user class path, source path entries are separated by colons (:) on Oracle Solaris and semicolons on Windows and can be directories, JAR archives, or ZIP archives. If packages are used, then the local path name within the directory or archive must reflect the package name.

    Note: Classes found through the class path might be recompiled when their source files are also found.

- verbose

    Uses verbose output, which includes information about each class loaded and each source file compiled.

- version

    Prints release information.

- werror

    Terminates compilation when warnings occur.

- X

    Displays information about nonstandard options and exits.

Cross-Compilation Options

By default, classes are compiled against the bootstrap and extension classes of the platform that javac shipped with. But javac also supports cross-compiling, where classes are compiled against a bootstrap and extension classes of a different Java platform implementation. It is important to use the -bootclasspath and -extdirs options when cross-compiling.

- target *version*

    Generates class files that target a specified release of the virtual machine. Class files will run on the specified target and on later releases, but not on earlier releases of the JVM. Valid targets are 1.1, 1.2, 1.3, 1.4, 1.5 (also 5), 1.6 (also 6), 1.7 (also 7), and 1.8 (also 8).

The default for the -target option depends on the value of the -source option:

- If the -source option is not specified, then the value of the -target option is 1.8

- If the -source option is 1.2, then the value of the -target option is 1.4

- If the -source option is 1.3, then the value of the -target option is 1.4

- If the -source option is 1.5, then the value of the -target option is 1.8

- If the -source option is 1.6, then the value of the -target is option 1.8

- If the -source option is 1.7, then the value of the -target is option 1.8

- For all other values of the -source option, the value of the -target option is the value of the -source option.

• bootclasspath *bootclasspath*

Cross-compiles against the specified set of boot classes. As with the user class path, boot class path entries are separated by colons (:) and can be directories, JAR archives, or ZIP archives.

Compact Profile Option

Beginning with JDK 8, the javac compiler supports compact profiles. With compact profiles, applications that do not require the entire Java platform can be deployed and run with a smaller footprint. The compact profiles feature could be used to shorten the download time for applications from app stores. This feature makes for more compact deployment of Java applications that bundle the JRE. This feature is also useful in small devices.

The supported profile values are compact1, compact2, and compact3. These are additive layers. Each higher-numbered compact profile contains all of the APIs in profiles with smaller number names.

• profile

When using compact profiles, this option specifies the profile name when compiling. For example:

```
javac -profile compact1 Hello.java
```

javac does not compile source code that uses any Java SE APIs that is not in the specified profile. Here is an example of the error message that results from attempting to compile such source code:

```
cd jdk1.8.0/bin
./javac -profile compact1 Paint.java
```

```
Paint.java:5: error: Applet is not available in profile 'com-
pact1'
import java.applet.Applet;
```

In this example, you can correct the error by modifying the source to not use the Applet class. You could also correct the error by compiling without the -profile option. Then the compilation would be run against the full set of Java SE APIs. (None of the compact profiles include the Applet class.)

An alternative way to compile with compact profiles is to use the -bootclasspath option to specify a path to an rt.jar file that specifies a profile's image. Using the -profile option instead does not require a profile image to be present on the system at compile time. This is useful when cross-compiling.

Nonstandard Options

•Xbootclasspath/p:*path*

Adds a suffix to the bootstrap class path.

•Xbootclasspath/a:*path*

Adds a prefix to the bootstrap class path.

•Xbootclasspath/:*path*

Overrides the location of the bootstrap class files.

•Xdoclint:[-]group [/access]

Enables or disables specific groups of checks, where group is one of the following values: accessibility, syntax, reference, html or missing. For more information about these groups of checks see the -Xdoclint option of the javadoc command. The -Xdoclint option is disabled by default in the javac command.

The variable access specifies the minimum visibility level of classes and members that the -Xdoclint option checks. It can have one of the following values (in order of most to least visible) : public, protected, package and private. For example, the following option checks classes and members (with all groups of checks) that have the access level protected and higher (which includes protected, package and public):

```
-Xdoclint:all/protected
```

The following option enables all groups of checks for all access levels, except it will not check for HTML errors for classes and members that have access level package and higher (which includes package and public):

```
-Xdoclint:all,-html/package
```

•Xdoclint:none

Disables all groups of checks.

• Xdoclint:all[/access]

> Enables all groups of checks.

• Xlint

> Enables all recommended warnings. In this release, enabling all available warnings is recommended.

• Xlint:all

> Enables all recommended warnings. In this release, enabling all available warnings is recommended.

• Xlint:none

> Disables all warnings.

• Xlint:*name*

> Disables warning name. for a list of warnings you can disable with this option.

• Xlint:-*name*

> Disables warning name. with the -Xlint option to get a list of warnings that you can disable with this option.

• Xmaxerrs *number*

> Sets the maximum number of errors to print.

• Xmaxwarns *number*

> Sets the maximum number of warnings to print.

• Xstdout *filename*

> Sends compiler messages to the named file. By default, compiler messages go to System.err.

• Xprefer:[*newer,source*]

> Specifies which file to read when both a source file and class file are found for a type. If the -Xprefer:newer option is used, then it reads the newer of the source or class file for a type (default). If the -Xprefer:source option is used, then it reads the source file. Use -Xprefer:source when you want to be sure that any annotation processors can access annotations declared with a retention policy of SOURCE.

• Xpkginfo:[*always,legacy,nonempty*]

> Control whether javac generates package-info.class files from package-info.java files. Possible mode arguments for this option include the following.

> always

Always generate a package-info.class file for every package-info.java file. This option may be useful if you use a build system such as Ant, which checks that each .java file has a corresponding .class file.

legacy

Generate a package-info.class file only if package-info.java contains annotations. Don't generate a package-info.class file if package-info.java only contains comments.

Note: A package-info.class file might be generated but be empty if all the annotations in the package-info.java file have RetentionPolicy.SOURCE.

nonempty

Generate a package-info.class file only if package-info.java contains annotations with RetentionPolicy.CLASS or RetentionPolicy.RUNTIME.

- Xprint

Prints a textual representation of specified types for debugging purposes. Perform neither annotation processing nor compilation. The format of the output could change.

- XprintProcessorInfo

Prints information about which annotations a processor is asked to process.

- XprintRounds

Prints information about initial and subsequent annotation processing rounds.

Enable or Disable Warnings with the -Xlint Option

Enable warning *name* with the -Xlint:name option, where name is one of the following warning names. Note that you can disable a warning with the -Xlint:-name: option.

- cast

Warns about unnecessary and redundant casts, for example:

```
String s = (String) "Hello!"
```

- classfile

Warns about issues related to class file contents.

- deprecation

Warns about the use of deprecated items, for example:

```
java.util.Date myDate = new java.util.Date();
int currentDay = myDate.getDay();
```

The method java.util.Date.getDay has been deprecated since JDK 1.1

- **dep ann**

    Warns about items that are documented with an @deprecated Javadoc comment, but do not have a @Deprecated annotation, for example:

    ```
    /**
      * @deprecated As of Java SE 7, replaced by {@link #newMeth-
    od()}
      */
    public static void deprecatedMethood() { }
    public static void newMethod() { }
    ```

- divzero

    Warns about division by the constant integer 0, for example:

    ```
    int divideByZero = 42 / 0;
    ```

- empty

    Warns about empty statements after if statements, for example:

    ```
    class E {
        void m() {
            if (true) ;
        }
    }
    ```

- Fallthrough

    Checks the switch blocks for fall-through cases and provides a warning message for any that are found. Fall-through cases are cases in a switch block, other than the last case in the block, whose code does not include a break statement, allowing code execution to fall through from that case to the next case. For example, the code following the case 1 label in this switch block does not end with a break statement:

    ```
    switch (x) {
    case 1:
      System.out.println("1");
      // No break statement here.
    case 2:
      System.out.println("2");
    }
    ```

    If the -Xlint: fallthrough option was used when compiling this code, then the compiler emits a warning about possible fall-through into case, with the line number of the case in question.

- finally

    Warns about finally clauses that cannot complete normally, for example:

    ```
    public static int m() {
        try {
            throw new NullPointerException();
        } catch (NullPointerException(); {
            System.err.println("Caught NullPointerException.");
            return 1;
        } finally {
            return 0;
        }
    }
    ```

    The compiler generates a warning for the finally block in this example. When the int method is called, it returns a value of 0. A finally block executes when the try block exits. In this example, when control is transferred to the catch block, the int method exits. However, the finally block must execute, so it is executed, even though control was transferred outside the method.

- options

    Warns about issues that related to the use of command-line options.

- overrides

    Warns about issues regarding method overrides. For example, consider the following two classes:

    ```
    public class ClassWithVarargsMethod {
        void varargsMethod(String... s) { }
    }


    public class ClassWithOverridingMethod extends ClassWith-
    VarargsMethod {
        @Override
        void varargsMethod(String[] s) { }
    }
    ```

    The compiler generates a warning similar to the following:.

    ```
    warning: [override] varargsMethod(String[]) in ClassWithOver-
    ridingMethod
    ```

overrides varargsMethod(String...) in ClassWithVarargsMethod;
overriding

method is missing '...'

When the compiler encounters a varargs method, it translates the varargs formal parameter into an array. In the method ClassWithVarargsMethod.varargsMethod, the compiler translates the varargs formal parameter String... s to the formal parameter String[] s, an array, which matches the formal parameter of the method ClassWithOverridingMethod.varargsMethod. Consequently, this example compiles.

- path

    Warns about invalid path elements and nonexistent path directories on the command line (with regard to the class path, the source path, and other paths). Such warnings cannot be suppressed with the @SuppressWarnings annotation, for example:

    ```
    javac -Xlint:path -classpath C:\nonexistentpath Example.java
    ```

- processing

    Warn about issues regarding annotation processing. The compiler generates this warning when you have a class that has an annotation, and you use an annotation processor that cannot handle that type of exception. For example, the following is a simple annotation processor:

    Source file AnnocProc.java:

    ```
    import java.util.*;

    import javax.annotation.processing.*;

    import javax.lang.model.*;

    import.javaz.lang.model.element.*;


    @SupportedAnnotationTypes("NotAnno")

    public class AnnoProc extends AbstractProcessor {

       public boolean process(Set<? extends TypeElement> elems,
    RoundEnvironment renv){

          return true;

      }


       public SourceVersion getSupportedSourceVersion() {

          return SourceVersion.latest();

        }

      }
    ```

Source file AnnosWithoutProcessors.java:

```
@interface Anno { }


@Anno
class AnnosWithoutProcessors { }
```

The following commands compile the annotation processor AnnoProc, then run this annotation processor against the source file AnnosWithoutProcessors.java:

```
javac AnnoProc.java

javac -cp . -Xlint:processing -processor AnnoProc -proc:only
AnnosWithoutProcessors.java
```

When the compiler runs the annotation processor against the source file AnnosWithout-Processors.java, it generates the following warning:

```
warning: [processing] No processor claimed any of these anno-
tations: Anno
```

To resolve this issue, you can rename the annotation defined and used in the class An-nosWithoutProcessors from Anno to NotAnno.

• rawtypes

Warns about unchecked operations on raw types. The following statement generates a raw-types warning:

```
void countElements(List l) { ... }
```

The following example does not generate a rawtypes warning

```
void countElements(List<?> l) { ... }
```

List is a raw type. However, List<?> is an unbounded wildcard parameterized type. Because List is a parameterized interface, always specify its type argument. In this example, the List formal argument is specified with an unbounded wildcard (?) as its formal type parameter, which means that the countElements method can accept any instantiation of the List interface.

• Serial

Warns about missing serialVersionUID definitions on serializable classes, for example:

```
public class PersistentTime implements Serializable
{
   private Date time;


   public PersistentTime() {
```

```
      time = Calendar.getInstance().getTime();
    }


    public Date getTime() {
      return time;
    }
  }
```

The compiler generates the following warning:

```
warning: [serial] serializable class PersistentTime has no
definition of

serialVersionUID
```

If a serializable class does not explicitly declare a field named serialVersionUID, then the serialization runtime environment calculates a default serialVersionUID value for that class based on various aspects of the class, as described in the Java Object Serialization Specification. However, it is strongly recommended that all serializable classes explicitly declare serialVersionUID values because the default process of computing serialVersionUID vales is highly sensitive to class details that can vary depending on compiler implementations, and as a result, might cause an unexpected InvalidClassExceptions during deserialization. To guarantee a consistent serialVersionUID value across different Java compiler implementations, a serializable class must declare an explicit serialVersionUID value.

- static

    Warns about issues relating to the use of statics, for example:

```
class XLintStatic {
    static void m1() { }
    void m2() { this.m1(); }
}
```

The compiler generates the following warning:

```
warning: [static] static method should be qualified by type
name,

XLintStatic, instead of by an expression
```

To resolve this issue, you can call the static method m1 as follows:

```
XLintStatic.m1();
```

Alternately, you can remove the static keyword from the declaration of the method m1.

- try

    Warns about issues relating to use of try blocks, including try-with-resources statements. For example, a warning is generated for the following statement because the resource ac declared in the try block is not used:

```
try ( AutoCloseable ac = getResource() ) {     // do nothing}
```

• unchecked

Gives more detail for unchecked conversion warnings that are mandated by the Java Language Specification, for example:

```
List l = new ArrayList<Number>();

List<String> ls = l;        // unchecked warning
```

During type erasure, the types ArrayList<Number> and List<String> become ArrayList and List, respectively.

The ls command has the parameterized type List<String>. When the List referenced by l is assigned to ls, the compiler generates an unchecked warning. At compile time, the compiler and JVM cannot determine whether l refers to a List<String> type. In this case, l does not refer to a List<String> type. As   a result, heap pollution occurs.

A heap pollution situation occurs when the List object l, whose static type is List<Number>, is assigned to another List object, ls, that has a different static type, List<String>. However, the compiler still allows this assignment. It must allow this assignment to preserve backward compatibility with releases of Java SE that do not support generics. Because of type erasure, List<Number> and List<String> both become List. Consequently, the compiler allows the assignment of the object l, which has a raw type of List, to the object ls.

• varargs

Warns about unsafe usages of variable arguments (varargs) methods, in particular, those that contain non-reifiable arguments, for example:

```
public class ArrayBuilder {

   public static <T> void addToList (List<T> listArg, T... el-
   ements) {

      for (T x : elements) {

        listArg.add(x);

      }

   }

}
```

Note: A non-reifiable type is a type whose type information is not fully available at runtime.

The compiler generates the following warning for the definition of the method ArrayBuilder.addToList

```
warning: [varargs] Possible heap pollution from parameterized
vararg type T
```

When the compiler encounters a varargs method, it translates the varargs formal parameter into an array. However, the Java programming language does not permit the creation of arrays of parameterized types. In the method ArrayBuilder.addToList, the compiler translates the varargs formal parameter T... elements to the formal parameter T[] elements, an array. However, because of type erasure, the compiler converts the varargs formal parameter to Object[] elements. Consequently, there is a possibility of heap pollution.

Command-Line Argument Files

To shorten or simplify the javac command, you can specify one or more files that contain arguments to the javac command (except -J options). This enables you to create javac commands of any length on any operating system.

An argument file can include javac options and source file names in any combination. The arguments within a file can be separated by spaces or new line characters. If a file name contains embedded spaces, then put the whole file name in double quotation marks.

File Names within an argument file are relative to the current directory, not the location of the argument file. Wild cards (*) are not allowed in these lists (such as for specifying *.java). Use of the at sign (@) to recursively interpret files is not supported. The -J options are not supported because they are passed to the launcher, which does not support argument files.

When executing the javac command, pass in the path and name of each argument file with the at sign (@) leading character. When the javac command encounters an argument beginning with the at sign (@), it expands the contents of that file into the argument list.

Example 1 - Single Argument File

You could use a single argument file named argfile to hold all javac arguments:

```
javac @argfile
```

This argument file could contain the contents of both files shown in Example 2

Example 2 - Two Argument Files

You can create two argument files: one for the javac options and the other for the source file names. Note that the following lists have no line-continuation characters.

Create a file named options that contains the following:

```
-d classes
-g
-sourcepath C:\java\pubs\ws\1.3\src\share\classes
```

Create a file named classes that contains the following:

```
MyClass1.java
MyClass2.java
```

```
MyClass3.java
```

Then, run the javac command as follows:

```
javac @options @classes
```

Example 3 - Argument Files with Paths

The argument files can have paths, but any file names inside the files are relative to the current working directory (not path1 or path2):

```
javac @path1/options @path2/classes
```

Jikes

Jikes™ is a compiler that translates Java™ source files as defined in The Java Language Specification into the bytecoded instruction set and binary format defined in The Java Virtual Machine Specification.

You may wonder why the world needs another Java compiler, considering that Sun provides javac free with its SDK. Jikes has five advantages that make it a valuable contribution to the Java community:

OSI certified

- Open source. Jikes is OSI Certified Open Source Software. OSI Certified is a certification mark of the Open Source Initiative.

- Strictly Java compatible. Jikes strives to adhere to both The Java Language Specification and The Java Virtual Machine Specification as tightly as possible, and does not support subsets, supersets, or other variations of the language. The FAQ describes some of the side effects of this strict language conformance.

- High performance. Jikes is a high performance compiler, making it ideal for use with larger projects.

- Dependency analysis. Jikes performs a dependency analysis on your code that provides two very useful features: Incremental builds and makefile generation.

- Constructive Assistance. Jikes strives to help the programmer write better code in two key ways. Jikes has always strived to provide clear error and warning text to assist the programmer in understanding problems, and now with release 1.19 Jikes helps point out common programming mistakes as documented in Effective Java.

The fact that Jikes is a high-performance, highly compatible Java compiler that can be used on almost any computing platform makes it an interesting program and worth investigating for almost any Java programmer. But Jikes is also notable because it lies at the center of two events: the adoption of open source philosophy and practice by large corporations, and the continued growth of Java for Linux.

It's worth pointing out that Jikes is not, and is not intended to be, a complete development environment -- it is simply a command line compiler. It should not be considered a replacement for more complete tools, such as Visual Slick Edit or Eclipse which provide sophisticated graphical IDEs (Integrated Development Environments).

The Jikes compiler was released in binary form in April 1997 on the IBM alphaWorks site. Jikes for Linux was released on 15 July 1998. The response was overwhelming -- Jikes had more downloads in the three months after the announcement than in the fifteen months before the announcement. Around the end of March 2002, IBM opened a fledgling community hosting location attached to their developerWorks site with Jikes as a founding member. Approximately 3 years later this server was decommissioned and the most active projects migrated into SourceForge.net hosting options. During those three years Jikes was the #1 most popular project every month, often by a large margin.

Release of Jikes for Linux was soon followed by requests to open up the source. Many notes and comments from users suggested this would be a good idea. The source was released under a liberal license in December 1998 to make a very visible demonstration of IBM's commitment to open standards and to Java Technology, to make Jikes more reliable and accessible, to encourage more widespread use of Java Technology, to encourage standardization of Java Technology, and to gain some experience actually running an open source project. This marked the start of one of IBM's first efforts in the open source arena.

The original alphaWorks version of Jikes was written by Philippe Charles and Dave Shields of the IBM T. J. Watson Research Center. For awhile after the release of the source they continued to work on the compiler as contributors; however, shortly after the project migrated to developer-Works' Open Source Server they were officially moved off onto other projects within IBM. Today there are no IBMers who work on Jikes as part of their job description. Jikes survives today soley based on the free time contributions of members of the open source community.

The source code is available under IBM's Public License, which has been approved by the OSI (Open Source Initiative) as a fully certified open source license. The project provides access to the complete CVS development tree, which includes not only Jikes, but also the source for the Jacks Test Suite and the Jikes Parser Generator used to build Jikes. Jikes is included in many Open Source Operating Systems. The Jacks Test Suite is a replacement for the Jikestst package.

Advantages

The major advantages of using the Jikes compiler are:Performance: Jikes offers high performance while compiling projects, which makes it an ideal choice for large projects. Language Conformance: Java strictly clings to both Java Language Specification and Java Virtual Machine Specification. Incremental Builds and Makefile Generation Features: These are very helpful feature provided by Jikes. Dependency Analysis: Jikes performs dependency analysis on the code. Better

Programming: Jikes helps to improve the quality of the code written by notifying errors and pointing out common mistakes made during programming.

Project Status

As of 2010 the project is no longer being actively developed. The last 1.22 version was released in October 2004 and partially supports Java 5.0 (with respect to new classes, but not new language features). As no further versions were released since, Java SE 6 is not supported.

While the free software community needed free Java implementations, the GNU Compiler for Java became the most commonly used compiler.

GNU Compiler for Java

The GNU Compiler for Java (GCJ) a radically traditional (*) Free Software implementation of the Java language, has been part of GCC since the 3.0 release in June 2001. Currently at version 3.2.1, it is supported on GNU/Linux on Pentium, Itanium, Alpha, PowerPC and AMD Hammer, FreeBSD on Pentium, Solaris on SPARC and more. Support for Windows using MinGW is also available.

It can compile Java source code to either Java bytecode (class files) or native machine code. It can also compile Java bytecode to native machine code. GCJ native code can be executables or shared libraries.

GCJ's Java implementation is not complete. Notable omissions include AWT and Swing. However most other Java features are supported, including collections, networking, reflection, serialization, JNI and RMI.

A First Look at GCJ

GCJ has two parts: the compiler and the runtime support library. The compiler includes these commands:

`gcj`

the GCJ compiler

`gcjh`

generates header files from Java class files

`jcf-dump`

prints information about Java class files

`jv-scan`

prints information about Java source files

The runtime support includes:

`libgcj.so.3`

GCJ runtime suppport library

```
libgcj-3.2.jar
```
Java class files of core GCJ classes, automatically searched when compiling Java sources

and commands:
```
gij
```
an interpreter for Java bytecode
```
grepjar
```
a grep utility that works on jar files
```
jar
```
Java archive tool
```
jv-convert
```
convert file from one encoding to another
```
rmic
```
generate stubs for Remote Method Invocation
```
rmiregistry
```
remote object registry

Compiling and Running Java Programs

The gcj command is very similar to the gcc command:

```
[weiqi@gao]$ gcj -c Hello.java                # compile to Hello.o
[weiqi@gao]$ gcj --main=Hello -o Hello Hello.o # link Hello.o to Hello
[weiqi@gao]$ ./Hello                           # run Hello
Hello, World!
```

Compiling and linking can be combined into one step:

```
[weiqi@gao]$ gcj --main=Hello -o Hello Hello.java # compile and link
```

The --main=Hello is needed to tell the linker which class's main() method is the entry point to the executable.

The -C switch tells gcj to compile to Java bytecode:

```
[weiqi@gao]$ gcj -C Hello.java   # compile to Hello.class
[weiqi@gao]$ gij Hello           # run Hello.class in the gij interpreter
Hello, World!
[weiqi@gao]$ java Hello          # run Hello.class in the Sun JIT
Hello, World!
```

The gcj compiler can compile Java class files, and even jar files to machine code:

```
[weiqi@gao]$ gcj -c Hello.class       # compile Hello.class to Hello.o
```

```
[weiqi@gao]$ jar cvf hi.jar Hello.class # create a jar
[weiqi@gao]$ gcj -c hi.jar              # compile hi.jar to hi.o
[weiqi@gao]$ gcj --main=Hello -o hi hi.o # link hi.o to hi
[weiqi@gao]$ ./hi                        # run hi
Hello, World!
```

```
1.    // A.java
2.    public class A {
3.        public void foo() {
4.            System.out.println("A.foo()");
5.        }
6.    }
7.    // B.java
8.    public class B {
9.        public static void main(String[] args) {
10.           new A().foo();
11.       }
12.   }
```

Shared Libraries

The -shared switch tells gcj to link into a shared library. Assume the following sources:

we can compile A.java into a shared library libA.so, and compile B.java into an executable B that is linked against libA.so:

```
[weiqi@gao]$ gcj -shared -o libA.so A.java      # compile to shared
library
[weiqi@gao]$ gcj --main=B -o B B.java -L. -lA  # link against libA.so
We have to put libA.so temporarily into the LD_LIBRARY_PATH before
executing B:
[weiqi@gao]$ LD_LIBRARY_PATH=. ./B
A.foo()
```

Debugging with GDB

Support for GCJ has been added to the GNU Debugger GDB. The full power of GDB can be used with Java programs. To make debugging symbols available to GDB, we need the -g switch on the gcj command line:

```
[weiqi@gao]$ gcj -g --main=C -o C C.java    # compile with debug sym-
bols
```

```
[wciyl@yao]$ gdb c                                      # debug it
(gdb)
```

In gdb, run starts the executable, break sets break points, step, next, cont controls flow of execution, print, display prints values of variables.

The gdb in Red Hat Linux 8.0 had trouble understanding the command

```
(gdb) break Foo.main
```

to set a break point at the main method on the class Foo. A work around is to type

```
(gdb) break 'Foo::main
```

and use tab completion to get

```
(gdb) break 'Foo::main(JArray<java::lang::String*>*)'
```

GCJ is sufficiently different from other Java implementations that we need to pay attention to how things are done with it.

Searching for Classes

In GCJ, Java classes may appear in .so files in addition to jar files and loose class files. When a Java class is dynamically loaded, libgcj searches for it in .so files first. For example, the class a.b.C is searched in the following order:

```
1.   lib-a-b-C.so
2.   lib-a-b.so
3.   lib-a.so
4.   the CLASSPATH
```

Note that if a class is loaded from the CLASSPATH, it is interpreted.

Setting Properties on InvoCATION

Since there is no JIT to invoke when running a GCJ compiled executable, properties are passed to the program at invocation time in an environment variable GCJ_PROPERTIES:

```
1.   // A.java
2.   public class A {
3.       public static void main(String[] args) {
4.           System.out.println(System.getProperty("a.b"));
5.           System.out.println(System.getProperty("c.d"));
6.       }
7.   }
}
```

```
[weiqi@gao]$ gcj --main=A -o A A.java
[weiqi@gao]$ GCJ_PROPERTIES="a.b=x c.d=y" ./A
x
y
```

Compiled Native Interface (CNI)

The Compiled Native Interface (CNI), previously named "Cygnus Native Interface", is a software framework for the GCJ that allows Java code to call, and be called by, native applications (programs specific to a hardware and operating-system platform) and libraries written in C++.

CNI closely resembles the JNI (Java Native Interface) framework which comes as a standard with various Java virtual machines.

Comparison of Language use

The authors of CNI claim for various advantages over JNI:

> We use CNI because we think it is a better solution, especially for a Java implementation that is based on the idea that Java is just another programming language that can be implemented using standard compilation techniques. Given that, and the idea that languages implemented using Gcc should be compatible where it makes sense, it follows that the Java calling convention should be as similar as practical to that used for other languages, especially C++, since we can think of Java as a subset of C++. CNI is just a set of helper functions and conventions built on the idea that C++ and Java have the *same* calling convention and object layout; they are binary compatible. (This is a simplification, but close enough.)

CNI depends on Java classes appearing as C++ classes. For example, given a Java class,

```
public class Int
{
    public int i;
    public Int(int i) { this.i = i; }
    public static Int zero = new Int(0);
}
```

one can use the class thus:

```
#include <gcj/cni.h>
#include <Int>


Int *mult(Int *p, int k)
{
    if (k == 0)
        return Int::zero;  // Static member access.
```

```
    return new Int(p >i * k),
}
```

Uses of GCJ

Since GCJ is a free software implementation of Java, many free software Java packages have been ported to work with GCJ. The rhug project provides a collection of such ports. Notable entries include Ant, Log4j, JUnit, Rhino, Xalan-Java, Xerces2-J.

GCJ is a capable, wide spread, free implementation of the Java platform. It offers some unique characteristics that make it viable to use the Java programming language in situations where using the J2SE SDK is not feasible.

Obvious advantages of GCJ over the J2SE SDK include faster startup time, smaller memory footprint, shared memory between different native Java processes, and easier interface with other languages. Disadvantages include the lack of AWT and Swing support.

GCJ is one more choice for Java and free software developers. Give it a try and see if it can solve some of your problems.

Graal Compiler

Graal is a new just-in-time compiler for the JVM focused on peak performance and multi-language support. Graal offers performance advantages not only to Java code, but also to scripting languages such as JavaScript, Ruby, Python, and R. Additionally, it enables the execution of native code on the JVM via an LLVM-based front end (project Sulong). Languages are executed by Graal via the Truffle framework, which comes with seamless interoperability and polyglot debugging and profiling functionality.

Usage

GraalVM is based on an Oracle Labs JDK 8 with JVMCI support. For a default download, the bin directory contains the following language execution binaries: java, js, node, lli, native-image. With the gu installer tool, additional languages can be installed, including ruby, python, and R.

Benefits

- Performance - Graal incorporates our research on compiler technology, and offers better peak performance on some workloads than a traditional JVM.

- Polyglot - Java, JavaScript, Ruby, Python, and R are all available at competitive performance within the same execution environment.

- Interoperability - Languages executed in Graal can call each other without overhead and libraries from other languages can be used.

- Embeddability - Embed dynamic languages and native code with sandboxing capabilities.

- Tooling - Graal benefits from JVM-based tooling and all languages share common tooling such as debugging and profiling.

Features of Graal (Compiler)

Graal is a state of the art optimising compiler. It sports the following features:

- Can run either just-in-time or ahead-of-time.

- Extremely advanced optimisations, like *partial escape analysis*. Escape analysis is a way of eliminating heap allocations of objects when they aren't actually necessary. EA was made famous by the JVM, but it's complicated and very few VMs support it. The Turbo-fan compiler that Chrome uses for Javascript only started getting EA at the end of 2015. Graal features an even more advanced form of the optimisation that lets it work in more cases.

- Recognises interpreters written using Truffle and can convert Truffle ASTs into optimised native code, using a technique called *partial evaluation*. Partial evaluation of a self-specialising interpreter is called the *first Futamura projection*.

- Comes with an advanced visualiser tool that lets you explore the compiler's intermediate representation as it passes through optimisation stages.

- Written in Java, which means it's significantly easier to hack on and extend than a traditional compiler written in C or C++.

- Starting with Java 9, it can be used as a JVM plugin.

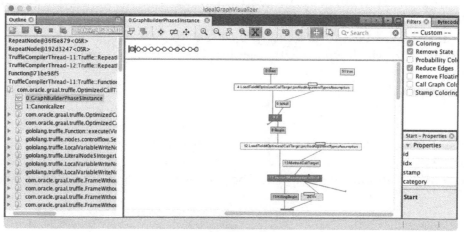

The IGV visualiser

Graal is designed from the start as a multi-language compiler, but its set of optimisation techniques is especially well suited to compiling programs with high levels of abstraction and dynamism. It runs Java as fast as the existing JVM compilers do, but when applied to Scala programs it runs them about 20% faster. Ruby programs get 400% faster than the *best* alternative runtime (i.e. not MRI).

Truffle

In association with GraalVM, Oracle developed a language abstract syntax tree interpreter called Truffle which would allow it to implement languages on top of the Graal framework.

The Truffle framework was released under GPL version 2 with the classpath exception to encourage use of the framework for projects which do not want to be bound by the viral, copyleft nature of the GPL, while the Graal compiler remains under GPLv2 only.

Ahead-of-Time Compilation

In September 2016, Oracle detailed plans to add ahead-of-time compilation to the OpenJDK using the Graal compiler for Java 9. This proposal, tracked by the JEP 295: Ahead-of-Time Compilation, was included in Java 9.

The experimental use of Graal as a Just-in-time compiler was added for the Linux x64 platform for Java 10.

As always in life, nothing is quite perfect. Graal & Truffle represent an almost complete wishlist of things you might want when implementing a new language from scratch, but they come with two big costs:

1. Warmup time

2. Memory usage

The process of converting an interpreter into fully optimised native code relies *heavily* on learning how the code being executed actually works in practice. This is of course hardly new: the notion of the code "warming up" i.e. getting faster as it runs is known to everyone who runs code on advanced VMs like HotSpot or V8. But Graal pushes speculative, profile-guided optimisation techniques far beyond the current state of the art and relies on profiling a whole lot more as a result.

That's why the research team behind it invariably only quotes *peak* performance numbers: the speed of a program after it's been running for a while. This way of measuring performance doesn't measure how long it takes to reach that peak performance. In server side applications this is often not a big deal as it's the peak performance that matters the most, but for other kinds of program, long warmup times can be a deal killer. We can easily see this problem in action by simply running the Octane benchmarks included with the tech preview JDK: the scores are a bit lower than Chrome even though Graal gives itself long (15–60 second) warmup times that it doesn't count towards its score.

The second issue is memory usage. Programs that rely heavily on speculative optimisations require tables of metadata to be generated by the compiler, so the program can be de-optimised—mapped back from CPU state to the state of the abstract interpreter. This metadata is typically the same size as the compiled code itself, even after compression and optimisation of the data structures. In addition, the original ASTs or bytecodes must also be kept around so there's something to fall back to if the native code bails out due to relying on an invalid assumption. All this adds up to a significant extra source of RAM consumption.

Compounding these problems is the fact that Graal, Truffle and the Truffle languages are themselves written in Java, meaning *the compilers themselves* need to warm up and become optimised. And as you go up the hierarchy of higher level languages, memory consumption of basic data structures tends to go up too, meaning the memory consumption of the base compiler infrastructure will also place additional load on the garbage collector.

The people writing Graal & Truffle are not unaware of these problems, and have solutions in mind. One is called the SubstrateVM. This is a whole virtual machine implemented in Java which is designed to be compiled ahead-of-time to native code using Graal & Truffle's AOT mode. The SubstrateVM is much less advanced than HotSpot is: such a VM can't do tricks like dynamically loading code over the internet or hotswapping, and the garbage collector is also pretty basic. But by doing a full AOT compile of not only the VM but the source code to be run along with it, the entire thing can be optimised as a whole, and a significant source of warmup time can be eliminated.

References

- "gcj to use Eclipse compiler as a front end". 2007-01-08. Archived from the original on 2007-05-09. Retrieved 2007-05-20

- Java-compiler, definition: theserverside.com, Retrieved 2018-04-21

- Campbell, Bill (2013). Introduction to Compiler Construction in a Java World. CRC Press Taylor & Francis Group. ISBN 978-1-4398-6088-5. Retrieved 2014-02-06

- Java-compiler, encyclopedia, term-45567: pcmag.com, Retrieved 2018-02-12

- Tromey, Tom (October 2, 2016). "The Deletion of gcj". The Cliffs of Inanity. Retrieved October 3, 2016

Java APIs

In programming, an API or application programming interface refers to a set of tools and protocols for building software. The topics elaborated in this chapter, such as Java Advanced Imaging, Java Persistence API, Java Naming and Directory Interface, Java 3D, etc. will help in providing a comprehensive understanding of Java APIs.

Application Programming Interface

API is the acronym for Application Programming Interface, which is a software intermediary that allows two applications to talk to each other. Each time you use an app like Facebook, send an instant message, or check the weather on your phone, you're using an API.

An *application program interface* (API) is a set of routines, protocols, and tools for building software applications. Basically, an API specifies how software components should interact. Additionally, APIs are used when programming graphical user interface (GUI) components. A good API makes it easier to develop a program by providing all the building blocks. A programmer then puts the blocks together

The API defines the correct way for a developer to write a program that requests services from an operating system (OS) or other application. APIs are implemented by function calls composed of verbs and nouns. The required syntax is described in the documentation of the application being called.

An Example of Application Programming interface

When you use an application on your mobile phone, the application connects to the Internet and sends data to a server. The server then retrieves that data, interprets it, performs the necessary actions and sends it back to your phone. The application then interprets that data and presents you with the information you wanted in a readable way. This is what an API is - all of this happens via API.

To explain this better, let us take a familiar example.

Imagine you're sitting at a table in a restaurant with a menu of choices to order from. The kitchen is the part of the "system" that will prepare your order. What is missing is the critical link to communicate your order to the kitchen and deliver your food back to your table. That's where the waiter or API comes in. The waiter is the messenger – or API – that takes your request or order and tells the kitchen – the system – what to do. Then the waiter delivers the response back to you; in this case, it is the food.

Here is a real-life API example. You may be familiar with the process of searching flights online. Just like the restaurant, you have a variety of options to choose from, including different cities, departure and return dates, and more. Let us imagine that you're booking you are flight on an airline website. You choose a departure city and date, a return city and date, cabin class, as well as other variables. In order to book your flight, you interact with the airline's website to access their database and see if any seats are available on those dates and what the costs might be.

However, what if you are not using the airline's website––a channel that has direct access to the information? What if you are using an online travel service, such as Kayak or Expedia, which aggregates information from a number of airline databases?

The travel service, in this case, interacts with the airline's API. The API is the interface that, like your helpful waiter, can be asked by that online travel service to get information from the airline's database to book seats, baggage options, etc. The API then takes the airline's response to your request and delivers it right back to the online travel service, which then shows you the most updated, relevant information.

Purpose

Just as a graphical user interface makes it easier for people to use programs, application programming interfaces make it easier for developers to use certain technologies in building applications. By abstracting the underlying implementation and only exposing objects or actions the developer needs, an API simplifies programming. While a graphical interface for an email client might provide a user with a button that performs all the steps for fetching and highlighting new emails, an API for file input/output might give the developer a function that copies a file from one location to another without requiring that the developer understand the file system operations occurring behind the scenes.

Uses

Libraries and Frameworks

An API is usually related to a software library. The API describes and prescribes the *expected behavior* (a specification) while the library is an *actual implementation* of this set of rules. A single API can have multiple implementations (or none, being abstract) in the form of different libraries that share the same programming interface. The separation of the API from its implementation can allow programs written in one language to use a library written in another. For example, because Scala and Java compile to compatible bytecode, Scala developers can take advantage of any Java API.

API use can vary depending on the type of programming language involved. An API for a procedural language such as Lua could primarily consist of basic routines to execute code, manipulate data or handle errors, while an API for an object-oriented language such as Java would provide a specification of classes and their class methods.

Language bindings are also APIs. By mapping the features and capabilities of one language to an interface implemented in another language, a language binding allows a library or service written in one language to be used when developing in another language. Tools such as SWIG and F2PY, a Fortran-to-Python interface generator, facilitate the creation of such interfaces.

An API can also be related to a software framework: a framework can be based on several libraries implementing several APIs, but unlike the normal use of an API, the access to the behavior built into the framework is mediated by extending its content with new classes plugged into the framework itself. Moreover, the overall program flow of control can be out of the control of the caller and in the hands of the framework by inversion of control or a similar mechanism.

Operating Systems

An API can specify the interface between an application and the operating system.POSIX, for example, specifies a set of common APIs that aim to enable an application written for a POSIX conformant operating system to be compiled for another POSIX conformant operating system. Linux and Berkeley Software Distribution are examples of operating systems that implement the POSIX APIs.

Microsoft has shown a strong commitment to a backward-compatible API, particularly within their Windows API (Win32) library, so older applications may run on newer versions of Windows using an executable-specific setting called "Compatibility Mode".

An API differs from an application binary interface (ABI) in that an API is source code based while an ABI is binary based. For instance, POSIX provides APIs, while the Linux Standard Base provides an ABI.

Remote APIs

Remote APIs allow developers to manipulate remote resources through protocols, specific standards for communication that allow different technologies to work together, regardless of language or platform. For example, the Java Database Connectivity API allows developers to query many different types of databases with the same set of functions, while the Java remote method invocation API uses the Java Remote Method Protocol to allow invocation of functions that operate remotely, but appear local to the developer. Therefore, remote APIs are useful in maintaining the object abstraction in object-oriented programming; a method call, executed locally on a proxy object, invokes the corresponding method on the remote object, using the remoting protocol, and acquires the result to be used locally as return value. A modification on the proxy object will also result in a corresponding modification on the remote object.

Web APIs

Web APIs are the defined interfaces through which interactions happen between an enterprise and applications that use its assets, which also is a Service Level Agreement (SLA) to specify the functional provider and expose the service path or URL for its API users, An API approach is an architectural approach that revolves around providing a program interface to a set of services to different applications serving different types of consumers. When used in the context of web development, an API is typically defined a set of specifications , such as Hypertext Transfer Protocol (HTTP) request messages, along with a definition of the structure of response messages, which is usually in an Extensible Markup Language (XML) or JavaScript Object Notation (JSON) format. An example might be a shipping company API that can be added to an eCommerce-focused website, to facilitate ordering shipping services and automatically include current shipping rates, without the site developer having to enter the shipper's rate table into a web database. While "web API" historically has been virtually synonymous for web service, the recent trend (so-called Web 2.0) has been moving away from Simple Object Access Protocol (SOAP) based web services and service-oriented architecture (SOA) towards more direct representational state transfer (REST) style web resources and resource-oriented architecture (ROA). Part of this trend is related to the Semantic Web movement toward Resource Description Framework (RDF), a concept to promote web-based ontology engineering technologies. Web APIs allow the combination of multiple APIs into new applications known as mashups. In the social media space, web APIs have allowed web communities to facilitate sharing content and data between communities and applications. In this way, content that is created in one place can be dynamically posted and updated in multiple locations on the web. For example, Twitter's REST API allows developers to access core Twitter data and the Search API provides methods for developers to interact with Twitter Search and trends data.

Design

The design of an API has significant impact on its usage. The principle of information hiding describes the role of programming interfaces as enabling modular programming by hiding the implementation details of the modules so that users of modules need not understand the complexities inside the modules. Thus, the design of an API attempts to provide only the tools a user would expect. The design of programming interfaces represents an important part of software architecture, the organization of a complex piece of software.

Several authors have created recommendations for how to design APIs, such as Joshua Bloch, Kin Lane, and Michi Henning.

Release Policies

APIs are one of the most common ways technology companies integrate with each other. Those that provide and use APIs are considered as being members of a business ecosystem.

The main policies for releasing an API are:

- Private: The API is for internal company use only.

- Partner: Only specific business partners can use the API. For example, car service companies such as Uber and Lyft allow approved third-party developers to directly order rides from within their apps. This allows the companies to exercise quality control by curating which apps have access to the API, and provides them with an additional revenue stream.

- Public: The API is available for use by the public. For example, Microsoft makes the Microsoft Windows API public, and Apple releases its APIs Carbon and Cocoa, so that software can be written for their platforms.

Public API Implications

An important factor when an API becomes public is its *interface stability*. Changes by a developer to a part of it—for example adding new parameters to a function call—could break compatibility with clients that depend on that API.

When parts of a publicly presented API are subject to change and thus not stable, such parts of a particular API should be explicitly documented as *unstable*. For example, in the Google Guava library the parts that are considered unstable, and that might change in the near future, are marked with the Java annotation.

A public API can sometimes declare parts of itself as *deprecated* or rescinded. This usually means that part of the API should be considered a candidate for being removed, or modified in a backward incompatible way. Therefore, these changes allows developers to transition away from parts of the API that will be removed or not supported in the future.

Documentation

API documentation describes what services an API offers and how to use those services, aiming to cover everything a client would need to know for practical purposes. Documentation is crucial for the development and maintenance of applications using the API. API documentation is traditionally found in documentation files but can also be found in social media such as blogs, forums, and Q&A websites. Traditional documentation files are often presented via a documentation system, such as Javadoc or Pydoc, that has a consistent appearance and structure. However, the types of content included in the documentation differs from API to API. In the interest of clarity, API documentation may include a description of classes and methods in the API as well as "typical usage scenarios, code snippets, design rationales, performance discussions, and contracts", but implementation details of the API services themselves are usually omitted. Restrictions and limitations on how the API can be used are also covered by the documentation. For instance, documentation for an API function could note that its parameters cannot be null, that the function itself is not thread safe, or that a decrement and cancel protocol averts self-trading. Because API documentation tends to be comprehensive, it is a challenge for writers to keep the documentation updated and for users to read it carefully, potentially yielding bugs.

API documentation can be enriched with metadata information like Java annotations. This metadata can be used by the compiler, tools, and by the *run-time* environment to implement custom behaviors or custom handling.

Copyright Controversy

In 2010, Oracle Corporation sued Google for having distributed a new implementation of Java embedded in the Android operating system. Google had not acquired any permission to reproduce the Java API, although permission had been given to the similar OpenJDK project. Judge William Alsup ruled in the *Oracle v. Google* case that APIs cannot be copyrighted in the U.S, and that a victory for Oracle would have widely expanded copyright protection and allowed the copyrighting of simple software commands:

To accept Oracle's claim would be to allow anyone to copyright one version of code to carry out a system of commands and thereby bar all others from writing their own different versions to carry out all or part of the same commands.

In 2014, however, Alsup's ruling was overturned on appeal, though the question of whether such use of APIs constitutes fair use was left unresolved.

In 2016, following a two-week trial, a jury determined that Google's reimplementation of the Java API constituted fair use, but Oracle vowed to appeal the decision. Oracle won on its appeal, with the Court of Appeals for the Federal Circuit ruling that Google's use of the APIs did not qualify for fair use

Java Advanced Imaging

Early versions of the Java AWT provided a simple rendering package suitable for rendering common HTML pages, but without the features necessary for complex imaging. The early AWT allowed the generation of simple images by drawing lines and shapes. A very limited number of image files, such as GIF and JPEG, could be read in through the use of a Toolkit object. Once read in, the image could be displayed, but there were essentially no image processing operators.

The Java 2D API extended the early AWT by adding support for more general graphics and rendering operations. Java 2D added special graphics classes for the definition of geometric primitives, text layout and font definition, color spaces, and image rendering. The new classes supported a limited set of image processing operators for blurring, geometric transformation, sharpening, contrast enhancement, and thresholding. The Java 2D extensions were added to the core Java AWT beginning with the Java Platform 1.2 release.

The Java Advanced Imaging (JAI) API further extends the Java platform (including the Java 2D API) by allowing sophisticated, high-performance image processing to be incorporated into Java applets and applications. JAI is a set of classes providing imaging functionality beyond that of Java 2D and the Java Foundation classes, though it is compatible with those APIs.

JAI implements a set of core image processing capabilities including image tiling, regions of interest, and deferred execution. JAI also offers a set of core image processing operators including many common point, area, and frequency-domain operators.

JAI is intended to meet the needs of all imaging applications. The API is highly extensible, allowing new image processing operations to be added in such a way as to appear to be a native part of it. Thus, JAI benefits virtually all Java developers who want to incorporate imaging into their applets and applications.

Need for Java Advanced Imaging

Several imaging APIs have been developed - a few have even been marketed and been fairly successful. However, none of these APIs have been universally accepted because they failed to address specific segments of the imaging market or they lacked the power to meet specific needs. As a consequence, many companies have had to "roll their own" in an attempt to meet their specific requirements.

Writing a custom imaging API is a very expensive and time-consuming task and the customized API often has to be rewritten whenever a new CPU or operating system comes along, creating a maintenance nightmare. How much simpler it would be to have an imaging API that meets everyone's needs.

Previous industry and academic experience in the design of image processing libraries, the usefulness of these libraries across a wide variety of application domains, and the feedback from the users of these libraries have been incorporated into the design of JAI.

JAI is intended to support image processing using the Java programming language as generally as possible so that few, if any, image processing applications are beyond its reach. At the same time, JAI presents a simple programming model that can be readily used in applications without a tremendous mechanical programming overhead or a requirement that the programmer be expert in all phases of the API's design.

JAI encapsulates image data formats and remote method invocations within a re-usable image data object, allowing an image file, a network image object, or a real-time data stream to be processed identically. Thus, JAI represents a simple programming model while concealing the complexity of the internal mechanisms.

Features of Java Advanced Imaging

JAI is intended to meet the requirements of all of the different imaging markets, and more. JAI offers several advantages for applications developers compared to other imaging solutions. Some of these advantages are described in the following paragraphs.

Cross-platform Imaging

Whereas most imaging APIs are designed for one specific operating system, JAI follows the Java run time library model, providing platform independence. Implementations of JAI applications will run on any computer where there is a Java Virtual Machine. This makes JAI a true cross-platform imaging API, providing a standard interface to the imaging capabilities of a platform. This means that you write your application once and it will run anywhere.

Distributed Imaging

JAI is also well suited for client-server imaging by way of the Java platform's networking architecture and remote execution technologies. Remote execution is based on Java RMI (remote method invocation). Java RMI allows Java code on a client to invoke method calls on objects that reside on another computer without having to move those objects to the client.

Object-oriented API

Like Java itself, JAI is totally object-oriented. In JAI, images and image processing operations are defined as objects. JAI unifies the notions of image and operator by making both subclasses of a common parent.

An operator object is instantiated with one or more image sources and other parameters. This operator object may then become an image source for the next operator object. The connections between the objects define the flow of processed data. The resulting editable graphs of image processing operations may be defined and instantiated as needed.

Flexible and Extensible

Any imaging API must support certain basic imaging technologies, such as image acquisition and display, basic manipulation, enhancement, geometric manipulation, and analysis. JAI provides a core set of the operators required to support the basic imaging technologies. These operators support many of the functions required of an imaging application. However, some applications require special image processing operations that are seldom, if ever, required by other applications. For these specialized applications, JAI provides an extensible framework that allows customized solutions to be added to the core API.

JAI also provides a standard set of image compression and decompression methods. The core set is based on international standards for the most common compressed file types. As with special image processing functions, some applications also require certain types of compressed image files. It is beyond the scope of any API to support the hundreds of known compression algorithms, so JAI also supports the addition of customized coders and decoders (codecs), which can be added to the core API.

Device Independent

The processing of images can be specified in device-independent coordinates, with the ultimate translation to pixels being specified as needed at run time. JAI's "renderable" mode treats all image sources as rendering-independent. You can set up a graph (or chain) of renderable operations without any concern for the source image resolution or size; JAI takes care of the details of the operations.

To make it possible to develop platform-independent applications, JAI makes no assumptions about output device resolution, color space, or color model. Nor does the API assume a particular file format. Image files may be acquired and manipulated without the programmer having any knowledge of the file format being acquired.

Powerful

JAI supports complex image formats, including images of up to three dimensions and an arbitrary number of bands. Many classes of imaging algorithms are supported directly, others may be added as needed.

JAI implements a set of core image processing capabilities, including image tiling, regions of interest, and deferred execution. The API also implements a set of core image processing operators, including many common point, area, and frequency-domain operations.

High Performance

A variety of implementations are possible, including highly-optimized implementations that can take advantage of hardware acceleration and the media capabilities of the platform, such as MMX on Intel processors and VIS on UltraSparc.

Interoperable

JAI is integrated with the rest of the Java Media APIs, enabling media-rich applications to be deployed on the Java platform. JAI works well with other Java APIs, such as Java 3D and Java component technologies. This allows sophisticated imaging to be a part of every Java technology programmer's tool box.

JAI is a Java Media API. It is classified as a Standard Extension to the Java platform. JAI provides imaging functionality beyond that of the Java Foundation Classes, although it is compatible with those classes in most cases.

An Example of Java Advanced Imaging

A simple example of a complete JAI program. This example reads an image, passed to the program as a command line argument, scales the image by 2x with bilinear interpolation, then displays the result.

Listing 1-1 Simple Example JAI Program

```java
import java.awt.Frame;

import java.awt.image.renderable.ParameterBlock;

import java.io.IOException;

import javax.media.jai.Interpolation;

import javax.media.jai.JAI;

import javax.media.jai.RenderedOp;

import com.sun.media.jai.codec.FileSeekableStream;

import javax.media.jai.widget.ScrollingImagePanel;
/**
 * This program decodes an image file of any JAI supported
 * formats, such as GIF, JPEG, TIFF, BMP, PNM, PNG, into a
 * RenderedImage, scales the image by 2X with bilinear
 * interpolation, and then displays the result of the scale
 * operation.
 */
public class JAISampleProgram {
    /** The main method. */
    public static void main(String[] args) {
        /* Validate input. */
        if (args.length != 1) {
            System.out.println("Usage: java JAISampleProgram " +
                                "input_image_filename");
            System.exit(-1);
        }
```

```
/*
 * Create an input stream from the specified file name
 * to be used with the file decoding operator.
 */
FileSeekableStream stream = null;
try {
    stream = new FileSeekableStream(args);
} catch (IOException e) {
    e.printStackTrace();
    System.exit(0);
}
/* Create an operator to decode the image file. */
RenderedOp image1 = JAI.create("stream", stream);
/*
 * Create a standard bilinear interpolation object to be
 * used with the "scale" operator.
 */
Interpolation interp = Interpolation.getInstance(
                        Interpolation.INTERP_BILINEAR);
/**
 * Stores the required input source and parameters in a
 * ParameterBlock to be sent to the operation registry,
 * and eventually to the "scale" operator.
 */
ParameterBlock params = new ParameterBlock();
params.addSource(image1);
params.add(2.0F);          // x scale factor
params.add(2.0F);          // y scale factor
params.add(0.0F);          // x translate
params.add(0.0F);          // y translate
params.add(interp);        // interpolation method
/* Create an operator to scale image1. */
RenderedOp image2 = JAI.create("scale", params);
/* Get the width and height of image2. */
```

```
int width = image2.getWidth();
int height = image2.getHeight();
/* Attach image2 to a scrolling panel to be displayed. */
ScrollingImagePanel panel = new ScrollingImagePanel(
                                    image2, width, height);
/* Create a frame to contain the panel. */
Frame window = new Frame("JAI Sample Program");
window.add(panel);
window.pack();
window.show();
   }
 }
```

Java Naming and Directory Interface

Naming and directory services play a vital role in intranets and the Internet by providing net-work-wide sharing of a variety of information about users, machines, networks, services, and applications.

The Java Naming and Directory Interface™ (JNDI) is an application programming interface (API) that provides naming and directory functionality to applications written using the Java™ programming language. It is defined to be independent of any specific directory service implementation. Thus a variety of directories -new, emerging, and already deployed can be accessed in a common way.

It is designed especially for the Java platform using Java's object model. Using JNDI, applications based on Java technology can store and retrieve named Java objects of any type. In addition, JNDI provides methods for performing standard directory operations, such as associating attributes with objects and searching for objects using their attributes.

JNDI is also defined independent of any specific naming or directory service implementation. It enables applications to access different, possibly multiple, naming and directory services using a common API. Different naming and directory service providers can be plugged in seamlessly behind this common API. This enables Java technology-based applications to take advantage of information in a variety of existing naming and directory services, such as LDAP, NDS, DNS, and NIS(YP), as well as enabling the applications to coexist with legacy software and systems.

Using JNDI as a tool, you can build new powerful and portable applications that not only take advantage of Java's object model but are also well-integrated with the environment in which they are deployed.

Basic Lookup

JNDI (Java Naming and Directory Interface) organizes its names into a hierarchy. A name can be any string such as "com.mydomain.ejb.MyBean". A name can also be an object that implements the Name interface; however a string is the most common way to name an object. A name is bound to an object in the directory by storing either the object or a reference to the object in the directory service identified by the name.

The JNDI API defines a context that specifies where to look for an object. The initial context is typically used as a starting point.

In the simplest case, an initial context must be created using the specific implementation and extra parameters required by the implementation. The initial context will be used to look up a name. The initial context is analogous to the root or top of a directory tree for a file system. Below is an example of creating an initial context:

```
Hashtable contextArgs = new Hashtable();


// First you must specify the context factory.
// This is how you choose between jboss implementation
// vs. an implementation from Sun or other vendors.
contextArgs.put( Context.INITIAL_CONTEXT_FACTORY, "com.jndiprovider.
TheirContextFactory" );


// The next argument is the URL specifying where the data store is:
contextArgs.put( Context.PROVIDER_URL, "jndiprovider-database" );


// (You may also have to provide security credentials)


// Next you create the initial context
Context myCurrentContext = new InitialContext(contextArgs);
```

A context is then used to look up previously bound names in that context. For example:

```
MyBean myBean = (MyBean)  myCurrentContext.lookup("com.mydomain.My-
Bean");
```

Alternative to above code is as below:

The Context object can also be configured by adding jndi.properties file in classpath containing initial context factory class name and provider URL. The above code will be reduced as shown below:

```
//just need to create initial context object, it will try to read
jndi.properties file from the classpath.
Context myCurrentContext = new InitialContext();
```

A context is then used to look up previously bound names in that context. For example:

```
MyBean myBean = (MyBean)   myCurrentContext.lookup("com.mydomain.My-
Bean");
```

Searching

Attributes may be attached to special entries called directories. Directories enable searching for objects by their associated attributes. Directories are a type of context; they restrict the name space much like a directory structure on a file system does

Architecture

The JNDI architecture consists of an API and a service provider interface (SPI). Java applications use the JNDI API to access a variety of naming and directory services. The SPI enables a variety of naming and directory services to be plugged in transparently, thereby allowing the Java application using the JNDI API to access their services. See the following figure:

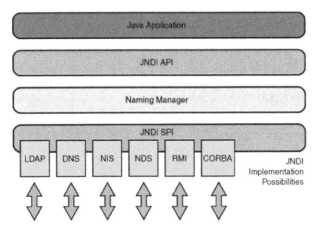

Packaging

JNDI is included in the Java SE Platform. To use the JNDI, you must have the JNDI classes and one or more service providers. The JDK includes service providers for the following naming/directory services:

- Lightweight Directory Access Protocol (LDAP)

- Common Object Request Broker Architecture (CORBA) Common Object Services (COS) name service

- Java Remote Method Invocation (RMI) Registry

- Domain Name Service (DNS)

The JNDI is divided into five packages:

- javax.naming

- javax.naming.directory

- javax.naming.ldap

- javax.naming.event

- javax.naming.spi

Java Persistence API

Data Persistence is a means for an application to persist and retrieve information from a non-volatile storage system. Persistence is vital to enterprise applications because of the required access to relational databases. Applications that are developed for this environment must manage persistence themselves or use third-party solutions to handle database updates and retrievals with persistence.

JPA

The Java™ Persistence API (JPA) provides a mechanism for managing persistence and object-relational mapping and functions since the EJB 3.0 specifications.

The JPA specification defines the object-relational mapping internally, rather than relying on vendor-specific mapping implementations. JPA is based on the Java programming model that applies to Java Enterprise Edition (Java EE) environments, but JPA can function within a Java SE environment for testing application functions.

JPA represents a simplification of the persistence programming model. The JPA specification explicitly defines the object-relational mapping, rather than relying on vendor-specific mapping implementations. JPA standardizes the important task of object-relational mapping by using annotations or XML to map objects into one or more tables of a database. To further simplify the persistence programming model:

- The EntityManager API can persist, update, retrieve, or remove objects from a database.

- The EntityManager API and object-relational mapping metadata handle most of the database operations without requiring you to write JDBC or SQL code to maintain persistence.

- JPA provides a query language, extending the independent EJB querying language (also known as JPQL), that you can use to retrieve objects without writing SQL queries specific to the database that you are working with.

JPA is designed to operate both inside and outside of a Java Enterprise Edition (Java EE) container. When you run JPA inside a container, the applications can use the container to manage the persistence context. If there is no container to manage JPA, the application must handle the persistence context management itself. Applications that are designed for container-managed persistence do not require as much code implementation to handle persistence, but these applications cannot be used outside of a container. Applications that manage their own persistence can function in a container environment or a Java SE environment.

Entities

A persistence entity is a lightweight Java class whose state is typically persisted to a table in a relational database. Instances of such an entity correspond to individual rows in the table. Entities typically have relationships with other entities, and these relationships are expressed through object/relational metadata. Object/relational metadata can be specified directly in the entity class file by using annotations, or in a separate XML descriptor file distributed with the application.

The Java Persistence Query Language

The Java Persistence Query Language (JPQL) makes queries against entities stored in a relational database. Queries resemble SQL queries in syntax, but operate against entity objects rather than directly with database tables.

Motivation

Prior to the introduction of EJB 3.0 specification, many enterprise Java developers used lightweight persistent objects, provided by either persistence frameworks (for example Hibernate) or data access objects instead of entity beans. This is because entity beans, in previous EJB specifications, called for too much complicated code and heavy resource footprint, and they could be used only in Java EE application servers because of interconnections and dependencies in the source code between beans and DAO objects or persistence framework. Thus, many of the features originally presented in third-party persistence frameworks were incorporated into the Java Persistence API, and, as of 2006, projects like Hibernate (version 3.2) and TopLink Essentials have become themselves implementations of the Java Persistence API specification.

Related Technologies

Enterprise Javabeans

The EJB 3.0 specification (itself part of the Java EE 5 platform) included a definition of the Java Persistence API. However, end-users do not need an EJB container or a Java EE application server in order to run applications that use this persistence API. Future versions of the Java Persistence API will be defined in a separate JSR and specification rather than in the EJB JSR/specification.

The Java Persistence API replaces the persistence solution of EJB 2.0 CMP (Container Managed Persistence).

Java Data Objects API

The Java Persistence API was developed in part to unify the *Java Data Objects API*, and the *EJB 2.0 Container Managed Persistence (CMP) API*. As of 2009 most products supporting each of those APIs support the Java Persistence API.

The Java Persistence API specifies persistence only for relational database management systems. That is, JPA focuses on object-relational mapping (ORM) (note that there are JPA providers who support other database models besides relational database, but this is outside the scope of what JPA was designed for). Refer to JPA 2 spec section 1 introduction for clarification of the role of

JPA, which states very clearly *"The technical objective of this work is to provide an object/relational mapping facility for the Java application developer using a Java domain model to manage a relational database."*

The Java Data Objects specification supports ORM, as well as persistence to other types of database models, for example flat file databases and NoSQL databases, including document databases, graph databases, as well as literally any other conceivable datastore.

Service Data Object API

The designers of the Java Persistence API aimed to provide for relational persistence, with many of the key areas taken from object-relational mapping tools such as Hibernate and TopLink. Java Persistence API improved on and replaced EJB 2.0, evidenced by its inclusion in EJB 3.0. The Service Data Objects (SDO) API (JSR 235) has a very different objective to the Java Persistence API and is considered complementary. The SDO API is designed for service-oriented architectures, multiple data formats rather than only relational data, and multiple programming languages. The Java Community Process manages the Java version of the SDO API; the C++ version of the SDO API is managed via OASIS.

Hibernate

Hibernate provides an open source object-relational mapping framework for Java. Versions 3.2 and later provide an implementation for the Java Persistence API. Gavin King founded the Hibernate project. He represented JBoss on JSR 220, the JCP expert group charged with developing JPA. This led to ongoing controversy and speculation surrounding the relationship between JPA and Hibernate. Sun Microsystems has stated that ideas came from several frameworks, including Hibernate and Java Data Objects

Spring Data JPA

An implementation of the repository abstraction that's a key building block of Domain-Driven Design based on the Java application framework Spring. Transparently supports all available JPA implementations and supports CRUD operations as well as the convenient execution of database queries.

JPA 2.0

Development of a new version of JPA 2.0 was started in July 2007 in the Java Community Process as JSR 317. JPA 2.0 was approved as final on 10 December 2009. The focus of JPA 2.0 was to address features that were present in some of the popular ORM vendors, but could not gain consensus approval for JPA 1.0.

Main features included were:

- Expanded object-relational mapping functionality
    - support for collections of embedded objects, linked in the ORM with a many-to-one relationship

- o   ordered lists
- o   combinations of access types
- A criteria query API
- standardization of SQL Hints
- standardization of additional metadata to support DDL generation
- support for validation
- Shared object cache support.
- Vendors supporting JPA 2.0:
- Batoo JPA
- DataNucleus (formerly JPOX)
- EclipseLink (formerly Oracle TopLink)
- IBM, for WebSphere Application Server
- JBoss with Hibernate
- Kundera
- ObjectDB
- OpenJPA
- OrientDB from Orient Technologies
- Versant Corporation JPA (not relational, object database)

JPA 2.1

Development of a new version of JPA 2.1 was started in July 2011 as JSR 338. JPA 2.1 was approved as final on 22 May 2013.

Main features included were:

- Converters - allowing custom code conversions between database and object types.
- Criteria Update/Delete - allows bulk updates and deletes through the Criteria API.
- Entity Graphs - allow partial or specified fetching or merging of objects.
- JPQL/Criteria enhancements - arithmetic sub-queries, generic database functions, join ON clause, TREAT option.
- Schema Generation

- Stored Procedures - allows queries to be defined for database stored procedures.

Vendors supporting JPA 2.1

- DataNucleus
- EclipseLink
- Hibernate

JPA 2.2

Development of a maintenance release as JPA 2.2 was started in 2017 under JSR 338.

Main features included were:

- Add @Repeatable to all relevant annotations
- Allow all JPA annotations to be used in meta-annotations.
- Add ability to stream a query result
- Allow AttributeConverters to be CDI injectable
- Support Java 8 Date and Time types

Vendors supporting JPA 2.2

- DataNucleus
- EclipseLink (from version 2.7)
- Hibernate (from version 5.3)

JPA Future Work

Future JPA specification information is available here:

- JPA Specification Mailing Lists
- JPA Specification JIRA

Java Speech API

The Java Speech API allows Java applications to incorporate speech technology into their user interfaces. It defines a cross-platform API to support command and control recognizers, dictation systems and speech synthesizers.

The Java™ Speech API is a standard extension to the Java platform that enables Java applications and applets to use speech input and output.

Java Speech API

The Java Speech API defines a standard, easy-to-use, cross-platform software interface to state-of-the-art speech technology. Two core speech technologies are supported through the Java Speech API: speech recognition and speech synthesis.

Enterprises and individuals can benefit from a wide range of applications of speech technology using the Java Speech API. For instance, interactive voice response systems are an attractive alternative to touch-tone interfaces over the telephone; dictation systems can be considerably faster than typed input for many users; speech technology improves accessibility to computers for many people with physical limitations.

Speech interfaces give Java application developers the opportunity to implement distinct and engaging personalities for their applications and to differentiate their products. Java application developers will have access to state-of-the-art speech technology from leading speech companies. With a standard API for speech, users can choose the speech products which best meet their needs and their budget.

The Java Speech API was developed through an open development process. With the active involvement of leading speech technology companies, with input from application developers and with months of public review and comment, the specification has achieved a high degree of technical excellence. As a specification for a rapidly evolving technology, Sun will support and enhance the Java Speech API to maintain its leading capabilities.

The Java Speech API is an extension to the Java platform. Extensions are packages of classes written in the Java programming language (and any associated native code) that application developers can use to extend the functionality of the core part of the Java platform.

Design Goals

Along with the other Java Media APIs, the Java Speech API lets developers incorporate advanced user interfaces into Java applications. The design goals for the Java Speech API included:

- Provide support for speech synthesizers and for both command-and-control and dictation speech recognizers.

- Provide a robust cross-platform, cross-vendor interface to speech synthesis and speech recognition.

- Enable access to state-of-the-art speech technology.

- Support integration with other capabilities of the Java platform, including the suite of Java Media APIs.

- Be simple, compact and easy to learn.

Core Technologies

Two core speech technologies are supported through the Java Speech API: *speech synthesis* and *speech recognition*.

Speech Synthesis

Speech synthesis provides the reverse process of producing synthetic speech from text generated by an application, an applet, or a user. It is often referred to as text-to-speech technology.

The major steps in producing speech from text are as follows:

- Structure analysis: Processes the input text to determine where paragraphs, sentences, and other structures start and end. For most languages, punctuation and formatting data are used in this stage.

- Text pre-processing: Analyzes the input text for special constructs of the language. In English, special treatment is required for abbreviations, acronyms, dates, times, numbers, currency amounts, e-mail addresses, and many other forms. Other languages need special processing for these forms, and most languages have other specialized requirements.

The result of these first two steps is a spoken form of the written text. Here are examples of the differences between written and spoken text:

```
St. Matthew's hospital is on Main St.

-> "Saint Matthew's hospital is on Main Street"


Add $20 to account 55374.

-> "Add twenty dollars to account five five, three seven four."
```

The remaining steps convert the spoken text to speech:

- Text-to-phoneme conversion: Converts each word to phonemes. A phoneme is a basic unit of sound in a language.

- Prosody analysis: Processes the sentence structure, words, and phonemes to determine the appropriate prosody for the sentence.

- Waveform production: Uses the phonemes and prosody information to produce the audio waveform for each sentence.

Speech synthesizers can make errors in any of the processing steps described above. Human ears are well-tuned to detecting these errors, but careful work by developers can minimize errors and improve the speech output quality. While the Java Speech API 1 relied on the Java Speech API Markup Language (JSML), the newer release utilizes SSML to provide many ways for you to improve the output quality of a speech synthesizer.

Speech Recognition

Speech recognition provides computers with the ability to listen to spoken language and determine what has been said. In other words, it processes audio input containing speech by converting it to text.

The major steps of a typical speech recognizer are as follows:

- Grammar design: Defines the words that may be spoken by a user and the patterns in which they may be spoken.

- Signal processing: Analyzes the spectrum (i.e., the frequency) characteristics of the incoming audio.

- Phoneme recognition: Compares the spectrum patterns to the patterns of the phonemes of the language being recognized.

- Word recognition: Compares the sequence of likely phonemes against the words and patterns of words specified by the active grammars.

- Result generation: Provides the application with information about the words the recognizer has detected in the incoming audio.

A *grammar* is an object in the Java Speech API that indicates what words a user is expected to say and in what patterns those words may occur. Grammars are important to speech recognizers because they constrain the recognition process. These constraints make recognition faster and more accurate because the recognizer does not have to check for bizarre sentences.

The Java Speech API 1 supports two basic grammar types: rule grammars and dictation grammars. These types differ in various ways, including how applications set up the grammars; the types of sentences they allow; how results are provided; the amount of computational resources required; and how they are used in application design. Rule grammars are defined in JSAPI 1 by JSGF, the Java Speech Grammar Format. The newer JSAPI 2 supports the more recent SRGS format. JSAPI 2 does not offer support for dictation.

The Java Speech API's classes and Interfaces

The different classes and interfaces that form the Java Speech API are grouped into the following three packages:

- javax.speech: Contains classes and interfaces for a generic speech engine

- javax.speech.synthesis: Contains classes and interfaces for speech synthesis.

- javax.speech.recognition: Contains classes and interfaces for speech recognition.

The EngineManager class is like a factory class that all Java Speech API applications use. It provides static methods to enable the access of speech synthesis and speech recognition engines. The Engine interface encapsulates the generic operations that a Java Speech API-compliant speech engine should provide for speech applications.

Speech applications can primarily use methods to perform actions such as retrieving the properties and state of the speech engine and allocating and deallocating resources for a speech engine. In addition, the Engine interface exposes mechanisms to pause and resume the audio stream generated or processed by the speech engine. Streams can be manipulated by the AudioManager. The

Engine interface is subclassed by the Synthesizer and Recognizer interfaces, which define additional speech synthesis and speech recognition functionality. The Synthesizer interface encapsulates the operations that a Java Speech API-compliant speech synthesis engine should provide for speech applications.

The Java Speech API is based on event-handling. Events generated by the speech engine can be identified and handled as required. Speech events can be handled through the EngineListener interface, and more specifically through the RecognizerListener and the SynthesizerListener.

Related Specifications

The Java Speech API was written before the Java Community Process (JCP) and targeted the Java Platform, Standard Edition (Java SE). Subsequently, the Java Speech API 2 (JSAPI2) was created as JSR 113 under the JCP. This API targets the Java Platform, Micro Edition (Java ME), but also complies with Java SE.

Speech-Enabled Java Applications

The existing capabilities of the Java platform make it attractive for the development of a wide range of applications. With the addition of the Java Speech API, Java application developers can extend and complement existing user interfaces with speech input and output. For existing developers of speech applications, the Java platform now offers an attractive alternative with:

- Portability: the Java programming language, APIs and virtual machine are available for a wide variety of hardware platforms and operating systems and are supported by major web browsers.

- Powerful and compact environment: the Java platform provides developers with a powerful, object-oriented, garbage collected language which enables rapid development and improved reliability.

- Network aware and secure: from its inception, the Java platform has been network aware and has included robust security.

Speech and other Java APIs

The Java Speech API is one of the Java Media APIs, a suite of software interfaces that provide cross-platform access to audio, video and other multimedia playback, 2D and 3D graphics, animation, telephony, advanced imaging, and more. The Java Speech API, in combination with the other Java Media APIs, allows developers to enrich Java applications and applets with rich media and communication capabilities that meet the expectations of today's users, and can enhance person-to-person communication.

The Java Speech API leverages the capabilities of other Java APIs. The Internationalization features of the Java programming language plus the use of the Unicode character set simplify the development of multi-lingual speech applications. The classes and interfaces of the Java Speech API follow the design patterns of JavaBeans™. Finally, Java Speech API events integrate with the event mechanisms of AWT, JavaBeans and the Java Foundation Classes (JFC).

Java 3D

The Java 3D API is an application programming interface used for writing three-dimensional graphics applications and applets. It gives developers high-level constructs for creating and manipulating 3D geometry and for constructing the structures used in rendering that geometry. Application developers can describe very large virtual worlds using these constructs, which provide Java 3D with enough information to render these worlds efficiently.

Java 3D delivers Java's "write once, run anywhere" benefit to developers of 3D graphics applications. Java 3D is part of the JavaMedia suite of APIs, making it available on a wide range of platforms. It also integrates well with the Internet because applications and applets written using the Java 3D API have access to the entire set of Java classes.

The Java 3D API draws its ideas from existing graphics APIs and from new technologies. Java 3D's low-level graphics constructs synthesize the best ideas found in low-level APIs such as Direct3D, OpenGL, QuickDraw3D, and XGL. Similarly, its higher-level constructs synthesize the best ideas found in several scene graph-based systems. Java 3D introduces some concepts not commonly considered part of the graphics environment, such as 3D spatial sound. Java 3D's sound capabilities help to provide a more immersive experience for the user.

Goals

Java 3D was designed with several goals in mind. Chief among them is high performance. Several design decisions were made so that Java 3D implementations can deliver the highest level of performance to application users. In particular, when trade-offs were made, the alternative that benefited runtime execution was chosen.

Other important Java 3D goals are to

- Provide a rich set of features for creating interesting 3D worlds, tempered by the need to avoid nonessential or obscure features. Features that could be layered on top of Java 3D were not included.

- Provide a high-level object-oriented programming paradigm that enables developers to deploy sophisticated applications and applets rapidly.

- Provide support for runtime loaders. This allows Java 3D to accommodate a wide variety of file formats, such as vendor-specific CAD formats, interchange formats, VRML 1.0, and VRML 2.0

Features

- Multithreaded scene graph structure

- Cross-platform

- Generic real-time API, usable for both visualization and gaming

- Support for retained, compiled-retained, and immediate mode rendering

- Includes hardware-accelerated JOGL, OpenGL, and Direct3D renderers (depending on platform)

- Sophisticated virtual-reality-based view model with support for stereoscopic rendering and complex multi-display configurations

- Native support for head-mounted display

- CAVE (multiple screen projectors)

- 3D spatial sound

- Programmable shaders, supporting both GLSL and CG

- Stencil buffer

- Importers for most mainstream formats, like 3DS, OBJ, VRML, X3D, NWN, and FLT

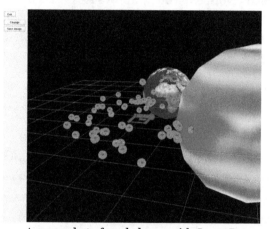

A screenshot of work drawn with Java 3D

Competing Technologies

Java 3D is not the only high-level API option to render 3D in Java. In part due to the pause in development during 2003 and 2004, several competing Java scene graph technologies emerged:

General purpose:

- Ardor3D

- JavaFX

Gaming:

- jMonkeyEngine

- Espresso3D

Visualization:

- Jreality

In addition to those, many other C or C++ scene graph APIs offer Java support through JNI.

At a lower level, the JOGL (JSR 231) OpenGL bindings for Java are a popular alternative to scene graph APIs such as Java 3D. LWJGL is another such binding.

Pros of Java 3D

- It provides a high-level, object-oriented view of 3D graphics. Java 3D accomplishes this in part by using a scene graph-based 3D graphics model. This approach is intended to help programmers without much graphics or multimedia programming experience use 3D in their applications. In stark contrast to lower-level, procedural 3D APIs like OpenGL, which are designed to optimize for the best possible speed and give programmers the greatest possible control over the rendering process, Java 3D is meant to be straightforward enough for any experienced Java programmer to learn.

- If you don't need low-level access to rendering operations, Java 3D may be an option. Rendering access is limited to requests via attributes andcapability bits, similar in form and function to Java 2D's rendering hints.

- Java 3D is optimized for speed where possible. The runtime uses rendering capability bits, in fact, to optimize the scene graph for the fastest possible renders. This approach makes Java 3D more applicable to interactive graphics environments (games, simulations, low-latency situations) than to offline, high-quality graphics applications (like render farms).

- A large and growing number of 3D loaders are available to import content into the Java 3D runtime. Sun has made a Java 3D VRML97 file loader and browser freely available with code. Look for next month's Media Programming column to explore Java 3D loaders in more detail.

- Java 3D requires vector math capabilities not available elsewhere in the Java platform. These math operations are currently located in thejavax.vecmath package and may be moved into the core platform in the future.

- Java 3D supports a number of exotic devices (wands, data gloves, and headsets, for example). The com.sun.j3d.utils.trackers package included with Sun's implementation provides classes for Fakespace, Logitech, and Polhemus devices.

Cons of Java 3D

- Java 3D is a standard extension API. Java platform licensees are given the option to implement the API if they like, but they're not required to implement it. Java 3D's positioning as a standard extension runs the risk of reducing the portability of Java 3D code across platforms -- most vendors have to struggle to keep up with changes and additions to the core platform alone.

- Java 3D has severe availability constraints. These are the result of Java 3D's status as an extension API. The only major vendor currently providing a Java 3D implementation is Sun, with its implementations for Solaris and Win32. Compared to OpenGL, which is available for every flavor of Unix, Windows, and many other operating systems, the cross-platform portability of Java 3D code looks questionable.

- Along with software availability problems come documentation deficits.Sun is making a valiant effort to provide developer training and support for Java 3D, but it is still falling short compared to the rest of the industry's efforts in documenting OpenGL and its use. The OpenGL Consortium's Web site is far deeper and broader than anything Sun has managed to put together for Java 3D so far. This is not a minor point: the relative complexity of 3D graphics APIs make good documentation a necessity.

- Java 3D hides rendering-pipeline details from the developer. Because Java 3D is a high-level API, it intentionally hides details of the rendering pipeline from the developer, which makes it unsuitable for a significant number of problems where such details are important.

- Java 3D components are heavyweight. That is, they have a native (non-Java) peer that actually does the rendering. This can complicate your GUI development if you use Java Swing and its all-Java, or lightweight, components. There are some special workarounds, but in general, lightweight and heavyweight components don't mix well in the same container objects and windows.

References

- Maalej, Waleed; Robillard, Martin P. (April 2012). "Patterns of Knowledge in API Reference Documentation" (PDF). IEEE TRANSACTIONS ON SOFTWARE ENGINEERING. Retrieved 22 July 2016

- Java Persistence with Hibernate. Manning Publications. ISBN 9781617290459. Retrieved 8 December 2013

- Monperrus, Martin; Eichberg, Michael; Tekes, Elif; Mezini, Mira (3 December 2011). "What should developers be aware of? An empirical study on the directives of API documentation" (PDF). Empirical Software Engineering. 17 (6): 703–737. arXiv:1205.6363. doi:10.1007/s10664-011-9186-4. Retrieved 22 July 2016

- Henning, Michi; Vinoski, Steve (1999). "Advanced CORBA Programming with C++". Addison-Wesley. ISBN 978-0201379273. Retrieved 16 June 2015

- Barreto, Charlton. "SDO and JPA". Digital Walkabout. Archived from the original on 13 August 2011. Retrieved 5 May 2011

6

Diverse Aspects of Java

Computer programming has undergone rapid developments in the past decade, which has resulted in the development of significant tools and techniques in the field of Java programming. This chapter discusses such diverse aspects including Java collections framework, Java Class Library, Java applet, Java servlet and JavaServer Pages, besides others.

Java Collections Framework

Collections are like containers that groups multiple items in a single unit. For example; a jar of chocolates, list of names etc. Collections are used almost in every programming language and when Java arrived, it also came with few Collection classes; Vector, Stack, Hashtable, Array. Java 1.2 provided Collections Frameworkthat is architecture to represent and manipulate Collections in java in a standard way. Java Collections Framework consists of following parts:

- Interfaces: Java Collections Framework interfaces provides the abstract data type to represent collection. java.util.Collection is the root interface of Collections Framework. It is on the top of Collections framework hierarchy. It contains some important methods such as size(), iterator(), add(), remove(), clear() that every Collection class must implement. Some other important interfaces are java.util.List, java.util.Set, java.util.Queue and java.util.Map. Map is the only interface that doesn't inherits from Collection interface but it's part of Collections framework. All the collections framework interfaces are present in java.util package.

- Implementation Classes: Collections in Java provides core implementation classes for collections. We can use them to create different types of collections in java program. Some important collection classes are ArrayList, LinkedList, HashMap, TreeMap, HashSet, TreeSet.These classes solve most of our programming needs but if we need some special collection class, we can extend them to create our custom collection class.

  Java 1.5 came up with thread-safe collection classes that allowed to modify Collections while iterating over it, some of them are CopyOnWriteArrayList, ConcurrentHashMap, CopyOnWriteArraySet. These classes are in java.util.concurrent package. All the collection classes are present in java.util and java.util.concurrent package.

- Algorithms: Algorithms are useful methods to provide some common functionalities, for example searching, sorting and shuffling.

Benefits of the Java Collections Framework

The Java Collections Framework provides the following benefits:

- Reduces programming effort: By providing useful data structures and algorithms, the Collections Framework frees you to concentrate on the important parts of your program rather than on the low-level "plumbing" required to make it work. By facilitating interoperability among unrelated APIs, the Java Collections Framework frees you from writing adapter objects or conversion code to connect APIs.

- Increases program speed and quality: This Collections Framework provides high-performance, high-quality implementations of useful data structures and algorithms. The various implementations of each interface are interchangeable, so programs can be easily tuned by switching collection implementations. Because you're freed from the drudgery of writing your own data structures, you'll have more time to devote to improving programs' quality and performance.

- Allows interoperability among unrelated APIs: The collection interfaces are the vernacular by which APIs pass collections back and forth. If my network administration API furnishes a collection of node names and if your GUI toolkit expects a collection of column headings, our APIs will interoperate seamlessly, even though they were written independently.

- Reduces effort to learn and to use new APIs: Many APIs naturally take collections on input and furnish them as output. In the past, each such API had a small sub-API devoted to manipulating its collections. There was little consistency among these ad hoc collections sub-APIs, so you had to learn each one from scratch, and it was easy to make mistakes when using them. With the advent of standard collection interfaces, the problem went away.

- Reduces effort to design new APIs: This is the flip side of the previous advantage. Designers and implementers don't have to reinvent the wheel each time they create an API that relies on collections; instead, they can use standard collection interfaces.

- Fosters software reuse: New data structures that conform to the standard collection interfaces are by nature reusable. The same goes for new algorithms that operate on objects that implement these interfaces.

Differences to Arrays

Collections and arrays are similar in that they both hold references to objects and they can be managed as a group. However, unlike arrays, collections do not need to be assigned a certain capacity when instantiated. Collections can also grow and shrink in size automatically when objects are added or removed. Collections cannot hold basic data type elements (primitive types) such as int, long, or double; instead, they hold Wrapper Classes such as Integer, Long, or Double.

Architecture

Almost all collections in Java are derived from the java.util.Collection interface. Collection defines the basic parts of all collections. The interface states the add() and remove() methods for adding to and removing from a collection respectively. Also required is the toArray() method, which converts the collection into a simple array of all the elements in the collection. Finally, the contains() method checks if a specified element is in the collection. The Collection interface is a subinterface of java. lang.Iterable, so any Collection may be the target of a for-each statement. (The Iterable interface provides the iterator() method used by for-each statements.) All collections have an iterator that goes through all of the elements in the collection. Additionally, Collection is a generic. Any collection can be written to store any class. For example, Collection<String> can hold strings, and the elements from the collection can be used as strings without any casting required. Note that the angled brackets < > can hold a type argument that specifies which type the collection holds.

Three Types of Collection

There are also three generic types of collection: ordered lists, dictionaries/maps, and sets. Ordered lists allows the programmer to insert items in a certain order and retrieve those items in the same order. An example is a waiting list. Two interfaces are included in the Ordered Lists which are the List Interface and the Queue Interface. Dictionaries/Maps store references to objects with a lookup key to access the object's values. One example of a key is an identification card. The Map Interface is included in the Dictionaries/Maps. Sets are unordered collections that can be iterated and where similar objects are not allowed. The Interface Set is included.

List Interface

Lists are implemented in the JCF via the java.util.List interface. It defines a list as essentially a more flexible version of an array. Elements have a specific order, and duplicate elements are allowed. Elements can be placed in a specific position. They can also be searched for within the list. Two examples for concrete classes that implement List are:

- java.util.ArrayList, which implements the list as an array. Whenever functions specific to a list are required, the class moves the elements around within the array in order to do it.

- java.util.LinkedList. This class stores the elements in nodes that each have a pointer to the previous and next nodes in the list. The list can be traversed by following the pointers, and elements can be added or removed simply by changing the pointers around to place the node in its proper place.

Stack Class

Stacks are created using java.util.Stack. The stack offers methods to put a new object on the stack (method push()) and to get objects from the stack (method pop()). A stack returns the object according to last-in-first-out (LIFO), e.g. the object which was placed latest on the stack is returned first. java.util.Stack is a standard implementation of a stack provided by Java. The Stack class represents a last-in-first-out (LIFO) stack of objects. It extends class java.util.Vector with five operations that allow a vector to be treated as a stack. The usual push and pop operations are provided, as well as a method to peek at the top item on the stack, a method to test for whether the stack is empty, and a method to search the stack for an item and discover how far it is from the top. When a stack is first created, it contains no items.

Queue Interfaces

The java.util.Queue interface defines the queue data structure, which stores elements in the order in which they are inserted. New additions go to the end of the line, and elements are removed from the front. It creates a first-in first-out system. This interface is implemented by java.util. LinkedList, java.util.ArrayDeque, and java.util.PriorityQueue. LinkedList, of course, also implements the List interface and can also be used as one. But it also has the Queue methods. ArrayDeque implements the queue as an array. Both LinkedList and ArrayDeque also implement the java. util.Deque interface, giving it more flexibility.

java.util.Queue can be used more flexibly with its subinterface, java.util.concurrent.BlockingQueue. The BlockingQueue interface works like a regular queue, but additions to and removals from the queue are blocking. If remove is called on an empty queue, it can be set to wait either a specified time or indefinitely for an item to appear in the queue. Similarly, adding an item is subject to an optional capacity restriction on the queue, and the method can wait for space to become available in the queue before returning.

java.util.PriorityQueue implements java.util.Queue, but also alters it. Instead of elements being ordered by the order in which they are inserted, they are ordered by priority. The method used to determine priority is either the compareTo() method in the elements or a method given in the constructor. The class creates this by using a heap to keep the items sorted.

Double-ended Queue (Deque) Interfaces

The java.util.Queue interface is expanded by the java.util.Deque subinterface. Deque creates a double-ended queue. While a regular queue only allows insertions at the rear and removals at the front, the deque allows insertions or removals to take place both at the front and the back. A deque is like a queue that can be used forwards or backwards, or both at once. Additionally, both a forwards and a backwards iterator can be generated. The Deque interface is implemented by java. util.ArrayDeque and java.util.LinkedList.

The java.util.concurrent.BlockingDeque interface works similarly to java.util.concurrent. BlockingQueue. The same methods for insertion and removal with time limits for waiting for the insertion or removal to become possible are provided. However, the interface also provides the flexibility of a deque. Insertions and removals can take place at both ends. The blocking function is combined with the deque function.

Set Interfaces

Java's java.util.Set interface defines the set. A set can't have any duplicate elements in it. Additionally, the set has no set order. As such, elements can't be found by index. Set is implemented by java.util.HashSet, java.util.LinkedHashSet, and java.util.TreeSet. HashSet uses a hash table. More specifically, it uses a java.util.HashMap to store the hashes and elements and to prevent duplicates. java.util.LinkedHashSet extends this by creating a doubly linked list that links all of the elements by their insertion order. This ensures that the iteration order over the set is predictable. java.util.TreeSet uses a red-black tree implemented by a java.util.TreeMap. The red-black tree makes sure that there are no duplicates. Additionally, it allows TreeSet to implement java.util.SortedSet.

The java.util.Set interface is extended by the java.util.SortedSet interface. Unlike a regular set, the elements in a sorted set are sorted, either by the element's compareTo() method, or a method provided to the constructor of the sorted set. The first and last elements of the sorted set can be retrieved, and subsets can be created via minimum and maximum values, as well as beginning or ending at the beginning or ending of the sorted set. The SortedSet interface is implemented by java.util.TreeSet.

java.util.SortedSet is extended further via the java.util.NavigableSet interface. It's similar to SortedSet, but there are a few additional methods. The floor(), ceiling(), lower(), and higher() methods find an element in the set that's close to the parameter. Additionally, a descending iterator over the items in the set is provided. As with SortedSet, java.util.TreeSetimplements NavigableSet.

Map Interfaces

Maps are defined by the java.util.Map interface in Java. Maps are simple data structures that associate a key with an element. This lets the map be very flexible. If the key is the hash code of the element, the map is essentially a set. If it's just an increasing number, it becomes a list. Maps are implemented by java.util.HashMap, java.util.LinkedHashMap, and java.util.TreeMap. HashMap uses a hash table. The hashes of the keys are used to find the elements in various buckets. Linked-HashMap extends this by creating a doubly linked listbetween the elements, allowing them to be accessed in the order in which they were inserted into the map. TreeMap, in contrast to HashMap and LinkedHashMap, uses a red-black tree. The keys are used as the values for the nodes in the tree, and the nodes point to the elements in the map.

The java.util.Map interface is extended by its subinterface, java.util.SortedMap. This interface defines a map that's sorted by the keys provided. Using, once again, the compareTo() method or a method provided in the constructor to the sorted map, the key-element pairs are sorted by the keys. The first and last keys in the map can be called. Additionally, submaps can be created from minimum and maximum keys. SortedMap is implemented by java.util.TreeMap.

The java.util.NavigableMap interface extends java.util.SortedMap in various ways. Methods can be called that find the key or map entry that's closest to the given key in either direction. The map can also be reversed, and an iterator in reverse order can be generated from it. It's implemented by java.util.TreeMap.

Extensions to the Java Collections Framework

Java collections framework is extended by the Apache Commons Collections library, which adds collection types such as a bag and bidirectional map, as well as utilities for creating unions and intersections.

Google has released its own collections libraries as part of the guava libraries.

Interface Java

An interface is a reference type in Java. It is similar to class. It is a collection of abstract methods. A class implements an interface, thereby inheriting the abstract methods of the interface.

Along with abstract methods, an interface may also contain constants, default methods, static methods, and nested types. Method bodies exist only for default methods and static methods.

Writing an interface is similar to writing a class. But a class describes the attributes and behaviors of an object. And an interface contains behaviors that a class implements.

Unless the class that implements the interface is abstract, all the methods of the interface need to be defined in the class.

An interface is similar to a class in the following ways –

- An interface can contain any number of methods.

- An interface is written in a file with a .java extension, with the name of the interface matching the name of the file.

- The byte code of an interface appears in a .class file.

- Interfaces appear in packages, and their corresponding bytecode file must be in a directory structure that matches the package name.

However, an interface is different from a class in several ways, including

- You cannot instantiate an interface.

- An interface does not contain any constructors.

- All of the methods in an interface are abstract.

- An interface cannot contain instance fields. The only fields that can appear in an interface must be declared both static and final.

- An interface is not extended by a class; it is implemented by a class.

- An interface can extend multiple interfaces.

Interfaces are used to encode similarities which the classes of various types share, but do not necessarily constitute a class relationship. For instance, a human and a parrot can both whistle; however, it would not make sense to represent Humans and Parrots as subclasses of a Whistler class. Rather they would most likely be subclasses of an Animal class (likely with intermediate classes), but both would implement the Whistler interface.

Another use of interfaces is being able to use an object without knowing its type of class, but rather only that it implements a certain interface. For instance, if one were annoyed by a whistling noise, one may not know whether it is a human or a parrot, because all that could be determined is that a whistler is whistling. The call whistler.whistle() will call the implemented method whistle of object whistler no matter what class it has, provided it implements Whistler. In a more practical example, a sorting algorithm may expect an object of type Comparable. Thus, without knowing the specific type, it knows that objects of that type can somehow be sorted.

For example:

```
interface Bounceable {
```

```
        double pi=3.1415;

        void setBounce(); // Note the semicolon
                                // Interface methods are public, abstract and
    never final.
                                // Think of them as prototypes only; no imple-
    mentations are allowed.

    }
```

An interface:

- declares only method headers and public constants.

- cannot be instantiated.

- can be implemented by a class.

- cannot extend a class.

- can extend several other interfaces.

Usage

Defining an Interface

Interfaces are defined with the following syntax (compare to Java's class definition):

```
[visibility] interface InterfaceName [extends other interfaces] {
        constant declarations
        abstract method declarations

}
```

Example: public interface Interface1 extends Interface2;

The body of the interface contains abstract methods, but since all methods in an interface are, by definition, abstract, the abstract keyword is not required. Since the interface specifies a set of exposed behaviors, all methods are implicitly public.

Thus, a simple interface may be

```
public interface Predator {
        boolean chasePrey(Prey p);
        void eatPrey(Prey p);

}
```

The member type declarations in an interface are implicitly static, final and public, but otherwise they can be any type of class or interface.

Implementing Interfaces in a Class

The syntax for implementing an interface uses this formula:

```
... implements InterfaceName[, another interface, another, ...] ...
```

Classes may implement an interface. For example,

```
public class Lion implements Predator {


        @Override
        public boolean chasePrey(Prey p) {
                // programming to  chase prey p (specifically for a lion)
        }


        @Override
        public void eatPrey(Prey p) {
                // programming to eat prey p (specifically for a lion)
        }

}
```

If a class implements an interface and does not implement all its methods, it must be marked as abstract. If a class is abstract, one of its subclasses is expected to implement its unimplemented methods, though if any of the abstract class' subclasses do not implement all interface methods, the subclass itself must be marked again as abstract.

Classes can implement multiple interfaces:

```
public class Frog implements Predator, Prey { ... }
```

Interfaces can share common class methods:

```
class Animal implements LikesFood, LikesWater
{boolean likes() {return true;}
}
```

However a given class cannot implement the same or a similar interface multiple times:

```
class Animal implements Shares<Boolean>, Shares<Integer> ...
// error: repeated interface
```

Interfaces are commonly used in the Java language for callbacks, as Java does not allow multiple inheritance of classes, nor does it allow the passing of methods (procedures) as arguments. Therefore, in order to pass a method as a parameter to a target method, current practice is to define and pass a reference to an interface as a means of supplying the signature and address of the parameter method to the target method rather than defining multiple variants of the target method to accommodate each possible calling class.

Subinterfaces

Interfaces can extend several other interfaces, using the same formula as described below. For example,

```
public interface VenomousPredator extends Predator, Venomous {
        //interface body
}
```

is legal and defines a subinterface. Note how it allows multiple inheritance, unlike classes. Note also that Predator and Venomous may possibly define or inherit methods with the same signature, say kill(Prey p). When a class implements VenomousPredator it will implement both methods simultaneously.

Examples

Some common Java interfaces are:

- `Comparable` has the method `compareTo`, which is used to describe two objects as equal, or to indicate one is greater than the other. Generics allow implementing classes to specify which class instances can be compared to them.

- `Serializable` is a marker interface with no methods or fields - it has an empty body. It is used to indicate that a class can be serialized. Its Javadoc describes how it should function, although nothing is programmatically enforced

Java Class Library

Java is an object oriented programming language, so in java programming, main two features are supported that is class and object. Basically we know that class is collection of objects and object is an instance of class. The uses of the java libraries of class spread the programmer efficiency by allowing computer programmer to focus on the functionality unique to their job. The library classes are generally planned with some typical usage pattern in observance, and the performance may be suboptimal if the actual usage differs. We deliver an approach for rewriting applications to use different customized versions of library classes that are generated using a combination of static analysis and profile information.

The java programming supports different type of classes as User defines class [A class which is created by user is known as user defined class.] and also there are some classes available with java system that provide some important support to the java programmer for developing their programming logic as well as their programming architecture with very smooth and very fine way. These classes are called Library Classes. In Java support thousands of library classes and also each class contains various types of functions. The availability of a large numbers of libraries of standardized classes is a vital reason for popularity of Java as a standard programming language in modern software world. The use of class libraries grows for the programmer productivity by allowing programmers to focus on the characteristics for that are unique to their application without being burdened with the unexciting task of building and debugging of the standard infrastructure. This java library classes are often designed and executed with some typical usage pattern in real life job profile.

The common case of unnecessary overhead occurs when single-threaded applications are used by library classes that are modified with multi-threaded clients in concept. For example, we find out that many Java programs frequently concatenate with strings via calls to the synchronized method/function like java.lang.StringBuffer.append()[Java compiler translate using +- operator on String manipulated objects is called StringBuffer.append()]. This points show that a lock must be developed for each call to this method, which is unnecessary for single-threaded applications. The performances of the programming concept can better-quality in such cases by rewriting the application to use convention, unsynchronized String Buffers.

Advantages of Library Classes in Java:

- The type constraints are used to control where the java library classes can be replaced with routine versions without affecting type perfection of programs.

- Static analysis is then used to control those applicants for which unused library functionality and synchronization can be removed safely from the allocated types.

- The profile data is collected about the usage features of the customization candidates to determine where the allocation of custom library classes is likely to be cost-effective.

- To base on the static analysis results and the profiling information the custom library classes are automatically generated from a template.

- The bytecode of the client application is rewritten to use the generated custom classes. This bytecode rewriting is completely see-through to the programmer.

List of Library Classes in Java:

Library classes	Purpose of the class
Java.io	Use for input and output functions.
Java.lang	Use for character and string operation.
Java.awt	Use for windows interface.
Java.util	Use for develop utility programming.
Java.applet	Use for applet.
Java.net	Used for network communication.
Java.math	Used for various mathematical calculations like power, square root etc.

We will come across different library classes, which basically deal with input/output operation, which can be applied for characters and string manipulations.

Process to Input/Output Operation in JAVA

Java languages do not provide specific statement to input a value from the keyboard or to print the result on the visual display unit [VDU]. It uses the functions read() to accept a character from the keyboard and print() or println() to display the result on the screen.

To input a character the function can be written as shown below:

a= System.in.read();

The Sytem.in.read() is an input stream belonging to the system class, which is, in turn an object of the input stream class available in Java.io Package.

To print the result the print function can be written as shown below:

System.out.print(x);

Here, System.out is an output stream of a system class, which is in turn an object of print stream class available in Java.io library package. Print stream class allow the users to display the result either by using print() or println() function.

Listing 1: Sample showing Example using package import java.util

```java
import java.util.*;
class WordUtil{
    public static void main(String[] args){
        Scanner input=new Scanner(System.in);
        System.out.println("Enter Word: ");
        String word = input.next();
        char ch=word.charAt(0);
        String newWord=word+Character.toString(ch);
        System.out.println(newWord);
    }
}
```

Listing 2: Sample showing Example using package import java.io

```java
import java.io.*;
class WordImport{
    public static void main(String[] args){
        int a,b,c;
        InputStreamReader isr=new InputStreamReader(System.in);
        BufferedReader br=new BufferedReader(isr);
        Sytem.out.println("Enter Digit");
        a=Integer.parseInt(br.readLine());
        Sytem.out.println("Enter Digit");
    b=Integer.parseInt(br.readLine());
        c=a+b;
```

```
        System.out.println("Sum of the data is.."+c);
    }
}
```

In the above two example we show that this packages are using for communication of data from keyboard as well as display on the Visual Display Unit.

Now we know that Java has defined many library classes for the use of the computer programmer. They contain highly useful methods/function.

Implementation and Configuration

Java Class Library (JCL) is almost entirely written in Java, except for the parts that need direct access to the hardware and operating system (such as for I/O, or bitmap graphics). The classes that give access to these functions commonly use Java Native Interface wrappers to access operating system APIs.

Almost all of JCL is stored in a single Java archive file called "rt.jar", which is provided with JRE and JDK distributions. The Java Class Library (rt.jar) is located in the default bootstrap classpath, and does not have to appear in the classpath declared for the application. The runtime uses the bootstrap class loader to find the JCL.

The upcoming Java Module System (planned for Java 9) will break the monolithic "rt.jar" Jar file, and modularize the Java Class Library itself in several modules with specified dependencies.

Conformance

Any Java implementation must pass the Java Technology Compatibility Kit tests for compliance, which includes JCL tests.

Main Features

JCL Features are accessed through classes provided in packages.

- java.lang contains fundamental classes and interfaces closely tied to the language and runtime system.

- I/O and networking access the platform file system, and more generally networks through the java.io, java.nio and java.net packages. For networking, SCTP is available through com.sun.nio.sctp.

- Mathematics package: java.math provides mathematical expressions and evaluation, as well as arbitrary-precision decimal and integer number datatypes.

- Collections and Utilities : built-in Collection data structures, and utility classes, for Regular expressions, Concurrency, logging and Data compression.

- GUI and 2D Graphics: the AWT package (java.awt) basic GUI operations and binds to the underlying native system. It also contains the 2D Graphics API. The Swing package (javax.

Swing) is built on AWT and provides a platform-independent widget toolkit, as well as a Pluggable look and feel. It also deals with editable and non-editable text components.

- Sound: interfaces and classes for reading, writing, sequencing, and synthesizing of sound data.

- Text: java.text deals with text, dates, numbers, and messages.

- Image package: java.awt.image and javax.imageio provide APIs to write, read, and modify images.

- XML: SAX, DOM, StAX, XSLT transforms, XPath and various APIs for Web services, as SOAP protocol and JAX-WS.

- CORBA and RMI APIs, including a built-in ORB

- Security is provided by java.security and encryption services are provided by javax.crypto.

- Databases: access to SQL databases via java.sql

- Access to Scripting engines: The javax.script package gives access to any conforming Scripting language.

- Applets: java.applet allows applications to be downloaded over a network and run within a guarded sandbox

- Java Beans: java.beans provides ways to manipulate reusable components.

- Introspection and reflection: java.lang.Class represents a class, but other classes such as Method and Constructor are available in java.lang.reflect.

Licensing

Prior Licenses

Before the release of OpenJDK, the JDK was based on a proprietary license.

Following their promise to release a fully buildable JDK based almost completely on free and open source code in the first half of 2007, Sun released the complete source code of the Class Library under the GPL on May 8, 2007, except some limited parts that were licensed by Sun from third parties who did not want their code to be released under an open source license. Sun's goal was to replace the parts that remain proprietary and closed source with alternative implementations and make the Class Library completely free and open source.

Until December 2010, the remaining encumbered part of the JDK was made available by Sun then Oracle as *Binary Plugs* which were required to build the JDK but not necessary to run it. as of May 2007, the only part of the Class library that remained proprietary and closed-source (4% as of May 2007 for OpenJDK 7, and less than 1% as of May 2008 and OpenJDK 6) was:

- The SNMP implementation.

Since the first May 2007 release, Sun, with the help of the community, released as open source or replaced with open source alternatives almost all the encumbered code:

- All the audio engine code, including the software synthesizer, became open source. The closed-source software synthesizer has been replaced by a new synthesizer developed specifically for OpenJDK called *Gervill*,

- All cryptography classes were released as open source,

- The code that scales and rasterizes fonts uses open source FreeType

- The native color management uses open source LittleCMS. There is a pluggable layer in the JDK, so that the commercial release of Java can use the original, proprietary color management system and OpenJDK can use LittleCMS.

- The anti-aliasing graphics rasterizer code uses the open source Pisces renderer used in the phoneME project.

- The JavaScript plugin is open source (the JavaScript engine itself was open source from the beginning).

Open Source Release

Beginning in December 2010, all the so-called *binary plugs* were replaced by open source replacements, making the entire JDK open.

Alternative Implementations

GNU Classpath is the other main free software class library for Java. Contrary to other implementations, it only implements the Class Library, and is used by many free Java runtimes (like Kaffe, SableVM, JamVM, CACAO).

Apache Harmony was another free software class library. Its aim was to implement the other parts of the Java stack (Virtual Machine, Compiler, and other tools required for any Java implementation).

Java Classloader

Java class loaders are used to load classes at runtime. ClassLoader in Java works on three principle: delegation,visibility and uniqueness. Delegation principle forward request of class loading to parent class loader and only loads the class, if parent is not able to find or load class. Visibility principle allows child class loader to see all the classes loaded by parent ClassLoader, but parent class loader can not see classes loaded by child. Uniqueness principle allows to load a class exactly once, which is basically achieved by delegation and ensures that child ClassLoader doesn't reload the class already loaded by parent. Correct understanding of class loader is must to resolve issues like NoClassDefFoundError in Java andjava.lang.ClassNotFoundException, which are related to class loading.

We know that Java programs run on Java Virtual Machine (JVM). When we compile a Java Class, it transforms into bytecode that is platform and machine independent. Compiled classes are stored as a .class file. When we try to use a Class, Java ClassLoader loads that class into memory. Classes are introduced into the Java environment when they are referenced by name in a class that is already running. Future attempts at loading classes are done by the class loader, once the first class is running. Running the first class is usually done by declaring and using a static main() method.

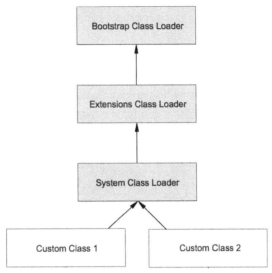

hierarchy of class loaders

Types of Java Class Loaders

1. Bootstrap Class Loader – It loads JDK internal classes, typically loads rt.jar and other core classes for example java.lang.* package classes

2. Extensions Class Loader – It loads classes from the JDK extensions directory, usually lib/ ext directory of the JRE.

3. System Class Loader –Loads classes from system classpath, that can be set while invoking a program using -cp or -classpath command line options.

Ways in which Classes are Loaded

When classes are loaded? There are exactly two cases:

1. when the new bytecode is executed (for example, MyClass *mc* = new MyClass()

2. when the bytecodes make a static reference to a class (for example, System.*out*).

Class loaders are hierarchical. The very first class is specially loaded with the help of static main() method declared in your class. All the subsequently loaded classes are loaded by the classes, which are already loaded and running.

Further classloaders follow this rules when loading classes:

1. Check if the class was already loaded.

2. If not loaded, ask parent class loader to load the class.

3. If parent class loader cannot load class, attempt to load it in this class loader.

User-defined Class Loaders

The Java class loader is written in Java. It is therefore possible to create your own class loader without understanding the finer details of the Java Virtual Machine. Every Java class loader has a parent class loader, defined when a new class loader is instantiated or set to the virtual machine's system default class loader.

This makes it possible (for example):

- to load or unload classes at runtime (for example to load libraries dynamically at runtime, even from an HTTP resource). This is an important feature for:
  - implementing scripting languages, such as Jython
  - using bean builders
  - allowing user-defined extensibility
  - allowing multiple namespaces to communicate. This is one of the foundations of CORBA / RMI protocols for example.
- to change the way the bytecode is loaded (for example, it is possible to use encrypted Java class bytecode).
- to modify the loaded bytecode (for example, for load-time weaving of aspects when using aspect-oriented programming).

Class Loaders in Java EE

Java Platform, Enterprise Edition (Java EE) application servers typically load classes from a deployed WAR or EAR archive by a tree of classloaders, isolating the application from other applications, but sharing classes between deployed modules. So-called "servlet containers" are typically implemented in terms of multiple classloaders.

JAR hell

JAR hell is a term similar to DLL hell used to describe all the various ways in which the classloading process can end up not working. Three ways JAR hell can occur are:

- Accidental presence of two different versions of a library installed on a system. This will not be considered an error by the system. Rather, the system will load classes from one or the other library. Adding the new library to the list of available libraries instead of replacing it may result in the application still behaving as though the old library is in use, which it may well be.

- Multiple libraries or applications require different versions of library foo. If versions of library foo use the same class names, there is no way to load the versions of library foo with the same classloader.

- The most complex JAR hell problems arise in circumstances that take advantage of the full complexity of the classloading system. A Java program is not required to use only a single "flat" classloader, but instead may be composed of several (potentially very many) nested, cooperating classloaders. Classes loaded by different classloaders may interact in complex ways not fully comprehended by a developer, leading to errors or bugs that are difficult to analyze, explain, and resolve.

The OSGi Alliance specified (starting as JSR 8 in 1998) a modularity framework that aims to solve JAR hell for current and future VMs in ME, SE, and EE that is widely adopted. Using metadata in the JAR manifest, JAR files (called bundles) are wired on a per-package basis. Bundles can export packages, import packages and keep packages private, providing the basic constructs of modularity and versioned dependency management.

To remedy the JAR hell problems, a Java Community Process — JSR 277 was initiated in 2005. The resolution — Java Platform Module System — intended to introduce a new distribution format, a modules versioning scheme, and a common modules repository (similar in purpose to Microsoft .NET's Global Assembly Cache). In December 2008, Sun announced that JSR 277 was put on hold. The Java Module System was later rebooted as "project Jigsaw" which was included in Java 9.

Java hashCode()

Hashing is a fundamental concept of computer science.

In Java, efficient hashing algorithms stand behind some of the most popular collections we have available – such as the *HashMap* and the *HashSet*.

The hashcode of a Java Object is simply a number, it is 32-bit signed int, that allows an object to be managed by a hash-based data structure. We know that hash code is an unique id number allocated to an object by JVM. But actually speaking, Hash code is not an unique number for an object. If two objects are equals then these two objects should return same hash code. So we have to implement hashcode() method of a class in such way that if two objects are equals, ie compared by equal() method of that class, then those two objects must return same hash code. If you are overriding hashCode you need to override equals method also.

hashCode() in General

All the classes inherit a basic hash scheme from the fundamental base class java.lang.Object, but instead many override this to provide a hash function that better handles their specific data. Classes which provide their own implementation must override the object method public int hashCode().

The general contract for overridden implementations of this method is that they behave in a way consistent with the same object's equals() method: that a given object must consistently report the same hash value (unless it is changed so that the new version is no longer considered "equal" to the old), and that two objects which equals() says are equal *must* report the same hash value. There's no requirement that hash values be consistent between different Java implementations, or even between different execution runs of the same program, and while two *unequal* objects having different hashes is very desirable, this is not mandatory (that is, the hash function implemented doesn't need to be a perfect hash).

For example, the class Employee might implement its hash function by composing the hashes of its members:

```
public class Employee {
        int         employeeId;
        String      name;
        Department dept;


        // other methods would be in here


        @Override
        public int hashCode() {
            int hash = 1;
            hash = hash * 17 + employeeId;
            hash = hash * 31 + name.hashCode();
            hash = hash * 13 + (dept == null ? 0 : dept.hashCode());
            return hash;
        }
    }
```

The Java.lang.String Hash Function

In an attempt to provide a fast implementation, early versions of the Java String class provided a hashCode() implementation that considered at most 16 characters picked from the string. For some common data this worked very poorly, delivering unacceptably clustered results and consequently slow hashtable performance.

From Java 1.2, java.lang.String class implements its hashCode() using a product sum algorithm over the entire text of the string. An instance s of the java.lang.String class, for example, would have a hash code $h(s)$ defined by

$$h(s) = \sum_{i=0}^{n-1} s[i] \cdot 31^{n-1-i}$$

where terms are summed using Java 32-bit int addition, i denotes the UTF-16 code unit of the nth character of the string, and $s[i]$ is the length of s.

Usage of *hashCode()* in Data Structures

The simplest operations on collections can be inefficient in certain situations.

For example, this triggers a linear search which is highly ineffective for lists of huge sizes:

```
1    List<String> words = Arrays.asList("Welcome", "to", "Baeldung");
2    if (words.contains("Baeldung")) {
3        System.out.println("Baeldung is in the list");
4    }
```

Java provides a number of data structures for dealing with this issue specifically – for example, several *Map* interface implementations are hash tables.

When using a hash table, these collections calculate the hash value for a given key using the *hashCode()* methodand use this value internally to store the data – so that access operations are much more efficient.

Understanding How *hashCode()* Works

Simply put, *hashCode()* returns an integer value, generated by a hashing algorithm.

Objects that are equal (according to their equals()) must return the same hash code. It's not required for different objects to return different hash codes.

The general contract of *hashCode()* states:

- Whenever it is invoked on the same object more than once during an execution of a Java application, *hashCode()*must consistently return the same value, provided no information used in equals comparisons on the object is modified. This value needs not remain consistent from one execution of an application to another execution of the same application

- If two objects are equal according to the equals(Object) method, then calling the *hashCode()* method on each of the two objects must produce the same value

- It is not required that if two objects are unequal according to the *equals(java.lang.Object)* method, then calling the *hashCode* method on each of the two objects must produce distinct integer results. However, developers should be aware that producing distinct integer results for unequal objects improves the performance of hash tables

Standard *hashCode()* Implementations

The better the hashing algorithm that we use to compute hash codes, the better will the performance of hash tables be.

Let's have a look at a "standard" implementation that uses two primes numbers to add even more uniqueness to computed hash codes:

```
1   @Override
2   public int hashCode() {
3       int hash = 7;
4       hash = 31 * hash + (int) id;
5       hash = 31 * hash + (name == null ? 0 : name.hashCode());
6       hash = 31 * hash + (email == null ? 0 : email.hashCode());
7       return hash;
8   }
```

While it's essential to understand the roles that *hashCode()* and *equals()* methods play, we don't have to implement them from scratch every time, as most IDEs can generate custom *hashCode()* and *equals()* implementations and since Java 7, we got an Objects.hash() utility method for comfortable hashing:

```
1   Objects.hash(name, email)
```

IntelliJ IDEA generates the following implementation:

```
1   @Override
2   public int hashCode() {
3       int result = (int) (id ^ (id >>> 32));
4       result = 31 * result + name.hashCode();
5       result = 31 * result + email.hashCode();
6       return result;
7   }
```

And Eclipse produces this one:

```
1   @Override
2   public int hashCode() {
3       final int prime = 31;
4       int result = 1;
5       result = prime * result + ((email == null) ? 0 : email.hashCode());
6       result = prime * result + (int) (id ^ (id >>> 32));
7       result = prime * result + ((name == null) ? 0 : name.hashCode());
8       return result;
9   }
```

In addition to the above IDE-based *hashCode()* implementations, it's also possible to automatically generate an efficient implementation, for example using Lombok. In this case, the lombok-maven dependency must be added to pom.xml:

```
1   <dependency>
2       <groupId>org.projectlombok</groupId>
3       <artifactId>lombok-maven</artifactId>
4       <version>1.16.18.0</version>
5       <type>pom</type>
6   </dependency>
```

It's now enough to annotate the *User* class with *@EqualsAndHashCode*:

```
1   @EqualsAndHashCode
2   public class User {
3       // fields and methods here
4   }
```

Similarly, if we want Apache Commons Lang's *HashCodeBuilder* class to generate a *hashCode()* implementation for us, the commons-lang Maven dependency must be included in the pom file:

```
1   <dependency>
2       <groupId>commons-lang</groupId>
3       <artifactId>commons-lang</artifactId>
4       <version>2.6</version>
5   </dependency>
```

And *hashCode()* can be implemented like this:

```
1   public class User {
2       public int hashCode() {
3           return new HashCodeBuilder(17, 37).
4           append(id).
5           append(name).
6           append(email).
7           toHashCode();
8       }
9   }
```

In general, there's no universal recipe to stick to when it comes to implementing *hashCode()*. We highly recommend reading Joshua Bloch's Effective Java, which provides a list of thorough guidelines for implementing efficient hashing algorithms.

What can be noticed here is that all those implementations utilize number 31 in some form – this is because 31 has a nice property – its multiplication can be replaced by a bitwise shift which is faster than the standard multiplication:

```
1   31 * i == (i << 5) - i
```

Handling Hash Collisions

The intrinsic behavior of hash tables raises up a relevant aspect of these data structures: even with an efficient hashing algorithm, two or more objects might have the same hash code, even if they're unequal. So, their hash codes would point to the same bucket, even though they would have different hash table keys.

This situation is commonly known as a hash collision, and various methodologies exist for handling it, with each one having their pros and cons. Java's HashMap uses the separate chaining method for handling collisions:

"When two or more objects point to the same bucket, they're simply stored in a linked list. In such a case, the hash table is an array of linked lists, and each object with the same hash is appended to the linked list at the bucket index in the array.

In the worst case, several buckets would have a linked list bound to it, and the retrieval of an object in the list would be performed linearly."

Hash collision methodologies show in a nutshell why it's so important to implement hashCode() efficiently.

Java 8 brought an interesting enhancement to HashMap implementation – if a bucket size goes beyond the certain threshold, the linked list gets replaced with a tree map. This allows achieving O(logn) look up instead of pessimistic O(n).

Creating a Trivial Application

To test the functionality of a standard *hashCode()* implementation, let's create a simple Java application that adds some *User* objects to a *HashMap* and uses SLF4J for logging a message to the console each time the method is called.

Here's the sample application's entry point:

```
public class Application {

    public static void main(String[] args) {
        Map<User, User> users = new HashMap<>();
        User user1 = new User(1L, "John", "john@domain.com");
        User user2 = new User(2L, "Jennifer", "jennifer@domain.com");
        User user3 = new User(3L, "Mary", "mary@domain.com");

        users.put(user1, user1);
        users.put(user2, user2);
        users.put(user3, user3);
        if (users.containsKey(user1)) {
            System.out.print("User found in the collection");
        }
    }
}
```

And this is the *hashCode()* implementation:

```
1   public class User {
2
3       // ...
4
5       public int hashCode() {
6           int hash = 7;
7           hash = 31 * hash + (int) id;
8           hash = 31 * hash + (name == null ? 0 : name.hashCode());
9           hash = 31 * hash + (email == null ? 0 : email.hashCode());
10          logger.info("hashCode() called - Computed hash: " + hash);
11          return hash;
12      }
13  }
```

The only detail worth stressing here is that each time an object is stored in the hash map and checked with the *containsKey()* method, *hashCode()* is invoked and the computed hash code is printed out to the console:

```
1   [main] INFO com.baeldung.entities.User - hashCode() called - Computed
    hash: 1255477819
2   [main] INFO com.baeldung.entities.User - hashCode() called - Computed
    hash: -282948472
3   [main] INFO com.baeldung.entities.User - hashCode() called - Computed
    hash: -1540702691
4   [main] INFO com.baeldung.entities.User - hashCode() called - Computed
    hash: 1255477819
5   User found in the collection
```

It's clear that producing efficient *hashCode()* implementations often requires a mixture of a few mathematical concepts, (i.e. prime and arbitrary numbers), logical and basic mathematical operations.

Regardless, it's entirely possible to implement *hashCode()* effectively without resorting to these techniques at all, as long as we make sure the hashing algorithm produce different hash codes for unequal objects and is consistent with the implementation of *equals()*.

Java Package

A java package is a group of similar types of classes, interfaces and sub-packages.

Package in java can be categorized in two form, built-in package and user-defined package.

There are many built-in packages such as java, lang, awt, javax, swing, net, io, util, sql etc.

A package is a namespace that organizes a set of related classes and interfaces. Conceptually you can think of packages as being similar to different folders on your computer. You might keep HTML pages in one folder, images in another, and scripts or applications in yet another. Because software written in the Java programming language can be composed of hundreds or *thousands* of individual classes, it makes sense to keep things organized by placing related classes and interfaces into packages.

The Java platform provides an enormous class library (a set of packages) suitable for use in your own applications. This library is known as the "Application Programming Interface", or "API" for short. Its packages represent the tasks most commonly associated with general-purpose programming. For example, a String object contains state and behavior for character strings; a File object allows a programmer to easily create, delete, inspect, compare, or modify a file on the filesystem; a Socket object allows for the creation and use of network sockets; various GUI objects control buttons and checkboxes and anything else related to graphical user interfaces. There are literally thousands of classes to choose from. This allows you, the programmer, to focus on the design of your particular application, rather than the infrastructure required to make it work.

Packages are used for:

- Preventing naming conflicts. For example there can be two classes with name Employee in two packages, college.staff.cse.Employee and college.staff.ee.Employee

- Making searching/locating and usage of classes, interfaces, enumerations and annotations easier

- Providing controlled access: protected and default have package level access control. A protected member is accessible by classes in the same package and its subclasses. A default member (without any access specifier) is accessible by classes in the same package only.

- Packages can be considered as data encapsulation (or data-hiding).

All we need to do is put related classes into packages. After that we can simply write a import a class from existing packages and use it in our program. A packages is container of group of related classes where some of the classes are accessible are exposed and others are kept for internal purpose. We can reuse existing classes from the packages as many time as we need it in our program.

Programmers can define their own packages to bundle group of classes/interfaces, etc. It is a good practice to group related classes implemented by you so that a programmer can easily determine that the classes, interfaces, enumerations, and annotations are related.

Creating a Package

While you should choose a name for the package and include a package statement along with that name at the top of every source file that contains the classes, interfaces, enumerations, and annotation types that you want to include in the package.

The package statement should be the first line in the source file. There can be only one package statement in each source file, and it applies to all types in the file.

If a package statement is not used then the class, interfaces, enumerations, and annotation types will be placed in the current default package.

To compile the Java programs with package statements, you have to use -d option as shown below.

```
javac -d Destination_folder file_name.java
```

Then a folder with the given package name is created in the specified destination, and the compiled class files will be placed in that folder.

Example

Let us look at an example that creates a package called animals. It is a good practice to use names of packages with lower case letters to avoid any conflicts with the names of classes and interfaces.

Following package example contains interface named *animals* –

```
/* File name : Animal.java */
package animals;


interface Animal {
   public void eat();
   public void travel();
}
```

Now, let us implement the above interface in the same package *animals* –

```
package animals;
/* File name : MammalInt.java */


public class MammalInt implements Animal {

   public void eat() {
      System.out.println("Mammal eats");
   }

   public void travel() {
      System.out.println("Mammal travels");
   }

   public int noOfLegs() {
      return 0;
```

```
    }

    public static void main(String args[]) {
        MammalInt m = new MammalInt();
        m.eat();
        m.travel();
    }
}
```

Now compile the java files as shown below –

```
$ javac -d . Animal.java
$ javac -d . MammalInt.java
```

Now a package/folder with the name animals will be created in the current directory and these class files will be placed in it as shown below.

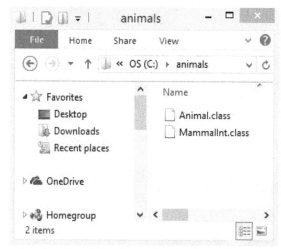

You can execute the class file within the package and get the result as shown below.

Mammal eats

Mammal travels

Using Packages

In a Java source file, the package that this file's class or classes belong to is specified with the package keyword. This keyword is usually the first keyword in the source file. At most one package declaration can appear in a source file.

```
package java.awt.event;
```

To use a package's classes inside a Java source file, it is convenient to import the classes from the package with an import declaration. The following declaration

```
import java.awt.event.*;
```

imports all classes from the java.awt.event package, while the next declaration

```
import java.awt.event.ActionEvent;
```

imports only the ActionEvent class from the package. After either of these import declarations, the ActionEvent class can be referenced using its simple class name:

```
ActionEvent myEvent = new ActionEvent();
```

Classes can also be used directly without an import declaration by using the fully qualified name of the class. For example,

```
java.awt.event.ActionEvent myEvent = new java.awt.event.ActionEvent();
```

does not require a preceding import declaration.

The Unnamed Package

Note that if you do not use a package declaration, your class ends up in an unnamed package. Classes in an unnamed package cannot be imported by classes in any other package.

The official Java Tutorial advises against this:

> Generally speaking, an unnamed package is only for small or temporary applications or when you are just beginning the development process. Otherwise, classes and interfaces belong in named packages.

Package Access Protection

Public members and classes are visible everywhere and private members are visible only in the same class. Classes within a package can access classes and members declared with *default* (*package-private*) access as well as class members declared with the *protected* access modifier. Default (package-private) access is enforced when a class or member has not been declared as public, protected or private. By contrast, classes in other packages cannot access classes and members declared with default access. However, class members declared as protected can be accessed from the classes in the same package as well as classes in other packages that are subclasses of the declaring class.

Creation of JAR Files

JAR files are created with the jar command-line utility. The command

```
jar cf myPackage.jar *.class
```

compresses all .class files into the JAR file *myPackage.jar*. The 'c' option on the command line tells the jar command to "create new archive." The ' f ' option tells it to create a file. The file's name comes next before the contents of the JAR file.

Package Naming Conventions

Packages are usually defined using a hierarchical naming pattern, with some levels in the hierarchy separated by periods (., pronounced "dot"). Although packages lower in the naming hierarchy are often referred to as "subpackages" of the corresponding packages higher in the hierarchy, there is almost no semantic relationship between packages. The Java Language Specification establishes package naming conventions to avoid the possibility of two published packages having the same name. The naming conventions describe how to create unique package names, so that packages that are widely distributed will have unique namespaces. This allows packages to be separately, easily and automatically installed and catalogued.

In general, a package name begins with the top level domain name of the organization and then the organization's domain and then any subdomains, listed in reverse order. The organization can then choose a specific name for its package. Subsequent components of the package name vary according to an organization's own internal naming conventions.

For example, if an organization in Canada called MySoft creates a package to deal with fractions, naming the package ca.mysoft.fractions distinguishes the fractions package from another similar package created by another company. If a German company named MySoft also creates a fractions package, but names it de.mysoft.fractions, then the classes in these two packages are defined in a unique and separate namespace.

Core Packages in Java SE 8

java.lang	— basic language functionality and fundamental types
java.util	— collection data structure classes
java.io	— file operations
java.math	— multiprecision arithmetics
java.nio	— the Non-blocking I/O framework for Java
java.net	— networking operations, sockets, DNS lookups, ...
java.security	— key generation, encryption and decryption
java.sql	— Java Database Connectivity (JDBC) to access databases
java.awt	— basic hierarchy of packages for native GUI components
java.text	— Provides classes and interfaces for handling text, dates, numbers, and messages in a manner independent of natural languages.
java.rmi	— Provides the RMI package.
java.time	— The main API for dates, times, instants, and durations.
java.beans	— The java.beans package contains classes and interfaces related to JavaBeans components.

The java.lang package is available without the use of an import statement.

Modules

In Java 9, "modules", a kind of collection of packages, are planned as part of Project Jigsaw; these were earlier called "superpackages" and originally planned for Java 7.

Modules will describe their dependencies in a module declaration which will be placed in a file named *module-info.java* at the root of the module's source-file hierarchy. The JDK will be able to check them both at compile-time and runtime. The JDK itself will be modularized for Java 9.

Java Applet

An applet is a small Internet-based program written in Java, a programming language for the Web, which can be downloaded by any computer. The applet is also able to run in HTML. The applet is usually embedded in an HTML page on a Web site and can be executed from within a browser.

An applet must be a subclass of the java.applet.Applet class. The Applet class provides the standard interface between the applet and the browser environment.

Swing provides a special subclass of the Applet class called javax.swing.JApplet. The JApplet class should be used for all applets that use Swing components to construct their graphical user interfaces (GUIs).

The browser's Java Plug-in software manages the lifecycle of an applet.

Life cycle of an applet :

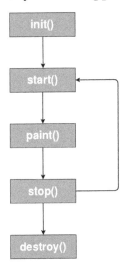

It is important to understand the order in which the various methods shown in the above image are called. When an applet begins, the following methods are called, in this sequence:

1. init( )
2. start( )
3. paint( )

When an applet is terminated, the following sequence of method calls takes place:

1. stop( )
2. destroy( )

Let's look more closely at these methods.

1. init( ) : The init( ) method is the first method to be called. This is where you should initialize variables. This method is called only once during the run time of your applet.

2. start( ) : The start( ) method is called after init( ). It is also called to restart an applet after it has been stopped. Note that init( ) is called once i.e. when the first time an applet is loaded whereas start( ) is called each time an applet's HTML document is displayed onscreen. So, if a user leaves a web page and comes back, the applet resumes execution at start( ).

3. paint( ) : The paint( ) method is called each time an AWT-based applet's output must be redrawn. This situation can occur for several reasons. For example, the window in which the applet is running may be overwritten by another window and then uncovered. Or the applet window may be minimized and then restored.

   paint( ) is also called when the applet begins execution. Whatever the cause, whenever the applet must redraw its output, paint( ) is called.

   The paint( ) method has one parameter of type Graphics. This parameter will contain the graphics context, which describes the graphics environment in which the applet is running. This context is used whenever output to the applet is required.

4. stop( ) : The stop( ) method is called when a web browser leaves the HTML document containing the applet—when it goes to another page, for example. When stop( ) is called, the applet is probably running. You should use stop( ) to suspend threads that don't need to run when the applet is not visible. You can restart them when start( )is called if the user returns to the page.

5. destroy( ) : The destroy( ) method is called when the environment determines that your applet needs to be removed completely from memory. At this point, you should free up any resources the applet may be using. The stop( ) method is always called before destroy( ).

The Applets are used to provide interactive features to web applications that cannot be provided by HTML alone.They can capture mouse input and also have controls like buttons or check boxes. In response to user actions, an applet can change the provided graphic content. This makes applets well-suited for demonstration, visualization, and teaching. There are online applet collections for studying various subjects, from physics to heart physiology.

An applet can also be a text area only; providing, for instance, a cross-platform command-line interface to some remote system. If needed, an applet can leave the dedicated area and run as a separate window. However, applets have very little control over web page content outside the applet's dedicated area, so they are less useful for improving the site appearance in general, unlike other types of browser extensions (while applets like news tickers or WYSIWYG editors are also known). Applets can also play media in formats that are not natively supported by the browser.

Pages coded in HTML may embed parameters within them that are passed to the applet. Because of this, the same applet may have a different appearance depending on the parameters that were passed.

As applets were available before CSS and DHTML were standard, they were also widely used for trivial effects such as rollover navigation buttons. This approach, which posed major problems for accessibility and misused system resources, is no longer in use and was strongly discouraged even at the time.

Technical Information

Java applets are executed in a *sandbox* by most web browsers, preventing them from accessing local data like the clipboard or file system. The code of the applet is downloaded from a web server, after which the browser either embeds the applet into a web page or opens a new window showing the applet's user interface.

A Java applet extends the class java.applet.Applet, or in the case of a Swing applet, javax.swing. JApplet. The class which must override methods from the applet class to set up a user interface inside itself (Applet) is a descendant of Panel which is a descendant of Container. As applet inherits from container, it has largely the same user interface possibilities as an ordinary Java application, including regions with user specific visualization.

The first implementations involved downloading an applet class by class. While classes are small files, there are often many of them, so applets got a reputation as slow-loading components. However, since .jars were introduced, an applet is usually delivered as a single file that has a size similar to an image file (hundreds of kilobytes to several megabytes).

The domain from where the applet executable has been downloaded is the only domain to which the usual (unsigned) applet is allowed to communicate. This domain can be different from the domain where the surrounding HTML document is hosted.

Java system libraries and runtimes are backwards-compatible, allowing one to write code that runs both on current and on future versions of the Java virtual machine.

Similar Technologies

Many Java developers, blogs and magazines are recommending that the Java Web Start technology be used in place of applets. Java Web Start allows the launching of unmodified applet code, which then runs in a separate window (not inside the invoking browser).

A Java Servlet is sometimes informally compared to be "like" a server-side applet, but it is different in its language, functions, and in each of the characteristics described here about applets.

Embedding into a Web Page

The applet can be displayed on the web page by making use of the deprecated applet HTML element, or the recommended object element.The embed element can be used with Mozilla family browsers (embed was deprecated in HTML 4 but is included in HTML 5). This specifies the applet's source and location. Both object and embed tags can also download and install Java virtual machine (if required) or at least lead to the plugin page. applet and object tags also support loading of the serialized applets that start in some particular (rather than initial) state. Tags also specify the message that shows up in place of the applet if the browser cannot run it due to any reason.

However, despite object being officially a recommended tag, as of 2010, the support of the object tag was not yet consistent among browsers and Sun kept recommending the older applet tag for deploying in multibrowser environments, as it remained the only tag consistently supported by the most popular browsers. To support multiple browsers, the object tag currently requires JavaScript (that recognizes the browser and adjusts the tag), usage of additional browser-specific tags or delivering adapted output from the server side. Deprecating applet tag has been criticized. Oracle now provides a maintained JavaScript code to launch applets with cross platform workarounds.

The Java browser plug-in relies on NPAPI, which many web browser vendors are deprecating due to its age and security issues. In January 2016, Oracle announced that Java runtime environments based on JDK 9 will discontinue the browser plug-in.

Example

The following example illustrates the use of Java applets through the java.applet package. The example also uses classes from the Java Abstract Window Toolkit (AWT) to produce the message "Hello, world!" as output.

```
import java.applet.*;
import java.awt.*;


// Applet code for the "Hello, world!" example.
// This should be saved in a file named as "HelloWorld.java".
public class HelloWorld extends Applet {
    // Print a message on the screen (x = 20, y = 10).
    public void paint(Graphics g) {
        g.drawString("Hello, world!", 20, 10);


        // Draws a circle on the screen (x = 40, y = 30).
        g.drawArc(40, 30, 20, 20, 0, 360);


        // Draws a rectangle on the screen (x1 = 100, y1 = 100, x2 =
300, y2 = 300).
        g.drawRect(100, 100, 300, 300);


        // Draws a square on the screen (x1 = 100, y1 = 100, x2 = 200,
y2 = 200).
        g.drawRect(100, 100, 200, 200);
    }
}
```

Simple applets are shared freely on the Internet for customizing applications that support plugins.

After compilation, the resulting .class file can be placed on a web server and invoked within an HTML page by using an <applet> or an <object> tag. For example:

```
<!DOCTYPE html>

<html>

<head>

  <title>HelloWorld_example.html</title>

</head>

<body>

  <h1>A Java applet example</h1>

  <p>

    Here it is:

    <applet code="HelloWorld.class" height="40" width="200">

      This is where HelloWorld.class runs.

    </applet>

  </p>

</body>

</html>
```

When the page is accessed it will read as follows:

A Java Applet Example

Here it is: Hello, world!

To minimize download time, applets can be delivered in the form of a jar file. In the case of this example, if all necessary classes are placed in the compressed archive *example.jar*, the following embedding code could be used instead:

```
<p>

  Here it is:

 <applet archive="example.jar" code="HelloWorld" height="40" width="200">

    This is where HelloWorld.class runs.

  </applet>

</p>
```

Applet inclusion is described in detail in Sun's official page about the APPLET tag.

Advantages

A Java applet can have any or all of the following advantages:

• It is simple to make it work on FreeBSD, Linux, Microsoft Windows and macOS – that is, to make it cross platform. Applets were supported by most web browsers through the first decade of the 21st century; since then, however, most browsers have dropped applet support for security reasons.

- The same applet can work on "all" installed versions of Java at the same time, rather than just the latest plug-in version only. However, if an applet requires a later version of the Java Runtime Environment (JRE) the client will be forced to wait during the large download.

- Most web browsers cache applets so they will be quick to load when returning to a web page. Applets also improve with use: after a first applet is run, the JVM is already running and starts quickly (the JVM will need to restart each time the browser starts afresh). It should be noted that JRE versions 1.5 and greater stop the JVM and restart it when the browser navigates from one HTML page containing an applet to another containing an applet.

- It can move the work from the server to the client, making a web solution more scalable with the number of users/clients.

- If a standalone program (like Google Earth) talks to a web server, that server normally needs to support all prior versions for users which have not kept their client software updated. In contrast, a properly configured browser loads (and caches) the latest applet version, so there is no need to support legacy versions.

- The applet naturally supports the changing user state, such as figure positions on the chessboard.

- Developers can develop and debug an applet directly simply by creating a main routine (either in the applet's class or in a separate class) and calling init() and start() on the applet, thus allowing for development in their favorite Java SE development environment. All one has to do after that is re-test the applet in the AppletViewer program or a web browser to ensure it conforms to security restrictions.

- An untrusted applet has no access to the local machine and can only access the server it came from. This makes such an applet much safer to run than a standalone executable that it could replace. However, a signed applet can have full access to the machine it is running on if the user agrees.

- Java applets are fast—and can even have similar performance to native installed software.

Disadvantages

A Java applet may have any of the following disadvantages compared to other client-side web technologies:

- Java applets depend on a Java Runtime Environment (JRE), which is a reasonably complex and heavy-weight software package. It also normally requires a plug-in for the web browser. Some organizations only allow software installed by an administrator. As a result, some users can only view applets that are important enough to justify contacting the administrator to request installation of the JRE and plug-in.

- If an applet requires a newer JRE than available on the system, or a specific JRE, the user running it the first time will need to wait for the large JRE download to complete.

- Mobile browsers on iOS or Android, do not run Java applets at all. As previously noted, desktop browsers have phased out Java applet support concurrently with the rise of mobile operating systems.

- Unlike the older applet tag, the object tag needs workarounds to write a cross-browser HTML document.

- There is no standard to make the content of applets available to screen readers. Therefore, applets can harm the accessibility of a web site to users with special needs.

- As with any client-side scripting, security restrictions may make it difficult or even impossible for an untrusted applet to achieve the desired goals. However, simply editing the java.policy file in the JAVA JRE installation, one can grant access to the local filesystem or system clipboard for example, or to other network sources other than the network source that served the applet to the browser.

Security

There are two applet types with very different security models: signed applets and unsigned applets. As of Java SE 7 Update 21 (April 2013) applets and Web-Start Apps are encouraged to be signed with a trusted certificate, and warning messages appear when running unsigned applets. Further starting with Java 7 Update 51 unsigned applets are blocked by default; they can be run by creating an exception in the Java Control Panel.

Unsigned

Limits on unsigned applets are understood as "draconian": they have no access to the local filesystem and web access limited to the applet download site; there are also many other important restrictions. For instance, they cannot access all system properties, use their own class loader, call native code, execute external commands on a local system or redefine classes belonging to core packages included as part of a Java release. While they can run in a standalone frame, such frame contains a header, indicating that this is an untrusted applet. Successful initial call of the forbidden method does not automatically create a security hole as an access controller checks the entire stack of the calling code to be sure the call is not coming from an improper location.

As with any complex system, many security problems have been discovered and fixed since Java was first released. Some of these (like the Calendar serialization security bug) persisted for many years with nobody being aware. Others have been discovered in use by malware in the wild.

Some studies mention applets crashing the browser or overusing CPU resources but these are classified as nuisances and not as true security flaws. However, unsigned applets may be involved in combined attacks that exploit a combination of multiple severe configuration errors in other parts of the system. An unsigned applet can also be more dangerous to run directly on the server where it is hosted because while code base allows it to talk with the server, running inside it can bypass the firewall. An applet may also try DoS attacks on the server where it is hosted, but usually people who manage the web site also manage the applet, making this unreasonable. Communities may solve this problem via source code review or running applets on a dedicated domain.

The unsigned applet can also try to download malware hosted on originating server. However it could only store such file into a temporary folder (as it is transient data) and has no means to complete the attack by executing it. There were attempts to use applets for spreading Phoenix and Siberia exploits this way, but these exploits do not use Java internally and were also distributed in several other ways.

Signed

A signed applet contains a signature that the browser should verify through a remotely running, independent certificate authority server. Producing this signature involves specialized tools and interaction with the authority server maintainers. Once the signature is verified, and the user of the current machine also approves, a signed applet can get more rights, becoming equivalent to an ordinary standalone program. The rationale is that the author of the applet is now known and will be responsible for any deliberate damage. This approach allows applets to be used for many tasks that are otherwise not possible by client-side scripting. However, this approach requires more responsibility from the user, deciding whom he or she trusts. The related concerns include a non-responsive authority server, wrong evaluation of the signer identity when issuing certificates, and known applet publishers still doing something that the user would not approve of. Hence signed applets that appeared from Java 1.1 may actually have more security concerns.

Self-signed

Self-signed applets, which are applets signed by the developer themselves, may potentially pose a security risk; java plugins provide a warning when requesting authorization for a self-signed applet, as the function and safety of the applet is guaranteed only by the developer itself, and has not been independently confirmed. Such self-signed certificates are usually only used during development prior to release where third-party confirmation of security is unimportant, but most applet developers will seek third-party signing to ensure that users trust the applet's safety.

Java security problems are not fundamentally different from similar problems of any client-side scripting platform. In particular, all issues related to signed applets also apply to Microsoft ActiveX components.

As of 2014, self-signed and unsigned applets are no longer accepted by the commonly available Java plugins or Java Web Start. Consequently, developers who wish to deploy Java applets have no alternative but to acquire trusted certificates from commercial sources.

Alternatives

Alternative technologies exist (for example, JavaScript) that satisfy all or more of the scope of what is possible with an applet. Of these, JavaScript is not always viewed as a competing replacement; JavaScript can coexist with applets in the same page, assist in launching applets (for instance, in a separate frame or providing platform workarounds) and later be called from the applet code. JavaFX is an extension of the Java platform and may also be viewed as an alternative.

Java Servlet

A servlet is a Java programming language class used to extend the capabilities of servers that host applications accessed by means of a request-response programming model. Although servlets can respond to any type of request, they are commonly used to extend the applications hosted by web servers. For such applications, Java Servlet technology defines HTTP-specific servlet classes.

The javax.servlet and javax.servlet.http packages provide interfaces and classes for writing servlets. All servlets must implement the Servlet interface, which defines lifecycle methods. When implementing a generic service, you can use or extend the GenericServlet class provided with the Java Servlet API. The HttpServlet class provides methods, such as doGet and doPost, for handling HTTP-specific services.

Using Servlets, you can collect input from users through web page forms, present records from a database or another source, and create web pages dynamically.

Java Servlets often serve the same purpose as programs implemented using the Common Gateway Interface (CGI). But Servlets offer several advantages in comparison with the CGI.

- Performance is significantly better.

- Servlets execute within the address space of a Web server. It is not necessary to create a separate process to handle each client request.

- Servlets are platform-independent because they are written in Java.

- Java security manager on the server enforces a set of restrictions to protect the resources on a server machine. So servlets are trusted.

- The full functionality of the Java class libraries is available to a servlet. It can communicate with applets, databases, or other software via the sockets and RMI mechanisms that you have seen already.

Servlets Architecture

The following diagram shows the position of Servlets in a Web Application.

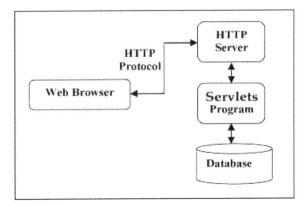

Servlets Tasks

Servlets perform the following major tasks –

- Read the explicit data sent by the clients (browsers). This includes an HTML form on a Web page or it could also come from an applet or a custom HTTP client program.

- Read the implicit HTTP request data sent by the clients (browsers). This includes cookies, media types and compression schemes the browser understands, and so forth.

- Process the data and generate the results. This process may require talking to a database, executing an RMI or CORBA call, invoking a Web service, or computing the response directly.

- Send the explicit data (i.e., the document) to the clients (browsers). This document can be sent in a variety of formats, including text (HTML or XML), binary (GIF images), Excel, etc.

- Send the implicit HTTP response to the clients (browsers). This includes telling the browsers or other clients what type of document is being returned (e.g., HTML), setting cookies and caching parameters, and other such tasks.

A Java servlet processes or stores a Java class in Java EE that conforms to the Java Servlet API, a standard for implementing Java classes that respond to requests. Servlets could in principle communicate over any client–server protocol, but they are most often used with the HTTP. Thus "servlet" is often used as shorthand for "HTTP servlet". Thus, a software developer may use a servlet to add dynamic content to a web server using the Java platform. The generated content is commonly HTML, but may be other data such as XML and more commonly, JSON. Servlets can maintain state in session variables across many server transactions by using HTTP cookies, or URL rewriting.

The Java servlet API has, to some extent, been superseded by two standard Java technologies for web services:

- the Java API for RESTful Web Services (JAX-RS 2.0) useful for AJAX, JSON and REST services, and

- the Java API for XML Web Services (JAX-WS) useful for SOAP Web Services.

To deploy and run a servlet, a web container must be used. A web container (also known as a servlet container) is essentially the component of a web server that interacts with the servlets. The web container is responsible for managing the lifecycle of servlets, mapping a URL to a particular servlet and ensuring that the URL requester has the correct access rights.

The Servlet API, contained in the Java package hierarchy javax.servlet, defines the expected interactions of the web container and a servlet.

A Servlet is an object that receives a request and generates a response based on that request. The basic Servlet package defines Java objects to represent servlet requests and responses, as well as objects to reflect the servlet's configuration parameters and execution environment. The package javax.servlet.http defines HTTP-specific subclasses of the generic servlet elements, including session management objects that track multiple requests and responses between the web server and a client. Servlets may be packaged in a WAR file as a web application.

Servlets can be generated automatically from JavaServer Pages (JSP) by the JavaServer Pages compiler. The difference between servlets and JSP is that servlets typically embed HTML inside Java code, while JSPs embed Java code in HTML. While the direct usage of servlets to generate HTML (as shown in the example below) has become rare, the higher level MVC web framework in Java EE (JSF) still explicitly uses the servlet technology for the low level request/response handling via the FacesServlet. A somewhat older usage is to use servlets in conjunction with JSPs in a pattern called "Model 2", which is a flavor of the model–view–controller.

Compared with other Web Application Models

The advantages of using servlets are their fast performance and ease of use combined with more power over traditional CGI (Common Gateway Interface). Traditional CGI scripts written in Java have a number of performance disadvantages:

- When an HTTP request is made, a new process is created each time the CGI script is called. The overhead associated with process creation can dominate the workload especially when the script does relatively fast operations. Thus, process creation will take more time for CGI script execution. In contrast, for servlets, each request is handled by a separate Java thread *within* the web server process, thereby avoiding the overhead associated with forking processes within the HTTP daemon.

- Simultaneous CGI requests will load the CGI script to be copied into memory once per request. With servlets, there is only one copy that persists across requests and is shared between threads.

- Only a single instance answers all requests concurrently. This reduces memory usage and eases the management of persistent data.

- A servlet can be run by a servlet container in a restrictive environment, called a sandbox. This is similar to an applet that runs in the sandbox of the web browser. This enables restricted use of potentially harmful servlets. CGI programs can of course also sandbox themselves, since they are simply OS processes.

Technologies like FastCGI and its derivatives (including SCGI, AJP) do not exhibit the performance disadvantages of CGI, incurred by the constant process spawning. They are, however, roughly as simple as CGI. They are therefore also in contrast with servlets which are substantially more complex.

Life Cycle of a Servlet

Three methods are central to the life cycle of a servlet. These are init(), service(), and destroy(). They are implemented by every servlet and are invoked at specific times by the server.

- During initialization stage of the servlet life cycle, the web container initializes the servlet instance by calling the init() method, passing an object implementing the javax.servlet.

ServletConfig interface. This configuration object allows the servlet to access name-value initialization parameters from the web application.

- After initialization, the servlet instance can service client requests. Each request is serviced in its own separate thread. The web container calls the service() method of the servlet for every request. The service() method determines the kind of request being made and dispatches it to an appropriate method to handle the request. The developer of the servlet must provide an implementation for these methods. If a request is made for a method that is not implemented by the servlet, the method of the parent class is called, typically resulting in an error being returned to the requester.

- Finally, the web container calls the destroy() method that takes the servlet out of service. The destroy() method, like init(), is called only once in the lifecycle of a servlet.

The following is a typical user scenario of these methods.

1. Assume that a user requests to visit a URL.

   o The browser then generates an HTTP request for this URL.

   o This request is then sent to the appropriate server.

2. The HTTP request is received by the web server and forwarded to the servlet container.

   o The container maps this request to a particular servlet.

   o The servlet is dynamically retrieved and loaded into the address space of the container.

3. The container invokes the init() method of the servlet.

   o This method is invoked only when the servlet is first loaded into memory.

   o It is possible to pass initialization parameters to the servlet so that it may configure itself.

4. The container invokes the service() method of the servlet.

   o This method is called to process the HTTP request.

   o The servlet may read data that has been provided in the HTTP request.

   o The servlet may also formulate an HTTP response for the client.

5. The servlet remains in the container's address space and is available to process any other HTTP requests received from clients.

   o The service() method is called for each HTTP request.

6. The container may, at some point, decide to unload the servlet from its memory.

   o The algorithms by which this decision is made are specific to each container.

7. The container calls the servlet's destroy() method to relinquish any resources such as file handles that are allocated for the servlet; important data may be saved to a persistent store.

8. The memory allocated for the servlet and its objects can then be garbage collected.

Example

The following example servlet prints how many times its service() method was called.

Note that HttpServlet is a subclass of GenericServlet, an implementation of the Servlet interface.

The service() method of HttpServlet class dispatches requests to the methods doGet(), doPost(), doPut(), doDelete(), and so on; according to the HTTP request. In the example below service() is overridden and does not distinguish which HTTP request method it serves.

```java
import java.io.IOException;

import javax.servlet.ServletConfig;
import javax.servlet.ServletException;
import javax.servlet.http.HttpServlet;
import javax.servlet.http.HttpServletRequest;
import javax.servlet.http.HttpServletResponse;

public class ServletLifeCycleExample extends HttpServlet {

    private int count;

    @Override
    public void init(final ServletConfig config) throws ServletException {
        super.init(config);
        getServletContext().log("init() called");
        count = 0;
    }

    @Override
    protected void service(final HttpServletRequest request, final HttpServletResponse response) throws ServletException, IOException {
        getServletContext().log("service() called");
        count++;
        response.getWriter().write("Incrementing the count to " + count);
    }
}
```

```
    @Override
    public void destroy() {
        getServletContext().log("destroy() called");
    }
}
```

The Servlet Container

Servlet container, also known as Servlet engine is an integrated set of objects that provide run time environment for Java Servlet components.

In simple words, it is a system that manages Java Servlet components on top of the Web server to handle the Web client requests.

Services provided by the Servlet container :

- Network Services : Loads a Servlet class. The loading may be from a local file system, a remote file system or other network services. The Servlet container provides the network services over which the request and response are sent.

- Decode and Encode MIME based messages : Provides the service of decoding and encoding MIME-based messages.

- Manage Servlet container : Manages the lifecycle of a Servlet.

- Resource management : Manages the static and dynamic resource, such as HTML files, Servlets and JSP pages.

- Security Service : Handles authorization and authentication of resource access.

- Session Management : Maintains a session by appending a session ID to the URL path.

JavaServer Pages

JavaServer Pages (JSP) is a server-side programming technology that enables the creation of dynamic, platform-independent method for building Web-based applications. JSP have access to the entire family of Java APIs, including the JDBC API to access enterprise databases.

A JavaServer Pages component is a type of Java servlet that is designed to fulfill the role of a user interface for a Java web application. Web developers write JSPs as text files that combine HTML or XHTML code, XML elements, and embedded JSP actions and commands.

Using JSP, you can collect input from users through Webpage forms, present records from a database or another source, and create Webpages dynamically.

JSP tags can be used for a variety of purposes, such as retrieving information from a database or registering user preferences, accessing JavaBeans components, passing control between pages, and sharing information between requests, pages etc.

Reasons for using JSP

JavaServer Pages often serve the same purpose as programs implemented using the Common Gateway Interface (CGI). But JSP offers several advantages in comparison with the CGI.

- Performance is significantly better because JSP allows embedding Dynamic Elements in HTML Pages itself instead of having separate CGI files.

- JSP are always compiled before they are processed by the server unlike CGI/Perl which requires the server to load an interpreter and the target script each time the page is requested.

- JavaServer Pages are built on top of the Java Servlets API, so like Servlets, JSP also has access to all the powerful Enterprise Java APIs, including JDBC, JNDI, EJB, JAXP, etc.

- JSP pages can be used in combination with servlets that handle the business logic, the model supported by Java servlet template engines.

Finally, JSP is an integral part of Java EE, a complete platform for enterprise class applications. This means that JSP can play a part in the simplest applications to the most complex and demanding.

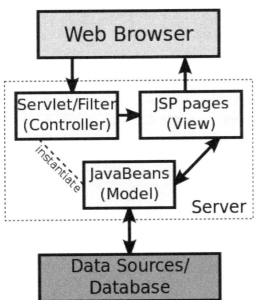

The JSP Model 2 architecture.

Architecturally, JSP may be viewed as a high-level abstraction of Java servlets. JSPs are translated into servlets at runtime, therefore JSP is a Servlet; each JSP servlet is cached and re-used until the original JSP is modified.

JSP can be used independently or as the view component of a server-side model–view–controller design, normally with JavaBeans as the model and Java servlets (or a framework such as Apache Struts) as the controller. This is a type of Model 2 architecture.

JSP allows Java code and certain pre-defined actions to be interleaved with static web markup content, such as HTML, with the resulting page being compiled and executed on the server to deliver a document. The compiled pages, as well as any dependent Java libraries, contain Java bytecode rather than machine code. Like any other Java program, they must be executed within a Java virtual machine (JVM) that interacts with the server's host operating system to provide an abstract, platform-neutral environment.

JSPs are usually used to deliver HTML and XML documents, but through the use of OutputStream, they can deliver other types of data as well.

The Web container creates JSP implicit objects like request, response, session, application, config, page, pageContext, out and exception. JSP Engine creates these objects during translation phase.

Syntax

JSP pages use several delimiters for scripting functions. The most basic is <% ... %>, which encloses a JSP *scriptlet*. A scriptlet is a fragment of Java code that is run when the user requests the page. Other common delimiters include <%= ... %> for *expressions,* where the scriptlet and delimiters are replaced with the result of evaluating the expression, and *directives*, denoted with <%@ ... %>.

Java code is not required to be complete or self-contained within a single scriptlet block. It can straddle markup content, provided that the page as a whole is syntactically correct. For example, any Java *if/for/while* blocks opened in one scriptlet must be correctly closed in a later scriptlet for the page to successfully compile.

Content that falls inside a split block of Java code (spanning multiple scriptlets) is subject to that code. Content inside an *if* block will only appear in the output when the *if* condition evaluates to true. Likewise, content inside a loop construct may appear multiple times in the output, depending upon how many times the loop body runs.

The following would be a valid for loop in a JSP page:

```
<p>Counting to three:</p>
<% for (int i=1; i<4; i++) { %>
    <p>This number is <%= i %>.</p>
<% } %>
<p>OK.</p>
```

The output displayed in the user's web browser would be:

Counting to three:

```
This number is 1.
This number is 2.
```

This number is 3.

OK.

Expression Language

Version 2.0 of the JSP specification added support for the Expression Language (EL), used to access data and functions in Java objects. In JSP 2.1, it was folded into the Unified Expression Language, which is also used in JavaServer Faces.

An example of EL Syntax:

The value of "variable" in the object "javabean" is ${javabean.variable}.

Additional Tags

The JSP syntax add additional tags, called JSP actions, to invoke built-in functionality. Additionally, the technology allows for the creation of custom JSP *tag libraries* that act as extensions to the standard JSP syntax. One such library is the JSTL, with support for common tasks such as iteration and conditionals (the equivalent of "for" and "if" statements in Java.)

Compiler

A JavaServer Pages compiler is a program that parses JSPs, and transforms them into executable Java Servlets. A program of this type is usually embedded into the application server and run automatically the first time a JSP is accessed, but pages may also be precompiled for better performance, or compiled as a part of the build process to test for errors.

Some JSP containers support configuring how often the container checks JSP file timestamps to see whether the page has changed. Typically, this timestamp would be set to a short interval (perhaps seconds) during software development, and a longer interval (perhaps minutes, or even never) for a deployed Web application.

Criticism

In 2000, Jason Hunter, author of "Java Servlet Programming", criticized JSP for either tempting or requiring the programmer to mix Java code and HTML markup, although he acknowledged it would "wean people off" of Microsoft's Active Server Pages. Later, he added a note to his site saying that JSP had improved since 2000, but also cited its competitors, Apache Velocity and Tea (template language).

Advantages of JSP

Following points lists out the other advantages of using JSP over other technologies –

- vs. Active Server Pages (ASP)

The advantages of JSP are twofold. First, the dynamic part is written in Java, not Visual Basic or other MS specific language, so it is more powerful and easier to use. Second, it is portable to other operating systems and non-Microsoft Web servers.

- vs. Pure Servlets

It is more convenient to write (and to modify!) regular HTML than to have plenty of println statements that generate the HTML.

- vs. Server-Side Includes (SSI)

SSI is really only intended for simple inclusions, not for "real" programs that use form data, make database connections, and the like.

- vs. JavaScript

JavaScript can generate HTML dynamically on the client but can hardly interact with the web server to perform complex tasks like database access and image processing etc.

- vs. Static HTML

Regular HTML, of course, cannot contain dynamic information.

References

- "Always override hashCode when you override equals" in Bloch, Joshua (2008), Effective Java (2nd ed.), Addison-Wesley, ISBN 978-0-321-35668-0

- Javase, Tutorial, Deployment, Applet, Index: docs.oracle.com, Retrieved 2018-04-05

- "What's new in Servlet 3.1 ? - Java EE 7 moving forward (Arun Gupta, Miles to go ...)". oracle.com. Retrieved 22 November 2016

- Crawford, William; Hunter, Jason (November 1998). "Preface". Java Servlet Programming (1st ed.). O'Reilly Media. p. ix–x. ISBN 978-1-56592-391-1

- Chang, Phil Inje (July 1, 1997). "Interview: The Java Web Server team gives you the skinny". JavaWorld. Retrieved 2018-07-25

Permissions

Index